# Open
## for Business

### Lessons in Chinese Commerce
### for the New Millennium

Volume One

Textbook and

Exercise Book

Jane C.M. Kuo

 **Cheng & Tsui Company**
**Boston**

2nd edition

13  12  11  10                8  7  6  5  4  3

ISBN-13: 978-0-88727-456-5
ISBN-10: 0-88727-456-0


Published by

Cheng & Tsui Company
25 West Street
Boston, MA 02111-1213 USA
Fax (617) 426-3669
www.cheng-tsui.com
"Bringing Asia to the World"™

Printed in Canada

# Publisher's Note

The Cheng & Tsui Company is pleased to announce the most recent addition to its Asian Language Series, *Open for Business: Lessons in Chinese Commerce for the New Millennium*. This new course program in business Chinese has been specifically designed for students with at least three years of experience in the language.

The *C&T Asian Language Series* is designed to publish and widely distribute quality language texts as they are completed by such leading institutions as the Beijing University of Language and Culture, as well as other significant works in the field of Asian languages developed in the United States and elsewhere.

We welcome readers' comments and suggestions concerning the publications in this series. Please contact the following members of the Editorial Board:

# Introduction

*Open for Business* is an advanced reading course designed for students who have an advanced level of Chinese language proficiency or who are in their third or fourth year of a Chinese language curriculum in the U.S. either at the undergraduate- or graduate-level. Upon finishing this textbook, students are expected to reach a higher level of proficiency in which they are able to read newspapers, magazines, or other business related documents as well as to make business presentations or conduct business negotiations.

This textbook consists of seven chapters containing a total of twenty-five lessons and corresponding exercises. In order to accommodate the typical 12-week semester in the U.S., the textbook has been divided into two volumes: Volume I (Chapters 1 to 3) and Volume II (Chapters 4 to 7). Topics covered in Volume I provide an overview of China's changing macro-economic environment and current business practices relating to finance and marketing. In Volume II, students will be exposed to Chinese management practices and foreign trade initiatives along with an overview of key industries and technology-related topics.

Source materials for the topics discussed in this textbook were gathered during several trips to China over the past few years. Such materials included articles from major Chinese newspapers, data from the State Statistics Bureau and China's Trade Bureau, and information obtained over the Internet from various online databases.

## Lesson Structure

As described below, each lesson includes a text reading and brief background on a specific topic, followed by a vocabulary list and explanation of important terms along with a section relating to the usage of synonyms. Each volume also includes comprehensive indexes of vocabulary, grammar terms, and synonyms for easy cross-referencing with the lessons. Exercises for each lesson are provided in a separate Exercise Book section.

**Text**

Each lesson begins with a text reading related to a specific subject matter. The text is presented in both simplified and traditional Chinese in order to expose students to both writing styles. An English translation is also provided so that students can verify their understanding of the material either in class or on their own.

**Background Information**
Each text reading is supplemented with background information relating to the topic at hand. Although brief, this additional information is useful in enhancing the reader's knowledge of the subject as well as generating additional classroom discussion.

**Vocabulary List**
Key words underlined in the text reading are listed in this section in both simplified and traditional Chinese. A *pinyin* spelling is also provided for pronunciation practice along with an English translation for additional reference.

**Explanation of Terms**
This section is aimed at enhancing the student's understanding of key expressions introduced in the text reading. Each term is explained briefly in English and then is used in a variety of sentences featuring practical, everyday business expressions.

**Distinguishing Synonyms**
Although fully understood by native speakers, Chinese synonyms often pose the biggest challenge for non-native speakers. Students will therefore find great interest in this section as it provides explanations and sample sentences illustrating the subtle differences among words or expressions with seemingly similar meanings.

**Exercises**
Practice exercises corresponding to each lesson can be found in the *Open for Business* Exercise Book. These exercises are designed to improve the student's ability to use Chinese business lexicon correctly. Particular emphasis is placed on sentence structure and reading comprehension. A Questions and Explorations section is also included to encourage students to perform further research on the Internet and present such information either orally or in writing for further discussion or debate.

# Acknowledgements

I would like to acknowledge the following people for their assistance, support, and encouragement. Their efforts made it possible to have this textbook published.

First of all, I would like to express my special appreciation to Jill Cheng, president of Cheng & Tsui Company, and her staff for their generous advice and faith in publishing this textbook. I am also very grateful to my reviewers, Vivian Ling, Olwen Bedford, and Jacques van Wersch, who kindly edited this book with their invaluable insight and knowledge of both Chinese and English. I also want to thank Yanmei Ji and Yan Zhu for helping me collect information from China.

My deepest thanks go to my home institution, Thunderbird, the American Graduate School of International Management, for providing me with graduate assistants and technical support during this project. My sincere thanks also go to my graduate assistants who spent an enormous amount of time helping me while also pursuing their graduate degrees at Thunderbird. I am most indebted to Victor Hoerst, Alan Jin, Kristi Kramersmeier, Li Niu, and Yong Yu for their patience and efforts in compiling, editing, and formatting this textbook.

Finally, my special thanks go to my dearest parents, Mr. and Mrs. Hsueh-Hu Kuo for their understanding and encouragement, and to my brother, Sunny Kuo, for creating the cover design. I would also like to thank my husband, Dr. Suguru Akutsu, for his inspiration and all-encompassing support while I was writing this textbook.

# Table of Contents

(continued on the next page)

# Table of Contents, continued

**Exercise Section**

# 第一章

# 改革开放

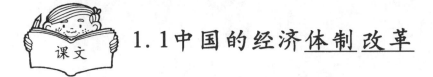

# 1.1中国的经济体制改革

从1949年中华人民共和国成立到1978年的30年中，中国一直实行计划经济体制，由中央政府分配资源、组织生产、统一供应。在这种经济体制下，资源不能有效利用，生产效率低下，市场缺乏活力，因此严重制约了经济的发展。为了克服计划经济的弊病，中国政府从1979年开始实行"对内改革、对外开放"政策，逐步建立了具有中国特色的社会主义市场经济体制。

对内改革的重点是改革国有企业和鼓励私有企业的发展。在过去20年，中国政府关闭了一批经营不善、长期亏损的国有企业，将部分国有企业转变为私有企业。此外，中国政府还加紧完善立法工作，进行了税收、金融、外贸等体制的改革，从而促进了私有企业的发展，加快了经济体制改革的步伐。

对外开放打开了中国的国门，也吸引了大量外资。越来越多的海外投资者看好中国市场，对在中国投资充满信心。目前，中国已经成为世界上资本流入量最大的发展中国家之一。

# 1.1中國的經濟體制改革

課文

從1949年中華人民共和國成立到1978年的30年中，中國一直實行計劃經濟體制，由中央政府分配資源、組織生產、統一供應。在這種經濟體制下，資源不能有效利用，生產效率低下，市場缺乏活力，因此嚴重制約了經濟的發展。爲了克服計劃經濟的弊病，中國政府從1979年開始實行"對內改革、對外開放"政策，逐步建立了具有中國特色的社會主義市場經濟體制。

對內改革的重點是改革國有企業和鼓勵私有企業的發展。在過去20年，中國政府關閉了一批經營不善、長期虧損的國有企業，將部分國有企業轉變爲私有企業。此外，中國政府還加緊完善立法工作，進行了稅收、金融、外貿等體制的改革，從而促進了私有企業的發展，加快了經濟體制改革的步伐。

對外開放打開了中國的國門，也吸引了大量外資。越來越多的海外投資者看好中國市場，對在中國投資充滿信心。目前，中國已經成爲世界上資本流入量最大的發展中國家之一。

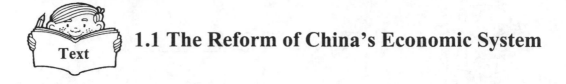

# 1.1 The Reform of China's Economic System

During the 30 years following the establishment of the People's Republic of China (from 1949 to 1978), the Chinese government implemented a planned economic system. The central government was in charge of distributing resources, organizing production, and centralizing distribution. Under this kind of economic system, resources were not effectively utilized, production efficiency dropped, and the market lacked strength; therefore, economic development was seriously constrained. In order to overcome the drawbacks of the planned economy, the Chinese government started implementing the "Reform and Open Door Policy" in 1979, and gradually established a socialist market system with Chinese characteristics.

The focal points of transforming China's domestic economic situation have been the reform of state-owned enterprises and encouraging the development of privately-owned enterprises. Over the past twenty years, the government has closed numerous state-owned enterprises that were managed poorly with long-standing deficits, and transformed some state-owned enterprises into privately-owned enterprises. Furthermore, the Chinese government has sped up the improvement of legislation and has carried out reforms in taxation, finance, and foreign trade, thereby promoting the development of private businesses and speeding up China's economic reform.

The "Open Door" policy has not only opened China's doors, but has also attracted a large amount of foreign capital. An increasing number of investors regard China's market favorably, showing confidence in Chinese investment. At present, the amount of capital inflow into China has become one of the largest among the world's developing countries.

**背景知识**

　　中国的经济体制改革也带来严重的失业问题。为了降低失业率，<u>维持</u>社会<u>稳定</u>，中国政府<u>推行</u>了"下岗职工再<u>就业工程</u>"，<u>引导</u>下岗职工到第三<u>产业</u>（即服务业）、中小企业和私营企业再就业。

**背景知識**

　　中國的經濟體制改革也帶來嚴重的失業問題。爲了降低失業率，<u>維持</u>社會<u>穩定</u>，中國政府<u>推行</u>了"下崗職工再<u>就業工程</u>"，<u>引導</u>下崗職工到第三<u>產業</u>（即服務業）、中小企業和私營企業再就業。

**Background Information**

　　Reform of the Chinese economic system has also brought about a serious unemployment problem. In order to lower the unemployment rate and maintain a stable society, the Chinese government carried out a program called "Reemployment of laid-off workers." This program guides laid-off workers to work for the 'Third Industry' (i.e. service industry), small and medium enterprises and privately owned businesses.

# 生词表

| 体制 | 體制 | tǐzhì | （名） | system |
| 改革 | 改革 | gǎigé | （名、动） | reform; to reform |
| 中央 | 中央 | zhōngyāng | （名、形） | center; central |
| 分配 | 分配 | fēnpèi | （动） | to distribute; to allocate; to assign |
| 统一 | 統一 | tǒngyī | （动、形） | to unify; to unite; centralized; unified |
| 供应 | 供應 | gōngyìng | （名、动） | supply; to supply |
| 有效 | 有效 | yǒuxiào | （形、副） | effective; valid; effectively |
| 缺乏 | 缺乏 | quēfá | （动） | to lack; to be short of |
| 活力 | 活力 | huólì | （名） | vitality; vigor; strength |
| 制约 | 制約 | zhìyuē | （动） | to restrict; to constrain |
| 克服 | 克服 | kèfú | （动） | to overcome; to conquer |
| 弊病 | 弊病 | bìbìng | （名） | drawback; shortcoming; problem |
| 政策 | 政策 | zhèngcè | （名） | policy |
| 建立 | 建立 | jiànlì | （动） | to build; to establish; to set up; to found |
| 具有 | 具有 | jùyǒu | （动） | to have; to possess |
| 特色 | 特色 | tèsè | （名） | unique characteristic; special feature |
| 关闭 | 關閉 | guānbì | （动） | to close; to shut down |
| 批 | 批 | pī | （量） | batch; group of (goods or people) |
| 不善 | 不善 | búshàn | （形） | bad; with ill intent; not good at |
| 亏损 | 虧損 | kuīsǔn | （名、动） | financial loss; deficit; to suffer a loss |

| | | | | |
|---|---|---|---|---|
| 部分 | 部分 | bùfen | （名） | part; portion |
| 转变 | 轉變 | zhuǎnbiàn | （动、名） | to change; transformation |
| 私有 | 私有 | sīyǒu | （形） | privately owned; private |
| 此外 | 此外 | cǐwài | （连） | in addition; besides; moreover |
| 加紧 | 加緊 | jiājǐn | （动） | to intensify; to step up; to speed up |
| 完善 | 完善 | wánshàn | （动） | to perfect; to improve |
| 立法 | 立法 | lìfǎ | （名、动、形） | legislation; to legislate; legislative |
| 税收 | 税收 | shuìshōu | （名） | tax revenue |
| 从而 | 從而 | cóng'ér | （连） | thus; thereby |
| 促进 | 促進 | cùjìn | （动） | to promote; to advance; to accelerate |
| 步伐 | 步伐 | bùfá | （名） | step; pace |
| 看好 | 看好 | kànhǎo | （动） | to seem good; to look promising |
| 成为 | 成爲 | chéngwéi | （动） | to become |
| 流入 | 流入 | liúrù | （动） | to flow into |
| 之一 | 之一 | zhīyī | （代） | one of ... |
| 维持 | 維持 | wéichí | （动） | to maintain; to keep; to preserve |
| 稳定 | 穩定 | wěndìng | （形、动） | stable; steady; to stabilize |
| 推行 | 推行 | tuīxíng | （动） | to carry out; to implement; to put into practice |
| 就业 | 就業 | jiùyè | （动） | to obtain employment |
| 工程 | 工程 | gōngchéng | （名） | project; engineering |
| 引导 | 引導 | yǐndǎo | （动） | to guide; to lead |
| 产业 | 産業 | chǎnyè | （名） | industry |

# 1. 由 "through; by"

*a. 由（介）is used to introduce the agent (i.e. a person or organization) that has an obligation or responsibility to perform an event or make a decision.*

1. 这个项目由他负责。
   He is responsible for this project.

2. 这个交易会由什么单位主办的？
   Which organization was in charge of the trade fair?

3. 从总公司来的技术人员是由王厂长陪着参观工厂的。
   It was Factory Manager Wang who accompanied the engineers sent by the headquarters on their tour of the factory.

4. 香港的水是由中国供应的。
   Hong Kong's water is provided by China.

*b. 由 is used to indicate a reason, way, or method which leads to a thing or event. Verbs used in this structure are usually limited to: 组成、构成、造成、决定、产生、引起, etc. 所 may be added before the verb.*

1. 水是由氢和氧构成的。
   Water is composed of hydrogen and oxygen.

2. 美国总统是由人民选举产生的。
   The President of the U.S.A. is chosen through a public election.

3. 这场火灾是由地震引起的。
   The fire was caused by the earthquake.

4. G-8是由八个先进工业国家（所）组成的。
   The G8 is formed by the eight most industrially advanced countries.

c. 由（动）is used in the colloquial form meaning "to be decided by someone; to be up to someone."

1. 由他去，别管他！
   Let him be! (Leave him alone, don't bother him!)

2. 这件事，信不信由你，反正我不信。
   It's up to you to believe it or not. At any rate, I do not believe it.

## 2. 在 ... 下 "under the circumstances of ..."

This structure 在 ... 下 is a conditional clause that sets the condition for the implementation of what is stated in the main clause.

1. 在任何情况下，他都不会答应你的请求。
   He would not agree to your request under any circumstances.

2. 在全体员工的合作下，工作进行得很顺利。
   Through the joint efforts of the entire crew, the project has progressed smoothly.

3. 在经济条件允许的情况下，很多人会考虑出国进修。
   Financial circumstances permitting, many people would consider going abroad to study.

## 3. 为了（介） "for the sake of; in order to"

a. 为了 is used to form a prepositional phrase or a clause expressing the objective or defining the cause of the following clause.

1. 为了您和家人的健康，请不要抽烟。
   For the sake of your health and that of your family, please do not smoke.

2. 为了鼓励私有企业的发展，政府制定了许多法规。

In order to encourage the development of privately-owned businesses, the government has set forth many laws and regulations.

3. 为了提高产量，公司决定增加几条生产线。

In order to increase production, the company has decided to add several production lines.

b. *The clause formed by* 为了 *can be placed at the end of a sentence to indicate the purpose or reason, and* 是 *is needed to complete the sentence.*

1. 实行"对外开放"政策是为了吸引外资。

The purpose of implementing the "Reform and Open Door Policy" is to attract foreign capital.

2. 公司进行改组是为了提高管理效率。

The company's purpose for implementing the restructuring is to improve management efficiency.

c. 为（了）*accompanied by* 起见 *indicates an objective or explains a reason. The function is the same as* 为了..., *except that this pattern can only be used with disyllabic adjectives and is usually limited to such adjectives as* 安全、方便、保险, *etc.*

1. 为了安全起见，每一个来工厂参观的人都得戴上安全帽。

For safety's sake, every visitor to the factory must wear a safety helmet.

2. 为了保密起见，所有文件都由经理保管。

In order to maintain confidentiality, all the documents are kept by the manager.

# 4. 转变（动、名） "to change; to transform; change"

转变 *refers to a change or transformation of a thought, form or circumstance. It is usually used when something turns for the better, but not the opposite. When used as a verb, it can have a complement, such as* 为, *which means "to change ... into ..."*

1. 在老板的面前，他的态度突然转变了。
   In the presence of his boss, his attitude suddenly changed.

2. 跟他做了这个项目以后，我对他的看法有了转变。
   After working with him on this project, I have changed my view of him.

3. 中国的经济体制由计划经济转变为市场经济了。
   China's economy is changing from a planned economy to a market economy.

# 5. 此外（连）"in addition to; besides; moreover"

a. *The* 此 *"this" in* 此外 *refers to what has just been mentioned.* 此外 *can be followed by a positive statement to indicate that there is something more in addition to what has been mentioned.*

1. 他上次到中国出差，考察了公司业务发展状况。此外，他还签了几份合同。
   On his last business trip to China, he reviewed the development of the company's operation. In addition, he also signed several contracts.

2. 中国的企业目前包括国有企业、私有企业，此外，还有合资企业。
   In addition to state-owned and privately-owned enterprises, there are also joint ventures presently in China.

b. 此外 *can also be followed by a negative form indicating that there is nothing more to add to what has already been mentioned.*

1. 我们只在上海建立了工厂，此外没有在别的地方投资。
   Except for the establishment of a factory in Shanghai, we have not invested in any other location.

2. 中国只有走市场经济的道路，此外没有别的出路。
   China has no other choice but to take the path toward a market economy.

# 6.从而（连）"thus; thereby"

*从而 is used to link clauses which have the same subject; the last clause introduces the result or a further action of the preceding clause.*

1. 两家公司互相交流，增进了解，从而加强了合作。
   Through mutual exchange and increased understanding, the two companies thereby strengthened their cooperation.

2. 政府实行改革开放，发展市场经济，从而提高了人民的生活水平。
   The government implemented the "Reform and Open Door Policy" and developed the market economy, thus improving people's living standards.

# 7.越来越多 "more and more"

*This pattern shows that the degree of a situation or condition has been intensified over time. It is also used as an adjective to modify a noun.*

1. 越来越多的外商对在中国投资具有信心。
   More and more foreign investors are becoming confident about investing in China.

2. 在政府的政策鼓励下，私有企业越来越多。
   With the encouragement of government policy, the number of privately-owned enterprises is increasing.

3. 越来越多的外国资金流入中国。
   More and more foreign capital is flowing into China.

# 8.看好（动）"to seem good; to look promising"

*看好 is a newly developed usage which is used to describe the marketing prospect of a product or business.*

1. 很多投资者看好网络公司未来的市场。
   Many investors think the future market of the Internet seems promising.

2. 笔记本电脑市场近来非常看好。
   The laptop computer market looks very promising lately.

3. 在零件供应短缺的情况下，公司下半年的营收不看好。
   With a short supply of components, the company's profit earnings for the
   second half of the year do not look good.

 词语辨析

# 1. 制度　体制

制度（名）"system"

1. 每个公司都有不同的财务制度。
   Each company has its own financial system.

2. 教育制度改革已经成为政府的重点工程。
   Reform of the educational system has become one of the government's key
   projects.

3. 制定严格的管理制度是为了提高公司的经营效率。
   Formulating a strict management system is for the purpose of enhancing
   the company's efficiency.

体制（名）"system; structure"

1. 经济体制改革发展了生产力，促进了经济的发展。
   Reform of the economic system has improved productivity and promoted
   the development of the economy.

2. 国有企业效率低下的原因之一是原有的经济体制缺乏市场活力。

One of the reasons for the low efficiency of the state-owned enterprises is that the original economic system lacked market vitality.

3. 中国正在积极推行经济、金融、政治等体制的改革。

China is actively undertaking reforms in economy, finance, and politics.

*Both 制度 and 体制 mean "system." However, 制度 is used at a micro level, whereas 体制 is used at a macro level.*

# 2. 实行　推行

实行（动）"to put into practice or effect; to carry out; to implement"

*实行 means to take action in order to implement or carry out a plan, policy, law, or regulation.*

1. 计划经济体制缺乏效率，因此不能再继续实行下去。

Due to the inefficiency of the planned economic system, it can no longer be implemented.

2. 中国正在实行新的税法。

China is implementing a new tax law.

3. 计划生育政策已经实行一段时间了。

Family planning has been implemented for a period of time.

推行（动）"to carry out; to pursue; to introduce"

*Since 推 means "to push," 推行 refers to policies or regulations that have been pushed to be carried out or to be put into practice.*

1. 公司正在推行新的奖惩制度。

Our company is in the midst of carrying out a new system of rewards and penalties.

2. 中国政府刚刚开始推行计划生育政策时，很多人不能接受。
When the Chinese government first implemented the family planning
policy, many people could not accept it.

# 3. 成为　变为

成为（动）"to become; to turn into"

*成为 is used in a written form. It is a verb and must have a noun as its object.*
*It cannot be used with 了、着, or 过. When 成为 is used as a complement of a*
*resultative verb, 为 can be omitted.*

1. 他已经成为一个很成功的企业家了。
He has become a very successful entrepreneur.

2. 解决下岗职工再就业问题成为热门的话题。
Solving the problem of re-employment for laid-off workers has become a
hot topic.

3. 我们要把中国建设成(为)一个具有中国特色的社会主义国
家。
We should build China into a Socialist country with Chinese
characteristics.

变为（动）"to change; to alter"

*变为 is always followed by a noun or an adjective. It cannot not be used*
*with 了、着, or 过. 变 and 为 can be used separately as "变 ... 为 ..." which*
*means "to change ... into ..."*

1. 技术革新可以把生产方法由低效率变为高效率。
Technological renovation can turn manufacturing methods from low to
high efficiency.

2. 目前很多国有企业已经变为私有企业了。
At present, many state-owned enterprises have been changed into
privately-owned enterprises.

3. 谈判的时候，我们应该变被动为主动。

We should take the initiative (lit. change from passive to active) during the negotiations.

*成为 should not be confused with 变为. 成为 means someone or something develops into another state of being or becomes something else. However, 变为 implies a change from the original quality, form, shape, or condition into a different one. In other words, 成为 means A becomes A' while 变为 means A changes to B.*

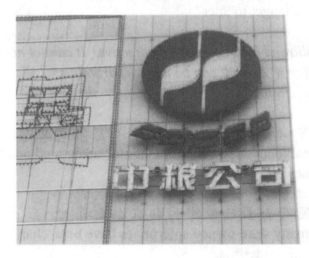

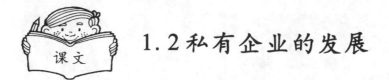 课文

# 1.2私有企业的发展

长期以来，国有企业一直在中国占主导地位，直到1979年改革开放以后，私有经济才开始得到政府的认可。经过20多年的发展，私有企业已取得了令人瞩目的成绩，企业规模也从过去单一的小手工作坊发展成不同规模的公司，其中有些甚至在国外设立了分公司或办事机构。

中国的私有企业有个体、合伙及有限责任公司等多种形式，此外还可以与外资企业组建公司，共同从事建筑、交通、商业及服务等行业。但是，政府不允许私有企业介入必须由国家垄断或涉及国家安全的经济领域。

目前，政府一方面对经营不善、效益不好的国有企业进行改组；另一方面还颁布了新的法规，允许私有企业以承包、租赁、兼并、购买等方式参与对国有企业的改革。一些实力雄厚的私有企业因此不断扩大规模，不仅购买了小型国有企业，甚至还成立了集团公司。

課文

# 1.2 私有企業的發展

長期以來，國有企業一直在中國佔主導地位，直到1979年改革開放以後，私有經濟才開始得到政府的認可。經過20多年的發展，私有企業已取得了令人矚目的成績，企業規模從過去單一的小手工作坊發展成爲不同規模的公司，其中有些甚至在國外設立了分公司或辦事機構。

中國的私有企業有個體、合伙及有限責任公司等多種形式，此外還可以與外資企業組建公司，共同從事建築、交通、商業及服務等行業。但是，政府不允許私有企業介入必須由國家壟斷或涉及國家安全的經濟領域。

目前，政府一方面對經營不善、效益不好的國有企業進行改組；另一方面還頒布了新的法規，允許私有企業以承包、租賃、兼併、購買等方式參與對國有企業的改革。一些實力雄厚的私有企業因此不斷擴大規模，不僅購買了小型國有企業，甚至還成立了集團公司。

# 1.2 The Development of Private Enterprises

Text

For a long time in China, state-owned enterprises played a leading role. Not until the "Reform and Open Door Policy" in 1979, did private enterprises start receiving government approval. After more than twenty years of development, private enterprises have obtained outstanding results. The scope of private business has also expanded from small handicraft workshops to companies of different sizes. Some have even set up foreign subsidiaries and offices overseas.

China's private enterprises take on many forms: sole proprietorships, partnerships, limited liability companies, etc. In addition, private enterprises can also form corporations with foreign companies and carry out business in the construction, transportation, trade, and service industries. However, the government does not allow private businesses to get involved in industries that must remain monopolized by the state or economic realms related with national security.

On one hand, the government is currently re-organizing poorly run, ineffective state-owned enterprises and, on the other hand, is issuing new regulations allowing private enterprises to participate in the reform of state-owned enterprises by means of contract, lease, merger, and acquisition. Some private enterprises with substantial strength have continuously expanded, not only purchasing small state-owned enterprises, but also setting up conglomerates.

在中国，多数私有企业都是从事轻工业、手工业、运输、建筑、商业、饮食和维修等与日常生活有关的生产和服务的小企业。虽然目前有40个私有企业资本超过1200万美元，但是平均<u>注册</u>资金只有6万美元，平均雇佣14人。

在中國，多數私有企業都是從事輕工業、手工業、運輸、建築、商業、飲食和維修等與日常生活有關的生產和服務的小企業。雖然目前有40個私有企業資本超過1200萬美元，但是平均<u>註冊</u>資金只有6萬美元，平均雇佣14人。

In China, most private enterprises are small enterprises engaged in industries related to daily life, such as light industries, handicrafts, transportation, construction, commerce, food service and maintenance. Although there are currently forty private enterprises with capital exceeding US$12 million, the average registered capital (of a private enterprise) is only US$60,000 and the average number of employees is 14.

生词表

| 主导 | 主導 | zhǔdǎo | （形、名） | leading; dominant; guiding principle |
| 认可 | 認可 | rènkě | （动、名） | to approve; to accept; to recognize; approval; acceptance |
| 取得 | 取得 | qǔdé | （动） | to obtain; to gain |
| 令 | 令 | lìng | （动） | to cause; to make |
| 瞩目 | 瞩目 | zhǔmù | （动） | to fix one's eyes on; to focus one's attention on |
| 坊 | 坊 | fáng | （名） | handicraftsman's workplace; workshop |
| 个体 | 個體 | gètǐ | （名、形） | sole proprietorship; individual (enterprise) |
| 合伙 | 合伙 | héhuǒ | （动） | to form a partnership |
| 有限 | 有限 | yǒuxiàn | （形） | limited; finite |
| 组建 | 組建 | zǔjiàn | （动） | to put together (a group); to organize |
| 从事 | 從事 | cóngshì | （动） | to go into (a profession or business); to be engaged in |
| 允许 | 允許 | yǔnxǔ | （动、名） | to permit; to allow; permission |
| 介入 | 介入 | jièrù | （动） | to intervene; to interpose |
| 垄断 | 壟斷 | lǒngduàn | （动、名） | to monopolize; monopoly |
| 涉及 | 涉及 | shèjí | （动） | to involve; to be related to |
| 领域 | 領域 | lǐngyù | （名） | domain; field; territory |
| 改组 | 改組 | gǎizǔ | （动、名） | to reorganize; reorganization |
| 颁布 | 頒布 | bānbù | （动） | to promulgate; to issue |
| 法规 | 法規 | fǎguī | （名） | laws and regulations |
| 承包 | 承包 | chéngbāo | （动） | to contract |
| 租赁 | 租賃 | zūlìn | （动、名） | to rent; to lease; lease |

| 兼并 | 兼併 | jiānbìng | （动、名） | to merge; to annex (territories); merger |
| 雄厚 | 雄厚 | xiónghòu | （形） | ample; substantial; solid; abundant |
| 集团 | 集團 | jítuán | （名） | conglomerate; a number of subsidiary companies |
| 注册 | 註冊 | zhùcè | （动、名） | to register; registration |

# 1. ... 以来（介）"Since ..."

*以来 is placed at the end of a clause to indicate that an action has been occurring or a situation has been in existence since a given point in time. 从，自 or 自从 can be added at the beginning of the clause.*

1. 改革开放以来，中国人民的生活方式有了很大的变化。
   Since the "Reform and Open Door Policy," Chinese people's lifestyles have changed significantly.

2. 自从进入黄梅季节以来，雨就一直下个不停。
   The rain has not stopped since the beginning of the rainy season.

3. 自从引进先进技术以来，我们公司的生产效益就不断提高。
   Since our company brought in the advanced technology, productivity has risen continuously.

4. 自从这两家公司合并以来，营业利润增加了一倍。
   Since these two companies merged, the operating profit has doubled.

# 2. 直到 "up to; until..."

*a.* （一）直到 ... 才 ... *"not until ... (then) ..."* *This pattern is used to express an action or situation that has been continuing without interruption until a new action is taken or a new situation arises.* 直 *is optional.*

1. 我经常在公司见到他，可是（直）到昨天才知道他就是公司的董事长。
   I often saw him at the office, but it was not until yesterday that I knew he was the Director of the Board.

2. 会议（一）直到天黑才结束。
   The meeting did not adjourn until it got dark.

3. 直到经济发展受到严重制约以后，政府才认识到计划经济体制的弊病。
   It was not until economic development had become seriously constrained that the government realized the drawbacks of the planned economic system.

*b.* 从 ... （一）直到 ... *"from ... to ...; from ... up to ..."* *indicates a continuous time span or distance between two places relevant to a certain situation or action. A verb can be placed between* 直 *and* 到 *to indicate that an action or situation extends from one point to another.*

1. 这家公司从筹备一直到开张只用了两个月的时间。
   It only took two months for this company to prepare for the grand opening.

2. 从这条街直到南京西路都是商店。
   There are stores from this street all the way to Nanjing West Road.

3. 丝绸之路从中国一直延伸到欧洲。
   The "Silk Road" starts in China and extends all the way to Europe.

4. 窗帘要是能从天花板一直挂到地上，房间会显得大一些。
   If the drapery can be hung from the ceiling to the floor, the room will seem bigger.

# 3. 令 "to make; to cause"

令（动）*indicates that a person's feelings are caused by a certain reason or condition. If the feeling is a more general phenomenon among a group of people,* 令人 *is used; otherwise a specific person is indicated, e.g.* 令他、令父母, *etc.*

1. 总经理所作的关于公司未来前景的演讲很令人鼓舞。
   People were inspired by the general manager's speech about the company's future prospects.

2. 公司的业务一直令他很失望。
   He has been disappointed by the company's business performance.

3. 他在学术上的成就很令人敬佩。
   His achievement in the academic field is admirable.

# 4. 甚至 "even; even to the point of"

a. 甚至（副）*is used in the second clause to intensify the tone of the expression and it is often accompanied by* 连、还, *or* 都 *before the verb.*

1. 总经理很少管这些杂事，有时候甚至连问都不问。
   The general manager seldom concerns him/herself with such trivial matters; sometimes he does not even bother to ask about them.

2. 有的人整天打麻将，不上班，甚至连家也不顾了。
   Some people play "majiang" all day long, and not only do they not go to work, but they also do not even pay attention to their families.

3. 有些实力雄厚的私有企业不仅跟外企成立合资公司，甚至还购买了国有企业。
   Some privately-owned enterprises with ample strength have not only set up joint ventures with foreign enterprises, but have also (even) purchased state-owned enterprises.

b. 甚至 *is placed at the end of a list of items in order to emphasize the extreme.*

1. 手机不但可以用来打电话、听收音机，甚至还可以上网和收发电子邮件。
   Not only can you make calls and listen to the radio with cellular phones, but you can also get on the Internet to receive and send e-mails.

2. 政府提供良好的投资环境，制定优惠政策，甚至还允许私有企业收购国有企业。
   The government is providing a good environment for investment, setting up favorable policies, and is even allowing privately-owned enterprises to purchase state-owned enterprises.

# 5. 以（介）"with; by means of"

a. 以 *is the written form of* 用 *or* 拿, *indicating the basis or means for an action or behavior, or the capacity in which a person is involved.*

1. 他以优秀的业绩得到了总经理的信任。
   Through his outstanding achievement in the company, he has gained the general manager's trust.

2. 经理以一般员工的身份参与了这次讨论。
   The manager participated in this discussion as an ordinary employee.

3. 他以总公司的名义参加此次国际论坛。
   He participated in the International Forum under his company's name.

b. 以... *occurs in some of the most commonly used four-character idioms that can be applied in business.*

1. 做生意除了会看准时机以外，还需要能够以理服人。
   Besides recognizing good business opportunities, in business one should also have the ability to convince people using good reasons.

2. 人事部门招聘员工时要避免以貌取人的现象。
   The HR department should avoid judging people by their appearance during the recruiting process.

3. 经理以身作则，这个月又是他的业绩最高。
   The manager himself set an example for others; his sales record for this month was again the highest.

c. *The pattern* 以...来说（讲 or 看）*meaning "based on ..., judging from ..." indicates a situation that can be estimated or anticipated based on what has been stated.*

1. 以目前的生产状况来说，今年的产量可望超过往年。
   Based on the present production situation, this year's output can be expected to exceed that of previous years.

2. 以今年的营业额来讲，我们的市场占有率将会远远超过竞争对手。
   Based on this year's sales volume, our company's market share will far exceed our competitors'.

d. *以 ... 来说 also means "for example" as in the following examples:*

1. 现在中国政府鼓励自由选择职业，以大学毕业生来说，以前工作是由国家分配的，现在可以自己作主。
   The Chinese government is now encouraging free employment choice. For example, while college graduates used to be assigned positions by the government, now they can search on their own.

2. 以中、小型规模的企业来说，公司的类型可以是个体、合伙或者是有限责任公司。
   Taking the small and medium sized enterprises as examples, they can be either sole proprietorships, partnerships, or limited liability corporations.

3. 国家减少了对经济的垄断，以私有企业来说，除了可以从事建筑业以外，还可以从事交通或服务行业。

   The government has reduced its economic monopoly. Take privately-owned enterprises for example, aside from being permitted to engage in the construction business, they may also engage in the transportation and service industries.

# 6. 不仅（连）"not only"

不仅 is the formal equivalent of 不但 and is used in the first clause of a sentence. The conjunctions 而且、还、也, or 反而 can be used in the second clause to emphasize that there is something else besides what has been mentioned.

1. 所有出口的货物，不仅要取得出口许可证，还必须办理海关手续。

   All exported goods not only must have export permits, but also must comply with customs procedures.

2. 目前国企面临的困难是不仅要跟外企，而且还要跟私营企业竞争。

   The difficulty currently confronting state-owned enterprises is that they have to compete not only with foreign enterprises, but also with privately-owned enterprises.

3. 这次会谈不仅没有解决问题，反而增加了矛盾。

   The meeting not only failed to solve the problem but, on the contrary, intensified the conflict.

 词语辨析

# 1. 认可 许可 允许

认可（动、名）"to approve; to accept; to recognize; approval; acceptance"

*认可 indicates that an authority in charge approves or gives approval to some request. It can also mean that an authoritative organization gives accreditation or credentials to academic or similar institutions. It usually does not have an object, if it is used as a verb.*

1. 他的研究结果得不到任何公司的认可。
   No company would recognize his research results.

2. 既然领导已经点头认可了，这件事就好办了。
   Since this project has been approved by the boss, it can proceed easily.

3. 如果你念的学校不是政府认可的话，就是得到了文凭也没用。
   If you attend a school that is not accredited, even if you receive a diploma, it will be useless.

4. 这个项目已经得到计划发展部的认可。
   This project has already received the approval of the Planning and Development Division.

许可(动、名)"to permit, to allow (by authorities or by circumstances)"

*许可 can almost be used interchangeably with 允许. However, 许可 is usually used in a written form and for a more formal situation. 许可 also occurs in the compound 许可证 meaning "permit or credentials." 许可证 is often modified by a specific term, e.g. 工作许可证 means "working permit."*

1. 为了避免造成市场垄断，政府没有许可这两家公司的合并计划。

   In order to avoid a monopoly situation, the government did not permit these two companies to merge.

2. 没有得到本公司书面许可，不能以任何形式出售本公司的产品。

   Without obtaining written permission from our company, one cannot sell the company's products by any means.

3. 在许可证没有下来以前，公司就已经开始做筹备工作了。

   Even before the permit was obtained, the company had already begun their preparatory work.

4. 未经许可（允许），不得入内。

   Entry without a permit is forbidden.

允许（动、名） "to permit; to allow; permission"

*允许 is usually used as a verb and can have a verb as its object. In some cases 允许 can be used interchangeably with 许可.*

1. 天气允许（许可）的话，我们可以去湖边烧烤。

   Weather permitting, we can barbecue by the lakeside.

2. 请允许我代表公司向大家道歉。

   Please allow me to apologize to all of you on behalf of the company.

3. 公司不允许员工随意迟到早退。

   The company does not allow employees to be late for work or to leave early.

# 2.领域　领土

领域

*a.* 领域（名）"territory"

*领域 refers to a territory where a nation has the right to exercise its sovereign rights .*

1. 一个国家的领域包括领土、领空、领海以及其它可以行使主权的范围。
   A nation's territory includes its land, air, and sea space as well as the area in which sovereign rights can be exercised.

*b.* 领域（名）"realm; field; sphere"

*领域 refers to areas of a special social activity or academic field. For example, 经济领域、政治领域、文化领域、科学领域、技术领域, etc.*

1. 经济发展起来以后，经济领域的活动也越来越多。
   Since the economy has developed, there are more and more activities in the field of economics.

2. 她在社会科学领域已经取得了令人瞩目的成就。
   Her outstanding achievement in the field of social science has attracted people's attention.

领土（名）"territory"

*It refers to a nation's land area.*

1. 前苏联是世界上领土最大的国家。
   The former Soviet Union was the nation with the largest territory in the world.

2. 每一个国家都可以在自己的领土上行使主权。
   Each country can exercise sovereign rights over its own land.

# 3. 颁布　公布

颁布（动）"to issue; to promulgate"

1. 为了促进私有企业以承包、租赁等方式参与国企改革，中国颁布了各种法律条例。
   In order to encourage private enterprises to become involved in the reform of the state-owned enterprises by means of contracts and leases, the Chinese government has promulgated various laws and regulations.

2. 自从城市扩建以来，政府颁布了许多交通法规。
   Since the city has expanded, the government has issued many traffic regulations.

公布（动）"to announce; to make public"

1. 公司必须每年公布财务报告。
   Companies must publish their financial reports every year.

2. 录取名单将在面试后一星期内公布。
   The list of selected candidates will be announced one week after the interviews have concluded.

3. 公司最近公布了一项裁员计划。
   The company recently announced a lay-off plan.

*Both 颁布 and 公布 have the meaning of "to announce." However, 颁布 is used for laws, orders, and regulations that are issued/promulgated by an authority or government, whereas 公布 refers to publicly announced news, regulations, or rules conveyed through written announcements.*

# 4. 扩大　扩充

扩大（动）"to expand; to enlarge; to enhance"

1. 参加新产品展销会可以扩大产品的知名度。
   Participating in the trade show could enhance the product's brand name recognition.

2. 兼并、购买是企业扩大规模的有效方式。
   Mergers and acquisitions are effective ways for companies to enlarge their scale.

3. 要扩大公司的影响，可以聘请电影或体育明星做广告。
   To promote a company, one can hire movie or sport celebrities to do commercials.

扩充（动） "to expand; to increase; to strengthen"

1. 为了满足市场需要，我们要不断扩充生产设备。
   In order to meet thc needs of the market, we must continuously expand production facilities.

2. 企业要不断发展，就必须扩充管理人才的队伍。
   In order to ensure continuous development, the company must strengthen its management team.

*Both* 扩大 *and* 扩充 *are verbs meaning "to expand." However,* 扩大 *indicates an increase in scope, whereas* 扩充 *indicates an increase in the size or substance of something.*

# 5. 方式　方法

方式（名） "way; fashion; style; pattern"

1. 从前中国人的生活方式是男主外、女主内。
   In the old days, the traditional Chinese lifestyle was for the man to rule the outside world, and the woman to be in charge of the household.

2. 在不同的国家和环境中，需要用不同的沟通方式，才能避免不必要的误会。
   To avoid unnecessary misunderstanding, one needs to adopt different communication styles in different countries or under different circumstances.

3. 买国库券和存银行一样，是最保守的投资方式。
Just like bank deposits, treasury bonds are the most conservative form of investment.

方法（名） "method; ways; means"

1. 解决问题的方法有很多种。
There are many ways to solve a problem.

2. 我们尝试了各种方法才完成这项计划。
This plan was not completed until we had tried various means.

3. 谈判双方还没能找出令大家都满意的付款方法。
The negotiating parties have not yet found a method of payment which is satisfactory to everyone.

*方法 emphasizes methods or means used to solve problems or achieve goals;*
*方式 emphasizes the style, manner, or mode employed in doing things.*

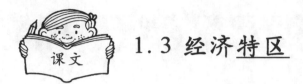

# 1.3 经济特区

　　中国政府为了<u>推进</u>改革开放，从1981年起，在沿海地区<u>先后</u><u>设立</u>了深圳、珠海、厦门、汕头和海南等五个经济特区。1984年底，又将大连、天津、上海、广州等十四个沿海港口工业城市<u>列</u>为沿海对外开放城市，<u>并</u><u>陆续</u>在主要<u>内陆</u>工业城市建立起许多经济技术开发区。<u>以上</u>这些区域经过十多年的开发<u>建设</u>，目前都已成为中国最<u>具</u>活力的经济区域。

　　经济特区和经济技术开发区都是中国政府重点<u>扶植</u>发展的经济区域，目的是为中外投资者提供理想的投资环境，以吸引国外的资金、技术、管理和人才。对来华投资的企业，中国政府不但给予最低的<u>所得税</u>税率，而且还在<u>财政</u>、<u>信贷</u>、资金等方面提供各项优惠政策。

　　经济特区和技术开发区都已成为中国吸引国内外投资的窗口。许多国际知名跨国企业纷纷来华投资设厂，如<u>消费品</u>产业的宝洁、可口可乐、雀巢；<u>制造业</u>的明尼苏达矿业、西门子；<u>制药</u>业的礼来、辉瑞；电子行业的松下、东芝、飞

# 1.3 經濟特區

　　中國政府爲了推進改革開放，從1981年起，在沿海地區先後設立了深圳、珠海、廈門、汕頭和海南等五個經濟特區。1984年底，又將大連、天津、上海、廣州等十四個沿海港口工業城市列爲沿海對外開放城市，並陸續在主要內陸工業城市建立起許多經濟技術開發區。以上這些區域經過十多年的開發建設，目前都已成爲中國最具活力的經濟區域。

　　經濟特區和經濟技術開發區都是中國政府重點扶植發展的經濟區域，目的是爲中外投資者提供理想的投資環境，以吸引國外的資金、技術、管理和人才。對來華投資的企業，中國政府不但給予最低的所得稅稅率，而且還在財政、信貸、資金等方面提供各項優惠政策。

　　經濟特區和技術開發區都已成爲中國吸引國內外投資的窗口。許多國際知名跨國企業紛紛來華投資設廠，如消費品產業的寶潔、可口可樂、雀巢；製造業的明尼蘇達礦業、西門子；製藥業的禮來、輝瑞；電子行業的松下、東芝、飛利浦；通讯行业的摩托罗拉、诺基亚、爱立信、朗讯等，投资项目<u>不胜枚举</u>。

利浦；通訊行業的摩托羅拉、諾基亞、愛立信、朗訊等，投資項目不勝枚舉。

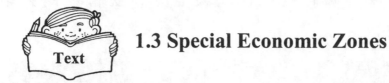

# 1.3 Special Economic Zones

From 1981, in order to promote the "Reform and Open Door Policy," the Chinese government successively set up five "Special Economic Zones (SEZs)" in Shenzhen, Zhuhai, Xiamen, Shantou, and Hainan. At the end of 1984, fourteen coastal ports and industrial cities including Dalian, Tianjin, Shanghai and Guangchou were listed as open cities to foreign investment. "Economic and Technological Development Zones" were also set up one after another in China's main inland industrial cities. After more than ten years of development and build-up, these aforementioned zones have become the most energized economic zones in China.

The "Special Economic Zones" and "Economic and Technological Development Zones" receive great support from the government. The goals in establishing these economic zones are to provide an ideal investment environment for foreign and domestic investors, as well as to attract foreign capital, technology, management, and talented professionals. The Chinese government offers not only the lowest income tax rates, but also preferential policies in terms of finance, credit, and capital to the investing companies.

"Special Economic Zones" and "Economic and Technological Development Zones" have become windows through which China attracts foreign and domestic investment. Many multinational corporations (MNCs) have invested and set up factories in China. For example: Proctor & Gamble, Coca-Cola, and Nescafe in consumer products; 3M and Siemens in manufacturing; Eli Lilly and Pfizer in pharmaceuticals; Panasonic, Toshiba, and Philips in electronics; and Motorola, Nokia, Ericsson, and Lucent in telecommunications, to name just a few.

投资环境包括硬环境和软环境。其中硬环境是指地理位置、自然、交通、能源等基础设施；软环境是指政策、管理水平、人员素质等。因此中国的经济特区都设在经济发达、交通便利、基础设施先进、工业基础雄厚的地区。为了克服目前沿海地区与内地经济差距日益拉大的问题，中国政府已大力推动西部大开发。

背 景 知 識

投資環境包括硬環境和軟環境。其中硬環境是指地理位置、自然、交通、能源等基礎設施；軟環境是指政策、管理水平、人員素質等。因此中國的經濟特區都設在經濟發達、交通便利、基礎設施先進、工業基礎雄厚的地區。爲了克服目前沿海地區與內地經濟差距日益拉大的問題，中國政府已大力推動西部大開發。

*Background Information*

The investment environment is composed of a "hard environment" and a "soft environment." The hard environment refers to the geographic location, natural environment, transportation, energy resources, and other infrastructures. The soft environment refers to policies, management skills, quality of personnel, etc. Thus, China set up its special economic zones in areas that are economically developed, with convenient transportation, advanced infrastructure, and a solid industrial base. To overcome the problems of the widening economic gap between coastal cities and inland areas, the government is vigorously promoting wide development of the western areas.

生词表

| 特区 | 特區 | tèqū | （名） | special zone |
|------|------|------|-------|--------------|
| 推进 | 推進 | tuījìn | （动） | to push forward; to promote |
| 先后 | 先後 | xiānhòu | （副、名） | one after another; successively; being early or late; priority |
| 设立 | 設立 | shèlì | （动） | to establish; to set up |
| 列 | 列 | liè | （动） | to list; to categorize |
| 陆续 | 陸續 | lùxù | （副） | one after another; in succession |
| 内陆 | 內陸 | nèilù | （名） | inland; interior |
| 以上 | 以上 | yǐshàng | （名） | the above mentioned; the foregoing; more than; over |
| 建设 | 建設 | jiànshè | （动） | to build; to construct |
| 具 | 具 | jù | （动） | to have; to possess |
| 扶植 | 扶植 | fúzhí | （动） | to foster; to support |
| 所得税 | 所得稅 | suǒdéshuì | （名） | income tax |
| 财政 | 財政 | cáizhèng | （名） | (public) finance |

| 信贷 | 信貸 | xìndài | （名） | credit and loans |
|---|---|---|---|---|
| 消费品 | 消費品 | xiāofèipǐn | （名） | consumer goods |
| 制造 | 製造 | zhìzào | （动） | to make; to manufacture |
| 制药 | 製藥 | zhìyào | （名） | pharmaceutical (industry) |
| 不胜枚举 | 不勝枚舉 | búshèng méijǔ | （成） | too numerous to mention one by one |
| 指 | 指 | zhǐ | （动） | to refer to; to point at; to point to |
| 位置 | 位置 | wèizhi | （名） | (geographical) location; place; position |
| 能源 | 能源 | néngyuán | （名） | energy resources |
| 基础设施 | 基礎設施 | jīchǔ shèshī | （名） | infrastructure |
| 推动 | 推動 | tuīdòng | （动） | to push forward; to give impetus to |

# 1. … 起

*起 means the starting point of a time or place. It is usually used with 从、由, or 自 to form a prepositional clause.*

1. 从1979年起，中国开始实行对外开放政策。
   China began implementing the "Reform and Open Door Policy" in 1979.

2. 很多成功的企业家都是从十几岁起就开始做生意了。
   Many successful entrepreneurs started doing business in their teens.

3. 买票的人从售票处起开始排队，一直排到马路对面。
The people buying tickets are lined up from the ticket window to the other side of the street.

4. 春节休假由大年夜起一直到正月初五。
The New Year's vacation is from New Year's Eve to January 5<sup>th</sup>.

# 2. 先后

*a.*（名）"being late or early; priority; order"

*When 先后 is used as a noun, it means something is established by sequence or order of importance or urgency.*

1. 请大家按先后顺序排队入场，对号入座。
Everybody, please line up and enter the arena in the order of your arrival, after which, please sit in your assigned seat.

2. 现在公司不再以进公司的先后提拔人才。
Nowadays companies no longer base promotions on seniority.

*b.*（副）"successively"

*先后 can be used as an adverb to indicate that multiple events have happened in succession or things have occurred one after another.*

1. 很多美国跨国公司为了实现全球化战略，先后在欧洲、亚洲和非洲成立了分公司。
For the purpose of globalization, many American MNCs have established branches successively in Europe, Asia, and Africa.

2. 他们公司先后聘请了很多海外留学归来的信息技术人才。
Their company has successively hired many talented people in information technology with overseas educational experience.

3. 许多海外公司先后来经济特区投资建厂。
One after another, many overseas companies have come to invest and set up factories in the special economic zones.

4. 他先后两次被评为优秀员工。
He was elected as an honorary employee twice in a row.

## 3. 以上（名） "the above; the above-mentioned"

1. 以上三点是我个人的意见。
The above three points are my personal opinions.

2. 以上报告的是这个项目的计划。
The report given above is the project plan.

3. 我完全同意以上几位发言人的建议。
I totally agree with the suggestions offered by the previous presenters.

## 4. 起（补）

*起 can be used as a complement to a verb and has various usages. This lesson focuses on the following three types of usages:*

*a. to indicate an action with an upward direction:*

1. 导游举起旗子，领着队伍参观每个景点。
The tour guide, holding a flag, led the tourists to visit each scenic point.

2. 到处是高楼大厦，就是抬起头也看不到屋顶。
There are skyscrapers all over the place and, even if you look up, you would not be able to see the roofs of the buildings.

3. 离起飞只差五分钟了，他提起箱子，拔腿就往登机口跑。
There were only five minutes before the flight's departure, so he picked up his luggage and ran to the gate.

4. 经过八小时的工作，他已经很疲劳了，不过还是提起精神参加培训。

He was tired after working for eight hours, but he still perked himself up to participate in the training session.

*b. to indicate the commencement and continuation of an action:*

1. 如果从明天写起，我们这个周末应该能把这篇报告写完。

If we start writing tomorrow, we should be able to finish the report by this weekend.

2. 主席一走上演讲台，会场上就响起了热烈的掌声。

As soon as the chairperson walked onto the stage, applause broke out throughout the hall.

3. 从总公司派来的美国职员组织起一支业余篮球队，定期和其它球队举行比赛。

The American employees sent from the headquarters have organized an amateur basketball team, which plays against other teams regularly.

*c. When used with verbs such as 想、提, or 说, the complement 起 means "to mention; to bring up something."*

1. 一想起自己做的第一笔生意，他就感慨万分。

Whenever he recalls his first business deal, he gets extremely emotional.

2. 他时常提起自己进公司以来同事们给予他的帮助。

He often mentioned the assistance that his colleagues gave him when he first entered this company.

# 5. 为（介）

*a. The usage of 为 here is to introduce the beneficiary of an action. It means 给 or 替.*

1. 我们公司愿意为顾客提供更好的服务。
   Our company is willing to provide customers with better service.

2. 公司在为员工创造良好的工作环境方面做了许多努力，例如在厂里设立餐厅和医疗室。
   The company has made tremendous effort to create a good working environment for its employees, such as setting up a cafeteria and a clinic inside the factory.

3. 政府的优惠政策为特区发展打下了雄厚的基础。
   The favorable policies enacted by the government laid a solid foundation for the development of the SEZs.

b. *为 (or 为了) is used to indicate the purpose, motive, or intention of an action. This usage was described in Lesson 1.1, Explanation of Terms, Section 3.*

1. 市政府为改变交通状况开辟了公车专行道。
   In order to improve traffic conditions, the city government has opened a special lane for buses only.

2. 为发展经济特区，政府颁布了很多优惠政策。
   The government has issued many preferential policies in order to develop the SEZs.

3. 为了提高员工的素质，公司的人力资源部不断为员工提供各种进修的机会。
   In order to raise the quality of the employees, the Human Resource Department of the company has continuously arranged various opportunities for employees to improve their professional skills.

# 6. 以（连）"in order to; so as to"

a. *In addition to the usage described in Lesson 1.2, Explanation of Terms, Section 5, 以 has another usage in which it is placed at the beginning of the second clause in a complex sentence, to indicate the aim or obligation.*

1. 政府允许经济特区免税引进新设备，以更新技术。
The government has allowed the SEZs to import equipment tax-free in order to replace older technology.

2. 公司决定采用电脑化生产，以减少开支、增进效益。
Our company has decided to implement computerized production in order to reduce expenses and increase efficiency.

3. 目前，很多公司提供住房贷款，以留住优秀技术人才。
At present, many companies offer housing loans in order to retain outstanding technicians.

b. 以便（连）"so that; in order to; so as to; for the purpose of"

*If the second clause in a sentence is an independent clause, then 以便 instead of 以 is used to connect the two clauses. This indicates that what is stated in the first clause will make the action in the second clause easier to be carried out.*

1. 每个项目完成以后应该及时进行评估，以便日后改进。
In order to make future progress, each project should be evaluated as soon as it has been finished.

2. 现在各大公司都设立网站，以便客户及时了解公司状况。
Now many large companies have set up web sites so that their clients can understand them quickly.

3. 我们应该采用廉价劳动力，以便（以）降低生产成本。
We should employ inexpensive labor in order to reduce the cost of production.

# 7. 纷纷

a. （形）"a lot of; numerous and confused"

1. 六月的江南，经常纷纷细雨，下个不停。
In the Jiangnan area in June, it usually drizzles ceaselessly.

2. 关于这项议案，全体组员意见纷纷，无法达成协议。
Regarding the proposal, everyone in the group had different opinions, so they could not reach an agreement.

b.（副）"continuously; one after another"

1. 公司领导纷纷出国考察，以了解当今世界技术发展的最新潮流。
In order to be updated on the new trend in technological development, a great number of company executives have traveled overseas one after another.

2. 参加会议的专家纷纷发表意见，肯定了这项工程的可行性。
Experts who attended the meeting presented their opinions one after another, and confirmed the feasibility of this project.

3. 不仅海外华人，甚至西方的企业家也纷纷来中国投资建厂。
Not only overseas Chinese, but also foreign businessmen have come one after another to China to invest and set up factories.

 词语辨析

# 1. 陆续　连续

陆续（副）"one after another; in succession"

1. 参加论坛的来宾陆续到齐了，下榻的宾馆今天一定很热闹。
   Almost all of the guests of the forum have arrived, so the hotel where they are staying must be very lively today.

2. 经过两年的研究调查，他积累了大批有关中国对外贸易发展的资料，并且陆续在国内外报刊上发表了数篇论文。
   After two years of investigation and research, he has collected a lot of information about China's foreign trade development, and has published several articles in succession in newspapers and magazines at home and abroad.

3. 公司的人力资源部门陆陆续续地举办了一系列有关电子商务的培训班，以提高管理人员的素质。
   The company's HR department has held a series of e-commerce training courses to raise the caliber of the management staff.

连续（副）"continuously; successively; in a row"

1. 在这篇最近发表的文章里，作者连续引用了两个实例来论述自己的观点。
   In the article that he published recently, the author cited two real life examples in succession to illustrate his point of view.

2. 出差回来后，他累得连续睡了整整两天。
   He was exhausted after the business trip and slept for two days straight.

3. 这家公司短短一年内连续收购了五家公司。
   Within the short period of a year, the company acquired five other companies successively.

*Both 陆续 and 连续 refer to the process of a continuous action or situation. However, if the action continues without interruption or cessation, then 连续 is used, and if the action is irregular or has interruptions and cessation, then 陆续 is used. 陆续 can be repeated as 陆陆续续, but 连续 cannot.*

# 2. 成立　建立　设立

*成立、建立, and 设立 are synonyms in their common meaning of "to build; to form; to set up," and are used with such nouns as 公司、学校、医院、研究所 and 研究机构. However, 成立 and 建立 each has an additional meaning as illustrated in the 'b' examples below, whereas 设立 does not have this additional meaning.*

成立

*a.（动）"to establish; to found; to set up; to form"*

*Since 成 has the meaning of "to become" or "to complete," 成立 implies that an organization or an institute has been set up or established from a certain point in time.*

1. 你们公司是在哪一年到中国成立分公司的呢？
   What year did your company go to China to set up a subsidiary?

2. 我们部门最近成立了一个工作小组专门研究这个问题。
   Recently, our department formed a task force to specifically research this problem.

*b.（动）"to establish; to form"*

*成立 is also used to express whether or not a theory, opinion, or argument is tenable or can withstand scrutiny.*

1. 没有根据的论点不能成立。
   Any argument without basis is untenable.

2. "产品周期" 理论已经成立很久了。
The theory of "product cycle" has been established for a long time.

建立 (动) "to build; to establish; to set up"

a. 建立 *refers to building up something over a period of time with effort and perseverance.*

1. 政府准备在全国各地建立老人院。
The government has decided to build nursing homes throughout the country.

2. 在大家的努力下，一所现代化的工厂终于建立了。
With everybody's hard work, a modern factory has finally been built.

3. 父母都希望自己的子女能建立美满的家庭。
All parents hope that their children are able to have (lit. build) happy families of their own.

b. 建立 *can be used with such abstract nouns as* 信心、信誉、友谊、感情、合作关系、友好关系、外交关系、邦交、体系、制度, *etc.*

1. 这家公司倒闭的主要原因是没有建立良好的信誉。
The main reason why the company went bankrupt was that it never established a good reputation.

2. 1949年新中国成立的时候还没有和美国建立外交关系。
When the new China was founded in 1949, it had not yet established diplomatic relations with the U.S.

3. 为了提高工作效率，公司一定要建立完善的管理制度。
In order to increase efficiency, the company must establish a comprehensive management system.

设立 (动) "to establish; to set up"

设立, *similar to* 成立 *and* 建立, *refers to the establishment of organizations such as companies, offices, and foundations.*

1. 中国政府在沿海地区设立了经济特区。
The Chinese government has established SEZs in coastal areas.

2. 为了配合国家开发西部的政策，公司在内地设立了办事处。
In order to cooperate with the government's policy of developing the west, the company has set up a representative office in the inland area.

3. 学校设立奖学金以帮助经济上有困难的学生取得学位。
The school has set up scholarships to help students with financial difficulties obtain degrees.

# 1.4 三 资 企 业

为了促进对外开放，中国政府<u>制定</u>了多项优惠政策，提供了多种投资形式，以吸引外商前来投资。目前，外国公司主要以中外合资、中外<u>合作</u>及外商<u>独资</u>等三种形式在中国进行投资，这三种形式的企业<u>统称</u>为"三资企业"。

中外合资经营企业是外国公司或个人同中国公司在中国<u>境内</u>设立的<u>股份</u>有限公司。双方共同投资、共同经营，按注册资本的投资比例（即股权）<u>分享利润</u>，同时也<u>分担风险</u>及亏损。

中外合作经营企业是外国公司或个人同中国公司在中国境内成立的<u>契约</u>式企业。合作各方的投资或合作条件可以不<u>折算</u>成股份；或者虽折算成股份，但<u>收益</u>分配、风险<u>承担</u>、<u>债务</u>分担及企业<u>终止</u>时<u>剩余</u>财产的分配等可不按投资时的股份比例来决定。

外商称独资企业是外国公司在中国境内设立的企业，全部资金由外国公司投资，所<u>获</u>利润也全部<u>归</u>外国投资者<u>所有</u>。

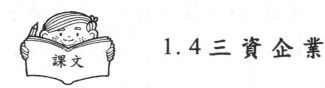

# 1.4 三資企業

爲了促進對外開放，中國政府制定了多項優惠政策，提供了多種投資形式，以吸引外商前來投資。目前，外國公司主要以中外合資、中外合作及外商獨資等三種形式在中國進行投資，這三種形式的企業統稱爲"三資企業"。

中外合資經營企業是外國公司或個人同中國公司在中國境內設立的股份有限公司。雙方共同投資、共同經營，按註冊資本的投資比例（即股權）分享利潤，同時也分擔風險及虧損。

中外合作經營企業是外國公司或個人同中國公司在中國境內成立的契約式企業。合作各方的投資或合作條件可以不折算成股份；或者雖折算成股份，但收益分配、風險承擔、債務分擔及企業終止時剩餘財產的分配等可不按投資時的股份比例來決定。

外商稱獨資企業是外國公司在中國境內設立的企業，全部資金由外國公司投資，所獲利潤也全部歸外國投資者所有。

三资企业的设立为中国引入了先进的技术、新的企业文化和管理经验。它不但加速了中国经济的国际化，而且促进了中国企业经营机制的转换。而对于跨国公司而言，建立三资企业则成为其开展全球经营的一种策略。

　　三資企業的設立爲中國引入了先進的技術、新的企業文化和管理經驗。它不但加速了中國經濟的國際化，而且促進了中國企業經營機制的轉換。而對於跨國公司而言，建立三資企業則成爲其開展全球經營的一種策略。

# 1.4 Three Capital Enterprises

In order to promote the "Reform and Open Door Policy," the Chinese government has formulated many preferential policies and provided many different forms of investment to attract foreign investors. At present, foreign companies' investments in China are primarily of three types: joint ventures, cooperative enterprises, and wholly-owned foreign enterprises. These three types of business operations were given the general name of "Three Capital Enterprises."

A "joint venture" is a limited stock corporation formed in China between a foreign company or individual and a Chinese company. The parties invest and manage (the company) together. According to their registered ratio (i.e. share) of invested capital, the two parties share in the profit, as well as in the risks and losses.

A "cooperative enterprise" is a contractual enterprise established between a foreign company or individual and a Chinese company inside China. The amount of investment or terms of cooperation for each side may not be converted into ownership shares. Even if they are converted to shares, the proportion of shares at the time of investment does not necessarily determine the apportionment of profit, risk, debt responsibilities, and surplus assets when the enterprise terminates.

"Wholly-owned foreign enterprises" are set up by foreign corporations inside China and are completely capitalized by foreign corporate investment. The resulting profits are also completely reverted to the foreign investors.

Establishing the "Three Capital Enterprises" has brought advanced technology, new corporate cultures, and management experience into China. It has not only accelerated the internationalization of the Chinese economy, but has also spurred the transformation of the operational mechanisms of China's enterprises. From the point of view of multinational corporations, establishing the "Three Capital Enterprises" is one kind of strategy for developing global operations.

改革初期，外商缺乏对中国市场的了解，需要中方合作伙伴的协助，因此合资企业成为外商投资的主要形式。90年代，随着中国开放程度的加深，外商希望独享在华投资收益；中国也期望通过设立更多的外商独资企业来提高出口总额。因此，外商独资企业逐渐取代了合资企业，成为外国公司在中国的主要投资方式。

改革初期，外商缺乏對中國市場的了解，需要中方合作夥伴的協助，因此合資企業成為外商投資的主要形式。90年代，隨著中國開放程度的加深，外商希望獨享在華投資收益；中國也期望通過設立更多的外商獨資企業來提高出口總額。因此，外商獨資企業逐漸取代了合資企業，成為外國公司在中國的主要投資方式。

**Background Information**

At the beginning of the reforms, foreign investors lacked understanding of the Chinese market and needed the assistance of Chinese partners. Thus, a joint venture was the primary type of foreign investment. With the deepening of the "Reform and Open Door Policy" in the 90's, more foreign investors wanted to earn profits by themselves, and China also wanted to increase their gross exports by setting up more foreign-owned businesses. Therefore, wholly-owned foreign enterprises gradually replaced joint ventures as the primary investment method of foreign corporations in China.

生词表

| 制定 | 制定 | zhìdìng | （动） | to formulate; to draw up |
|---|---|---|---|---|
| 合作 | 合作 | hézuò | （名、动） | cooperative (enterprises); to cooperate |
| 独资 | 獨資 | dúzī | （名） | wholly owned (foreign enterprise) |
| 统称 | 統稱 | tǒngchēng | （动、名） | to be called by a general name; a general term or name |
| 境内 | 境內 | jìngnèi | （名） | location within the borders of a country |
| 股份 | 股份 | gǔfèn | （名） | share; stock |
| 分享 | 分享 | fēnxiǎng | （动） | to share (joy, rights, etc.) |
| 利润 | 利潤 | lìrùn | （名） | profit |
| 分担 | 分擔 | fēndān | （动） | to share (burden / responsibility) |
| 风险 | 風險 | fēngxiǎn | （名） | risk; hazard |
| 契约 | 契約 | qìyuē | （名） | contract |

| 折算 | 折算 | zhésuàn | （动） | to convert |
|---|---|---|---|---|
| 收益 | 收益 | shōuyì | （名） | profit; earnings (in business) |
| 承担 | 承擔 | chéngdān | （动） | to undertake; to bear; to assume |
| 债务 | 債務 | zhàiwù | （名） | debt; liability |
| 终止 | 終止 | zhōngzhǐ | （名、动） | termination; to terminate |
| 剩余 | 剩餘 | shèngyú | （名、动） | surplus; remainder; to have a surplus |
| 财产 | 財產 | cáichǎn | （名） | property; assets |
| 获 | 獲 | huò | （动） | to gain; to obtain; to achieve |
| 归...所有 | 歸...所有 | guī ... suǒyǒu | （动） | to belong to ... |
| 机制 | 機制 | jīzhì | （名） | mechanism |
| 转换 | 轉換 | zhuǎnhuàn | （动） | to change; to transform |
| 开展 | 開展 | kāizhǎn | （动） | to develop; to launch |
| 全球 | 全球 | quánqiú | （形、名） | global; the whole world |
| 策略 | 策略 | cèlüè | （名） | strategy; tactics |
| 伙伴 | 夥伴 | huǒbàn | （名） | partner; companion |
| 协助 | 協助 | xiézhù | （动、名） | to assist; to help; assistance |
| 额 | 額 | é | （名） | a specified quantity |
| 取代 | 取代 | qǔdài | （动） | to replace; to substitute |

# 1. 为（动 ）

*a.* 为 *is pronounced with the second tone and is the written form of* 做*, meaning "to do, to act." It usually does not have an object, for example,* 为人 *or* 为难*, and often occurs in four-character expressions.*

1. 事在人为，只要努力坚持，总会成功。
It all depends on your effort; as long as you persevere, you will succeed.

2. 敢作敢为是成功创业者的共同点。
The courage to act is a common trait of all successful entrepreneurs.

3. 企业要下决心争第一，管理人员仅仅尽力而为是不够的。
If a company is determined to be number one, merely having managers who do their best may not be enough.

4. 经理的所作所为经常出人意料。
The manager often does the unexpected.

*b.* 为 *"to be called as ... ; serve as ... ; function as ..."*

*In this usage,* 为 *is attached to another verb to form a compound used primarily in written form, e.g.* 称为 *or* 当选为*. The first verb in the compound may or may not have an object.*

1. 上海的外滩被称为 " 东方华尔街 " 。
The Bund in Shanghai is referred to as the "Wall Street of the East."

2. 他当选为董事长以后，公司的经营有了改善。
Since he was elected chairman of the board, the company's operations have improved.

3. 他的武艺高强，拜他为师的人很多。
Because he excels in martial arts, many people honor him as their master.

c. 以 ... 为 ..., *a prepositional phrase, is a written form of* 把 ... 当作 ... *or* 认为 ... 是 ... *meaning to* "regard ... as ... " *or* "consider ... as ... " *or* "take ... as ... "

1. 我们公司这个月销售业绩又是以他为最高。
Again, his sales performance this month is regarded as the highest in our company.

2. 商业在发展的初期是以等价交换为标准的。
Trade in its early developmental stage used equal value bartering as a standard.

3. 日本员工对公司特别忠心，总是以公司为家。
Japanese employees are quite loyal to their companies; they always regard the company as their family.

4. 找实习工作时，应该以获得工作经验为主，以报酬为辅。
When looking for internship opportunities, one should consider gaining work experience as the primary goal, and getting paid as secondary.

# 2. 按（介）"according to; on the basis of"

a. 按 *indicates the reason or justification for a behavior or an action.*

1. 主席按事先拟定的议程主持会议。
The chair proceeded with the meeting according to the previously prepared agenda.

2. 供求双方按商定好的价格成交。
The supplier and buyer made a transaction according to the negotiated price.

b. *按 is used to introduce a condition or procedure upon which an action or behavior is based. The condition implies a quantity or quality, and may be expressed by the use of two adjectives that are paired antonyms (opposite in meaning).*

1. 供应商的名字是按字母的先后顺序排列的。
   The names of the suppliers are listed alphabetically.

2. 合唱团的成员是按身高（身材的高矮）排列的。
   The chorus members stand according to their heights.

3. 体育比赛是按年龄（大小）分组进行的。
   The sports competitions are conducted according to age groups.

c. *按 is also used to indicate the basis for calculating something.*

1. 在中国，长度是按公尺计算的，距离是按公里计算的。
   In China, length is measured in meters; distance is measured in kilometers.

2. 多数英联邦国家都是按英磅计算重量的。
   Weight is measured in pounds in the former British Commonwealth nations.

3. 很多企业为了减轻公司负担，采取"按件计酬"的方式。
   In order to reduce the financial burden, many companies have adopted a system of remuneration by project.

# 3. 或者

a. (副) "perhaps; maybe"

*或者, a synonym of 也许, indicates conjecture or prediction and is placed at the beginning of a sentence.*

1. 你再给他发一次电子邮件，或者还可以跟他联系上。
   Send him another e-mail, and perhaps you can still contact him.

2. 这批商品如果马上降价售出，或者还可以收回一些成本。
   If we can sell this batch of goods at a discount price right away, then perhaps we can still recover some of the costs.

3. 出了差错就应该尽快检讨，或者还可以取得谅解。
   When we make a mistake, we should re-examine ourselves as soon as possible, so that we may perhaps gain forgiveness and understanding.

b. (连) "or; either ... or ..."

*或者 can be used as a conjunction to link two or three elements in a sentence; it always occurs with the last element in the series, and may also occur with the preceding elements, including the first one. The first element may be introduced by 无论、不管, or 不论 to emphasize that all the options are included. When the verb following 或者 is 是, 或 can be used instead of 或者.*

1. 无论是合资，或(者)是独资，都可以享受中国政府所给予的优惠政策。
   Foreign investors can enjoy favorable policies granted by the Chinese government, regardless of whether the investment is made in the form of a joint venture or sole investment.

2. 不管是财务分析，或(者)是市场调查，他都很有经验。
   He has experience in financial analysis as well as in marketing research.

3. 或者赞成、或者反对、或者弃权，投票时必须选择一项。
   Whether you are in favor, opposed, or neutral, you must choose one of them when you vote.

# 4. 来

*来 is an optional element that may be used before a verbal construction or a verb to indicate the purpose of the action.*

1. 现在先由厂长来作工厂简介。
   Now, the plant manager will give a brief overview of the factory.

2. 如果公司以年资(来)决定年终奖金分配的话,会影响年轻员工的进取心。
   Young employees' motivation would be affected if year-end bonuses were based upon seniority within the company.

3. 合资双方发生矛盾时,通常请第三者来调解。
   A third party is usually asked to mediate when conflicts occur between joint venture partners.

4. 当董事会意见不一致的时候,就需要投票表决来决定。
   When a consensus cannot be reached among the board members, then a vote must be taken to reach a decision.

# 5. 所 + V + 的（名）

*所 is used before a transitive verb to form a compound which in turn can be used as an adjective to modify a noun. The noun can be omitted if understood.*

1. 在会议上总经理所提出的计划,因为没有得到半数以上的支持,所以没有通过。
   The plan proposed by the general manager didn't get passed at the meeting because it did not receive majority support.

2. 顾客对商品的质量所提的意见是我们不断改进的动力。
   Feedback from customers regarding quality problems is the impetus for our continuous improvement.

3. 投资者所考虑的因素有很多,其中利润回报和政治风险是他们最关心的。
   There are many factors that investors are concerned about (regarding their investment), among which the most important are returns and political risks.

4. 市民所关心的环保问题一直到现在都没有得到解决。
   To this day, environmental issues which concern the citizens have not been resolved.

5. 我所知道的都告诉你了。
   I have told you everything I know.

# 6. ～化（动）"-ization; -ized; -ify"

a. *化 is used as a suffix, and can be added to a noun, an adjective, or a verb to indicate the transformed state of the word to which it is added.*

1. 年轻化和专业化是目前企业提拔管理人才的重要标准之一。
   Some of the present criteria for promoting managers are age and professional competency.

2. 这个汽车厂的生产流程已经完全做到了电脑化。
   The manufacturing process of this automobile factory has already been completely computerized.

3. 中国的大城市也开始出现人口老龄化的问题。
   The problems of an aging population are beginning to show up in China's big cities.

4. 全球化的优势在于企业能够更有效地利用各地的人力和物力资源降低成本，还能为企业赢得更广阔的市场。
   The advantages of globalization are that companies can use the world's human and material resources more effectively to reduce cost, and they can also attain a wider market.

5. 专家预测再过十年，所有的书籍都将会电子化。
   According to the experts' predictions, all books will be computerized in ten years.

b. *There are only a few monosyllabic adjectives to which 化 is added and can be followed by an object, as shown in the following examples:*

1. 我们要美化城市，绿化街道。
   We should beautify the city and make the streets green.

2. 中国应该深化改革开放，强化领导阵容。
   China should deepen the "Reform and Open Door Policy" and strengthen the leadership team.

3. 政府简化审批程序以后，外商投资企业在中国注册所需要的时间大大地缩短了。
   After the government simplified the approval procedure, time required for foreign-owned enterprises to register in China shortened greatly.

# 7. 对于 ... 而言（来说）（介）"to ...; as for; from the perspective (viewpoint) of ... ; as far as ... is concerned"

*This prepositional structure is used to introduce the people or things from which a point of view or judgment is derived. 对于...而言 is used in written form, whereas 对于...来说 is a colloquial form.*

1. 对于创业者而言，公司上市会带来巨大的经济回报。
   From the perspective of startup entrepreneurs, the initial public offering will bring great financial returns.

2. 对于海外投资来说，政治风险分析是可行性研究的一部分。
   For foreign investors, political risk analysis is part of feasibility studies.

3. 对于跨国公司而言，结合全球化和本地化是他们获得最高经济效益的经营策略。
   As far as MNCs are concerned, the combination of globalization with localization is their management strategy for maximizing profit.

# 8. 则（副）"however; on the other hand"

*a. 则 is used in the second clause of a compound sentence to form a contrast with the first clause. It has the same meaning as 却.*

1. 这项合资计划看起来可行，实行起来则（却）困难重重。
   This joint venture project seems feasible; however, there are many difficulties in its implementation.

2. 北方已是冰天雪地，南方则（却）还是温暖如春。
   The north is already covered with snow; whereas, the south is still as warm as spring.

b. 则 *is also used in the second clause of a compound sentence to indicate the result derived from the reason or condition stated in the first clause. It has the same meaning as* 就.

1. 如果对产品质量控制不严的话，公司的声誉则(就)有可能受到影响。
   Improper control of product quality could ruin a company's reputation.

2. 如果利润分配不当，合资双方的关系则(就)很难维持。
   The relationship of the joint venture partners could be jeopardized when profits are not properly divided between them.

3. 如果得不到这笔贷款，公司则(就)无法继续运行。
   Without the bank loan, the company will not be able to continue its operations.

4. 资金运转不灵，轻则影响公司运行，重则导致公司破产。
   Cash flow difficulties could, at the very least, affect the company's operations or, in the worst case, lead to bankruptcy.

# 9. 其（代）

其 *is used in written form and not used at the beginning of a sentence, but within a sentence referring to someone or something just mentioned. It has the following usages.*

a. *to replace 'he' 'she' 'it,' or 'they'*

1. 既然美方代表已经签了意向书，就该促其尽早签合同。
   Since U.S. representatives have already signed the letter of intent, we should urge them to sign the contract ASAP.

2. 这个计划很理想，我们应该努力促其实现。
   This plan is very good, and we should work hard to put it into effect.

*b. to replace 'his' 'her' 'its,' or 'their'*

1. 政府在特区制定各项优惠政策，其目的是为了吸引外资。
   The government has formulated several preferential policies towards special zones, with the purpose of attracting foreign investments.

2. 政府有时会限制大公司的行为，其目的是保证市场自由竞争。
   The government sometimes will restrain large companies' behavior and the purpose is to guarantee free competition in the market.

3. 为减轻其财务负担，很多企业都采用按项目付款的方式。
   In order to reduce their financial burden, many companies have adopted the method of project-based pay.

4. 因为技术进步，原油的利用率已达到90%以上，可说是物尽其用。
   Thanks to the improvement in technology, the ratio of utilization of crude oil has reached over 90%, which could be considered maximum utilization.

*c. to replace "that" or "that one"*

1. 有其父，必有其子。
   Like father, like son.

2. 那家公司逃税的传闻经税务局调查证实确有其事。
   The rumor that the company evaded taxes was proven to be true after an investigation was conducted by the Tax Bureau.

 词语辨析

# 1. 形式　形状

形式（名）"form; shape"

1. 虽然这家公司花了很多钱做广告和装潢，可是这些都是形式而已，实际上经营情况还是一直不佳。
   The company has spent a lot of money on advertising and remodeling; however, these are just external changes.  In reality, the company's performance has remained lackluster.

2. 通过各种民间的交流形式增进两国人民的了解。
   Through different forms of non-governmental exchange, understanding between the people of the two countries will be enhanced.

3. 这次周年庆改用鸡尾酒会的形式。
   This time, the annual party will be held in the form of a cocktail party.

形状（名）"form; appearance; shape"

1. 桂林每--座山的形状都不一样。
   The shape of each and every mountain in Guilin is different.

2. 我们会照你所要求的形状制作这些玩具。
   We will manufacture these toys according to the shape that you requested.

*Both 形式 and 形状 mean "form; shape." However, the former has a more general scope than the latter. 形式 can be used for both concrete and abstract things, i.e. 表演形式 or 动画形式, whereas 形状 can only be used for concrete things to indicate the appearance or shape of things*

## 2. 分享　分担

分享（动）"to share (joy, rights, etc.)"

1. 成功的快乐应该和同事们一起分享。
   The joy of success should be shared with colleagues.

2. 企业合并的结果是分享信息和增加投资效益。
   The result of mergers is to enable companies to share information and increase profitability.

分担（动）"to share (responsibility, burden, etc.)"

1. 现代家庭大都是双职工家庭，家务事需要由夫妇两人一起分担。
   In modern times when both the husband and wife have jobs, housework should be shared by both of them.

2. 展销会的费用是由参展公司分担的。
   The cost of the trade exhibition is shared by the participating companies.

3. 合资企业由合资方分担经营风险。
   In joint ventures, the operating risks are shared by the joint venture partners.

*Both 分享 and 分担 mean to share. However, 分享 is to share a joyful thing such as happiness, victory, or accomplishments.  分担 is to share a burden such as worry, debt, or responsibility.*

## 3. 对于　对

对于（介）

*This prepositional structure is used to introduce people, things, situations, or actions which are under discussion.  The structure can be placed before or after the subject of a sentence.*

1. 由于刚受过培训，他对于(对)这种操作程序非常熟悉。
   Due to the training he has just received, he is very familiar with the operation of this program.

2. 对于（对）公司的财务状况，总经理十分担心。
   The general manager was very worried about the financial situation of the company.

3. 改革开放政策对于（对）中国的经济发展有很大的影响。
   The "Reform and Open Door Policy" has had a major impact on the development of China's economy.

4. 对于长期为公司作出贡献的人，公司都会奖励他们，让他们将来都有可能当上公司的高层经理。
   For those who have contributed to the company, the company will reward them with opportunities to become higher level managers in the future.

对于 *can be used interchangeably with* 对 *in the above examples; however, the following usages of* 对 *cannot be replaced by* 对于.

对

1. 在工作的时候，总经理对员工特别严格认真；下班后则平易近人。
   At work, the manager is very strict and serious toward the employees; after work, however, he is a very approachable person.

2. 总经理对他最信任，只有请他去游说才会管用。
   Since the general manager only trusts him, it will only work if we ask him to sell the idea.

3. 在商店里退货的时候需要对收据。
   When returning merchandise to a store, one needs to have the receipt for verification.

4. 我们出门之前先对一下表。
   Let's synchronize our watches before we leave.

5. 他对我点头说，"你说对了。"
   He nodded to me and said, "You are right."

# 第二章

# 金融发展

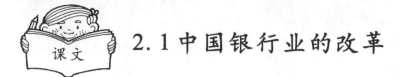

# 2.1中国银行业的改革

银行业是一国金融体系中最重要的组成部分。在以前的计划经济体制下，中国的银行业完全由政府垄断，银行仅仅承担执行国家财政和金融政策的任务，商业银行的功能很小，所以在经济发展中对企业没有真正起到促进及监督的作用。

1993年，中国政府对银行体制进行了改革。这次改革的重点是分离银行的政策职能与商业职能，从而使银行在中国经济中发挥更大的作用。

目前，中国的银行体系主要包括中央银行、政策性银行和商业银行。中国人民银行是中央银行，其职能是协助国务院制定国家金融政策，确定利率和贴现率等。政策性银行包括国家开发银行、中国农业发展银行和中国进出口银行。这些银行主要承担政策性职能，扶持农业政策，提供出口支持，以及对国家大型项目进行融资。商业银行包括中国工商银行、中国建设银行、中国银行和中国农业银行以及其它一些地方性银行和股份制银行。这些商业银行自主经营，自负盈亏。

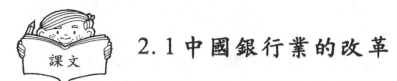

# 2.1中國銀行業的改革

銀行業是一國金融體系中最重要的<u>組成</u>部分。在以前的計劃經濟體制下，中國的銀行業完全由政府壟斷，銀行僅僅承擔<u>執行</u>國家財政和金融政策的<u>任務</u>，商業銀行的功能很小，所以在經濟發展中對企業沒有真正起到促進及<u>監督</u>的作用。

1993年，中國政府對銀行體制進行了改革。這次改革的重點是<u>分離</u>銀行的政策<u>職能</u>與商業職能，從而使銀行在中國經濟中<u>發揮</u>更大的作用。

目前，中國的銀行體系主要包括中央銀行、政策性銀行和商業銀行。中國人民銀行是中央銀行，其職能是協助<u>國務院</u>制定國家金融政策，<u>確定</u>利率和<u>貼現率</u>等。政策性銀行包括國家開發銀行、中國<u>農業</u>發展銀行和中國進出口銀行。這些銀行主要承擔政策性職能，<u>扶持農業政策</u>，提供出口支持，<u>以及</u>對國家大<u>型項目</u>進行<u>融資</u>。商業銀行包括中國工商銀行、中國建設銀行、中國銀行和中國農業銀行以及其它一些地方性銀行和股份制銀行。這些商業銀行自主經營，<u>自負盈虧</u>。

# 2.1 China's Banking Reforms

Banking is the most important sector of the financial system in any country. Formerly, under China's planned economy, the government exercised complete control over the banking sector. Banks were only responsible for the administration of the country's finances and financial policy. Commercial banking played a minimal role. Therefore, commercial banking did not play much of a promotional or supervisory role to enterprises in the course of economic development.

The Chinese government instituted banking reforms in 1993. The principal objective of these reforms was to separate the banking sector's functions with respect to policy and commerce, thus leveraging the role of banks in the Chinese economy.

Currently, the banking sector is divided into three banking systems: the central bank, policy-making banks, and commercial banks. The People's Bank of China is the nation's central bank. Its primary role is to assist the State Council in implementing national financial policy. It is responsible for controlling interest and discount rates. Policy banks include the State Development Bank, the Agricultural Development Bank of China, and the Import and Export Bank of China. These banks are primarily responsible for implementing (government) policies, supporting agricultural policies, and supporting exports, as well as providing major national projects with loans. Commercial banks include the Industrial and Commercial Bank of China, the Construction Bank of China, the Bank of China, and the Agricultural Bank of China, as well as several regional banks and joint-stock banks. Commercial banks operate independently and are solely responsible for their own profit or loss.

中国政府从1995年开始允许外国银行在华设立分行。象摩根·斯坦利、花旗银行、德意志银行都是最早进入中国市场的外资银行。起初，外资银行只能开展外币业务。随着改革的加深，目前已有多家外资银行<u>获准</u>经营人民币业务。

中國政府從1995年開始允許外國銀行在華設立分行。象摩根·斯坦利、花旗銀行、德意志銀行都是最早進入中國市場的外資銀行。起初，外資銀行只能開展外幣業務。隨著改革的加深，目前已有多家外資銀行<u>獲准</u>經營人民幣業務。

In 1995, the Chinese government began to permit foreign banks to establish branches in China. Morgan Stanley, Citibank, and Deutsche Bank were among the first foreign banks to move into the Chinese market. Initially, foreign banks were permitted to handle foreign currency transactions only. As reforms progressed, a number of foreign banks obtained permission to handle *Renminbi* transactions as well.

# 生词表

| 组成 | 組成 | zǔchéng | （动） | to form; to make up; to compose |
| 执行 | 執行 | zhíxíng | （动） | to implement; to carry out |
| 任务 | 任務 | rènwù | （名） | mission; assignment; task; job |
| 监督 | 監督 | jiāndū | （动） | to supervise; to control |
| 分离 | 分離 | fēnlí | （动） | to separate |
| 职能 | 職能 | zhínéng | （名） | function (of a person, thing, organization, etc.) |
| 发挥 | 發揮 | fāhuī | （动） | to bring into play; to give free rein to |
| 国务院 | 國務院 | guówùyuàn | （名） | the State Council (of China) |
| 确定 | 確定 | quèdìng | （动、形） | to determine; to decide; to confirm; definite; fixed |
| 贴现率 | 貼現率 | tiēxiànlǜ | （名） | discount rate |
| 农业 | 農業 | nóngyè | （名） | agriculture; farming |
| 扶持 | 扶持 | fúchí | （动） | to support |
| 以及 | 以及 | yǐjí | （连） | and; as well as, along with |
| 项目 | 項目 | xiàngmù | （名） | project; item |
| 融资 | 融資 | róngzī | （名） | financing; a loan |
| 自负盈亏 | 自負盈虧 | zìfù yíngkuī | （词组） | to assume sole responsibility for profit or loss |
| 获准 | 獲准 | huòzhǔn | （动） | to be permitted; to be allowed |

# 1. 仅（副）"only; merely; no more than ..."

a. 仅, *the written form of* 只, *is used to indicate that the item mentioned is within the limits of a certain scope or quantity.*

1. 这些意见，仅供参考。
   These suggestions are only for your reference.

2. 我们公司有很多高阶层经理，可是执行主管仅有一人。
   There are many scnior managers in our company, but there's only one CEO.

3. 生产流程完全电脑化后，仅二十分钟就可以组装一部汽车。
   Since the production process was completely computerized, it takes only twenty minutes to assemble a car.

b. 仅 *is also used before a noun or a noun phrase to indicate that the item mentioned is a special example.*

1. 制药公司以开发新产品为主，所以仅研发人员就占公司员工的百分之六十以上。
   Pharmaceutical companies emphasize new product development; therefore, R&D personnel alone often account for more than 60% of all employees.

2. 抚养孩子开销不少，仅教育费用就会占去家庭开支的三分之一。
   It costs a lot to raise children, and education expenses alone could account for one-third of household expenses.

c. 仅仅 *is the same as* 仅, *but the expression is much stronger.*

1. 仅仅去了两次，他对中国的投资情况就有了相当的了解。
   After visiting China only twice, he had already gained a fairly good understanding of the Chinese investment environment.

2. 他仅仅用了两个星期就完成了公司下半年度的预算方案。
   It took him only two weeks to prepare the company's budget for the second half of the year.

3. 董事会仅仅是表决机构，它不直接参与公司的日常运作。
   The board is only a voting body, and it isn't directly involved in the company's daily operations.

4. 你的可行性报告仅仅是一种预测，实际的情况还有待进一步证实。
   Your feasibility report is only a forecast, and the reality of the situation is yet to be determined.

# 2. 在 ... 中 "in the middle of ..."

在 ... 中 *indicates a certain time, place, scope, process, or condition in which an action occurs or a status exists.*

1. 在谈判过程中，会场气氛一直很融洽。
   An amicable atmosphere was maintained throughout the negotiation process.

2. 在犹豫不决中，我们失去了一次进入市场的好时机。
   We lost a great market-entry opportunity due to hesitation.

3. 他的性格特别坚强，就是在逆境中也从不轻易放弃。
   He has a very strong character, and he does not give up easily even under adverse circumstances.

4. 有关这笔坏帐的对策，银行各部门都在讨论中，所以还无法对外发布。

The decision on how to deal with this bad loan cannot be announced yet because the various departments of the bank are still in the process of discussing the issue.

# 3. 起

*In addition to the usage discussed in the Lesson 1.3, Explanation of Terms, Sections 1 and 4, 起 can also be used as follows:*

*a. When used in the pattern 起...作用, 起 is a verb meaning "发生、发挥." 起 can also have 到 or 了 as a verb complement and the pattern is used as a predicate in a sentence meaning "to play a ... role."*

1. 设立经济特区对中国的经济发展起了很大的作用。
Establishing SEZs had a strong impact on the development of the Chinese economy.

2. 降低利率，可以起到刺激消费的作用。
Lowering interest rates can stimulate consumer spending.

3. 过时的款式，就是降低价格也起不到促销的作用。
Lowering prices would not be an effective way to promote dated fashions.

*b. In the following examples, 起 means 发生 "to appear; to arise."*

1. 刚出门的时候天气还晴朗，突然起了一阵风，下起雨来了。
The weather was fine when I left the house, but then suddenly it became windy and started to rain.

2. 自从被骗以后，他对什么人都起疑心。
Ever since he was cheated, he has become suspicious of everyone.

3. 出国两年，他的人生观起了很大的变化。
Living overseas for two years has changed his outlook on life.

*c. The meaning of* 起 *in the following examples is* 长出 *"to develop something (on the body)."*

1. 空调开的太冷，他起了一身的鸡皮疙瘩。
   He got goose bumps all over his body when the air conditioner was turned up too much.

2. 他摔了一跤，头上起了个大包。
   He fell and got a huge bump on his forehead.

3. 天气湿热，身上很容易起痱子。
   When the weather is hot and humid it is easy to get a heat rash.

*d.* 起 *is also used as a measure word for incidents, cases, etc.*

1. 律师通常会同时处理三、四起案件。
   A lawyer usually handles three to four cases at a time.

2. 这条街路面狭窄，几乎每天都会发生几起交通事故。
   The street is very narrow, and several traffic accidents occur here practically every day.

3. 这起意外事件给公司带来了巨大的经济损失。
   This unexpected accident brought about a huge financial loss for the company.

# 4. 使 "to make (people) become; to cause to be or become; to enable"

*a.* 使 *is the written form of* 让 *or* 叫. 使 *can be replaced by* 让 *or* 叫, *except in imperative sentences. It must be used in a pivotal sentence and it cannot be used as an independent verb. The negative marker* 不 *should be placed before the main verb or adjective.*

1. 虚心使人进步，骄傲使人落后。
   Modesty leads to advances, while conceit leads one to fall behind.

2. 他的所作所为经常使我们感到意外。
What he does often surprises us.

3. 经理的过分要求使许多职员无法忍受。
The staff cannot tolerate the manager's excessive demands.

4. 提供良好的售后服务是使客户满意，从而提高对产品忠诚度的有效办法。
Providing good after-sales service is an effective way of satisfying customers and maintaining brand loyalty.

*b. 使 is used as a verb meaning 用 "to use."*

1. 日本的家用电器非常好使，所以在世界各国都很畅销。
Japanese electronic appliances sell well around the world because they are very user-friendly.

2. 我向你使眼色的时候，你就起身告辞。
When I give you the sign with my eyes, you get up and say goodbye.

3. 电脑技术发展迅速，经常是使用不到一年就得更新换代。
Computer technology develops so quickly that computers usually need to be upgraded in less than a year.

# 5. 随着(介、副) "following the event of; accordingly; as a result of"

*随着 has several usages, including the following:*

*a. To indicate that an event occurs as a result of another event.*

1. 随着市场的逐步成熟，顾客对产品的要求也越来越高。
As the market matures, customers' expectations of products increase steadily.

2. 随着金融体制改革的不断深入，中国政府开始逐步允许外资银行开展人民币业务。
   As banking reform in China continues to progress, the Chinese government has gradually begun to permit foreign banks to conduct RMB services.

3. 随着互联网技术的发展，无纸作业开始成为公司办公的主要方式。
   As Internet technology develops, the paperless office is becoming a reality.

b. *To indicate that an action occurs right after another has finished.*

1. 他喝完了一杯果汁，随着又喝了一杯咖啡。
   He drank a cup of coffee right after he finished a glass of juice.

2. 一阵雷电过后，随着就起了一场暴风雨。
   A heavy rainstorm followed the thunder and lightning.

3. 大通银行公布降息一个百分点以后，其它银行也随着纷纷调低了利率。
   As soon as Chase lowered the interest rate by one point, other banks followed suit.

c. *To indicate that one action follows another in the same direction.*

1. 大会主席进入会场以后，媒体工作人员也随着进入了会场。
   The media followed the chairperson into the conference room.

2. 比赛开始以后，观众的视线随着选手发出的球左右移动。
   After the game started, the audience's eyes moved back and forth following the ball being hit by the players.

3. 他也随着人潮赶去出事地点看到底发生了什么事。
   He followed the others to the scene of the accident to find out what had happened.

 词语辨析

# 1. 以及　及

以及（连）"and; as well as"

*a. The order of items listed is based on their relative importance. 以及 can be replaced by 及 in the following examples.*

1. 美国银行的服务一般包括支票存款、储蓄存款、结算以及（及）各种贷款。
   American bank services usually include checking accounts, savings accounts, settlements, and loans.

2. 现代通讯有固定通讯、移动通讯以及（及）卫星通讯等三种主要方式。
   Fixed, mobile, and satellite are the three primary modes of modern communication.

3. 这家电脑商店销售硬件、软件以及（及）其它配套元件。
   This computer store sells hardware, software, and other computer parts.

4. 在国民经济中应该优先发展水、电、路以及（及）其它各项基础设施。
   The development of water, electricity, roads, and other infrastructures must be given priority in the national economy.

*b. Items are listed according to the order of their occurrence.*

1. 出差回来的第二天，他就向公司详细汇报了此次出差去了哪些城市、拜访了些什么客户，以及谈了些什么项目。
   The day after returning from his business trip, he reported to his company with respect to where he had gone, what clients he had visited, and what projects they had discussed.

2. 从报考托福到申请学校，以及办理出国签证，你总共花了多少钱？

How much did you spend all together to take the TOEFL exam, apply to educational institutions, and arrange a visa?

3. 在会议开始之前，首先要做的是办理住宿、报到以及领取议程 。

Before the conference starts, one must first check-in, then register and get the conference program.

c. 以及 *also can be used to distinguish different categories.*

1. 这家商店卖的饮料包括茶、咖啡等热饮料以及果汁、可乐、雪碧等冷饮料。

This store sells hot beverages such as black tea, hot chocolate, and coffee, as well as cold drinks such as juice, Coke, and Sprite.

2. 跨国公司招聘人才的条件是：硕士以上学历、专业技术、三年以上的工作经验，以及懂汉语和愿意出差，最好还有居住海外的经验。

Most multinational corporations recruit staff who have the following qualifications: possess a masters degree or above, have professional skills, have three or more years of work experience, are fluent in Chinese, are willing to travel, and preferably have lived overseas previously.

及（连）

*The third person possessive pronoun* 其 *can follow* 及 *meaning "and his/her/their..."*

1. 八国元首及其随从出席了这次高峰会议。

Leaders from eight countries and their associates attended this summit.

2. 两位总统候选人及其助理们先后来到本地开展竞选活动。

The two presidential candidates and their campaign aides have come here one after another to campaign.

3. 公司总裁、总经理及其夫人们都参加了合资工厂的开工典
   礼。
   The president and general manager of the company and their wives
   attended the grand opening ceremony of the joint venture plant.

*Both* 以及 *and* 及 *are used in the written form to link a series of items that are listed according to their order of occurrence and relative importance, with the more important ones usually being listed first. However,* 以及 *can also be used to link clauses with a comma separating them, whereas* 及 *cannot have a comma before it.*

# 2. 开展　展开　发展

开展（动）"to develop; to launch"

1. 可行性报告完成后，这项计划就可以很快开展起来了。
   As soon as the feasibility report is finished, we can begin the project.

2. 员工的素质太差，很多活动开展不起来。
   Due to the poor quality of the employees, many activities cannot be
   launched.

3. 为了增强企业凝聚力，我们公司经常开展文娱活动。
   In order to increase cohesiveness, our company often holds entertainment
   activities.

展开（动）"to unfold; to launch; to carry out; to set off"

展 *means "to open; to unfold," and* 展开 *refers to opening something which has been scrolled up lengthwise, such as* 展开一幅画. 展开, *meaning "to carry out," also uses nouns such as* 讨论、战斗, *and* 竞赛 *as its objects.*

1. 会议的开幕式完毕后，会员们立刻分成了小组并展开了激烈
   的讨论。
   After the opening ceremony of the conference, delegates immediately
   divided into subcommittees and began their intense discussions.

2. 各项竞赛已全面展开了。
All contests are now in full swing.

3. 让贫穷地区的孩子也能接受教育的 " 希望工程 " 在中国全面展开了。
The "Hope Project," which develops educational opportunities for children in poor areas, has been launched throughout China.

发展 ( 动 ) "to develop; to expand"

1. 计划经济是阻碍经济发展的主要原因。
The planned economy was the main hindrance to economic development.

2. 由于没有及时采取对策，事情才会发展到不可收拾的地步。
Due to the delay of the adoption of the counter measure, things have been unmanageable.

3. 开发内地的目的是为了解决经济发展不平衡的问题。
The means of solving the unbalanced economic development is to develop the inner region.

*开展 means to start developing something from a small scale to a large scale.*
*展开 is to develop, launch, or begin a large scale project or activity.*
*发展 describes the process of advancement and change, with an emphasis on the change. 展开、开展, and 发展 can have an object or a complement. (Note: 展开 cannot have 起来 or 下去 as a complement.)*

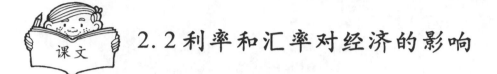

# 2.2 利率和汇率对经济的影响

利率和汇率是两个重要的经济<u>指标</u>，它们既受市场规律的<u>约束</u>，也受政府政策的影响，而两者的变化又会对经济<u>产生</u>重要的影响。

利率影响<u>货币</u>的价格。利率上升，会<u>提高</u>企业的融资成本，增加投资负担，从而降低经济的<u>增长</u>速度；利率下降会降低储蓄欲望、促使<u>居民</u>提高消费，从而加快经济的增长速度。所以每<u>当</u>经济<u>萧条时</u>，政府就下调利率，以<u>鼓励</u>更多的资金进入市场，刺激消费；<u>反之</u>，如果经济发展过热，政府往往会提高利率，<u>紧缩银根</u>，以冷却过热的经济，<u>抑制</u>通货膨胀。

汇率对一个国家经济的发展也起着非常重要的作用。<u>首先</u>，汇率的<u>变动</u>会影响一国的资本<u>流动</u>。比如，当本国货币<u>价值</u>下降时，为<u>防止</u>货币<u>贬值</u>的损失，国内资本会被投资者<u>调往</u>他国。<u>其次</u>，汇率变动对一国的对外贸易也有巨大的影响。当本币贬值时，以外币表示的出口商品价格降低，从而有助于扩大出口；当本币<u>升值</u>时，以本币表示的进口商品价格降低，从而起到扩大进口的作用。最后，

# 2.2 利率和匯率對經濟的影響

利率和匯率是兩個重要的經濟<u>指標</u>，它們既受市場規律的<u>約束</u>，也受政府政策的影響，而兩者的變化又會對經濟<u>產生</u>重要的影響。

利率影響<u>貨幣</u>的價格。利率上升，會<u>提高</u>企業的融資成本，增加投資負擔，從而降低經濟的<u>增長</u>速度；利率下降會降低儲蓄欲望、促使<u>居民</u>提高消費，從而加快經濟的增長速度。所以每當經濟<u>蕭條</u>時，政府就下調利率，以<u>鼓勵</u>更多的資金進入市場，刺激消費；<u>反之</u>，如果經濟發展過熱，政府往往會提高利率，<u>緊縮</u> <u>銀根</u>，以<u>冷卻</u>過熱的經濟，<u>抑制</u>通貨膨脹。

匯率對一個國家經濟的發展也起著非常重要的作用。<u>首先</u>，匯率的<u>變動</u>會影響一國的資本<u>流動</u>。比如，<u>當本國</u>貨幣<u>價值</u>下降<u>時</u>，為<u>防止</u>貨幣<u>貶值</u>的損失，國內資本會被投資者<u>調往</u>他國。<u>其次</u>，匯率變動對一國的對外貿易也有巨大的影響。當本幣貶值時，以外幣表示的出口商品價格降低，從而有助于擴大出口；當本幣<u>升值</u>時，以本幣表示的進口商品價格降低，從而起到擴大進口的作用。最後，如果汇率<u>波动</u>太大，则会增加进出口的风险，从而影响对外贸易的发展。

利率和汇率又有密切的联系。当一国利率上升时，投资<u>回报</u>率会<u>随之</u>提高，因而造成在国际货币市场上对<u>该国</u>货币的需求增大，从而使该国汇率上升。如何<u>运用</u>好这两个经济指标，是<u>控制</u>经济发展速度，保证经济良好<u>运行</u>的<u>关键</u>。

如果匯率波動太大，則會增加進出口的風險，從而影響對外貿易的發展。

利率和匯率又有密切的聯系。當一國利率上升時，投資回報率會隨之提高，因而造成在國際貨幣市場上對該國貨幣的需求增大，從而使該國匯率上升。如何運用好這兩個經濟指標，是控制經濟發展速度，保證經濟良好運行的關鍵。

# 2.2 The Influence of Interest Rates and Foreign Exchange Rates on the Economy

Interest rates and foreign exchange rates are two important economic indexes. They are restrained by both market forces and government policies. Changes in these two rates will have a substantial impact on the economy.

Interest rates influence the price of a currency. A rise in interest rates leads to an increase in financing cost and investment burden, thereby reducing the pace of economic growth. A drop in interest rates reduces the impetus to save and encourages spending, thereby speeding up economic growth. During economic recession, the government may lower interest rates to encourage more capital injection into the market and stimulate consumer spending. On the other hand, if the economy is overheated, the government will increase interest rates to tighten up the money market, in order to cool off the overheated economy and put a check on inflation.

Foreign exchange rates play a vital role in a nation's economy. First, the fluctuation of foreign exchange rates influences a country's capital flow. For example, if the domestic currency depreciates, local investors are likely to transport their capital to foreign countries to prevent losses from depreciation. Secondly, fluctuations in foreign exchange rates exert a major influence on a nation's foreign trade. When the domestic currency depreciates, the price of export goods denominated in foreign currency will decrease, which will expand exports. When domestic currency appreciates, the price of import goods denominated by domestic currency will decrease, which will lead to more imports. Finally, if the foreign exchange rate fluctuates with too much volatility, the risk in the import-export business will increase, and the development of international trade will be affected.

Interest rates and foreign exchange rates are tightly related. When interest rates in a country increase, investment returns will increase, and the demand for that country's currency will increase, thereby driving up its exchange rate. Utilizing these two indexes well is the key to controlling the economic growth rate and guaranteeing good economic operation.

中国货币，即人民币，目前还不能在国际市场自由兑换。国家对外汇控制严格，虽然经常项目下人民币已经放开，但在资本项目下如要换汇，仍须向国家及地方外汇<u>管理局</u>（简称外管局）申请，<u>获得</u>批准后才可以兑换所需的外汇。

中國貨幣，即人民幣，目前還不能在國際市場自由兌換。國家對外匯控制嚴格，雖然經常項目下人民幣已經放開，但在資本項目下如要換匯，仍須向國家及地方外匯<u>管理局</u>（簡稱外管局）申請，<u>獲得</u>批准後才可以兌換所需的外匯。

The Chinese currency, *Renminbi,* currently cannot be freely converted in international markets. The Chinese government exerts strict control over foreign exchange. Although conversion into *Renminbi* is permitted under current accounts now, conversion into foreign currency under capital accounts still needs approval from the State or local branches of the State Administration of Foreign Exchange ("SAFE").

# 生词表

| 指标 | 指標 | zhǐbiāo | （名） | index; target; quota |
| 约束 | 約束 | yuēshù | （名、动） | constraint; restriction; to restrain; to restrict; to keep within bounds; to bind |
| 产生 | 產生 | chǎnshēng | （动） | to produce; to engender; to give rise to |
| 货币 | 貨幣 | huòbì | （名） | currency |
| 提高 | 提高 | tígāo | （动） | to increase; to raise |
| 增长 | 增長 | zēngzhǎng | （动） | to increase; to rise; to grow |
| 居民 | 居民 | jūmín | （名） | resident |
| 当 … 时 | 當 … 時 | dāng ... shí | （介） | when; while |
| 萧条 | 蕭條 | xiāotiáo | （名） | depression |
| 鼓励 | 鼓勵 | gǔlì | （动、名） | to encourage; encouragement |
| 反之 | 反之 | fǎnzhī | （连） | conversely; whereas; on the other hand; on the contrary |
| 紧缩 | 緊縮 | jǐnsuō | （动） | to tighten; to reduce |
| 银根 | 銀根 | yíngēn | （名） | money supply |
| 冷却 | 冷卻 | lěngquè | （动） | to cool down |
| 抑制 | 抑制 | yìzhì | （动） | to restrain; to control; to check |
| 首先 | 首先 | shǒuxiān | （副） | first; first of all |
| 变动 | 變動 | biàndòng | （名、动） | change; to change; to alter |
| 流动 | 流動 | liúdòng | （名、动、形） | flow; circulation; to flow; to circulate; to be on the move; mobile; fluid |

| 价值 | 價值 | jiàzhí | （名） | value |
|---|---|---|---|---|
| 防止 | 防止 | fángzhǐ | （动） | to prevent; to keep something from occurring |
| 贬值 | 貶值 | biǎnzhí | （动、名） | to depreciate; depreciation |
| 调往 | 調往 | diàowǎng | （动） | to transfer to; to shift to |
| 其次 | 其次 | qícì | （连） | next; secondly; then |
| 升值 | 升值 | shēngzhí | （动、名） | to appreciate; appreciation |
| 波动 | 波動 | bōdòng | （动） | (price of goods) to fluctuate; to undulate |
| 回报 | 回報 | huíbào | （名、动） | return (on an investment); to repay; to reciprocate |
| 之 | 之 | zhī | （代） | him/her; it; them (used as a substitute for a person or thing) |
| 该 | 該 | gāi | （代） | the aforementioned |
| 运用 | 運用 | yùnyòng | （动） | to utilize; to make use of |
| 控制 | 控制 | kòngzhì | （动） | to control; to dominate |
| 运行 | 運行 | yùnxíng | （动） | to operate; to move in motion |
| 关键 | 關鍵 | guānjiàn | （名、形） | key (point or issue); crux; crucial; critical |
| 管理局 | 管理局 | guǎnlǐjú | （名） | administrative / management bureau |
| 获得 | 獲得 | huòdé | （动） | to obtain; to gain |
| 批准 | 批准 | pīzhǔn | （名、动） | approval; to approve; to ratify |

# 1.既 ... 也 ... （连） "not only ... but also ..."

*The pattern is used to link two similar structures indicating that two actions occur concurrently or two situations exist simultaneously. Usually, 既...也... is used if the two structures are opposite in meaning or have two different attributes.*

1. 每项决策都既有正面影响，也有负面影响。
   Every decision has both a positive and negative impact.

2. 任何项目的成功都既要有周密的计划，也要有灵活的措施。
   The success of any project requires a comprehensive plan as well as flexible methods.

3. 对待下属既要肯定成绩，也要指出缺点。
   One must not only acknowledge the achievements of subordinates, but also point out their shortcomings.

*The usage of 既 ... 又 ... is basically the same as 既...也... , but it is more appropriate to use 既 ... 又 ... when the two verbs that are linked have the same number of syllables and the two structures are parallel in meaning.*

1. 公司食堂供应的午餐既经济又实惠。
   The company's cafeteria provides an economical and substantial lunch.

2. 现代女性既要做家务，又要出外工作。
   Women nowadays not only have to do housework at home, but must also work outside of the house.

3. 利率变动既影响资本项目，又影响经常项目的资金流动。
   Interest rate fluctuations will have an impact on the flow of funds in both capital and current accounts.

4. 既有信誉又有经验的管理人才是我们聘请的对象。
   We would like to invite those who have both a good reputation and experience in management.

既…且… *is used to link a few monosyllabic adjectives.  Similar to* 既…又…, *it indicates that there are two aspects to the nature of something.  The pattern is used more often in written form.*

1. 他的办公桌既脏且乱。
   His desk is dirty and messy.

2. 新盖的楼房都既高且大。
   The newly built buildings are tall and large.

# 2. 每当 "Whenever ... ; each time when ... "

每 *can be used as an adverb indicating an action or situation that occurs or repeats on a regular basis.* 时 *is often used at the end of a clause.*

1. 每当国家调整利息，股票市场就会随着变动。
   Whenever the interest rate is adjusted, the stock market changes in response.

2. 每当公司资金周转不灵时，就需要总经理亲自出马向银行交涉。
   Whenever the company has cash flow problems, the general manager has to negotiate with the banks personally.

3. 每当发生天灾人祸，红十字会就会到灾区协助当地人民开展救灾活动。
   Whenever there is a natural disaster, the Red Cross will go to the affected site to help local citizens carry out relief efforts.

# 3. 反之（连） "conversely; on the contrary; otherwise; whereas"

a. *反之 is used in a written form to link two clauses or two sentences indicating that the situation described before and after 反之 are the opposite.*

1. 科技股股票过去几个月来不断上涨；反之，其它股票却不断下跌。
   For the past few months, technology stocks have continuously gone up, whereas other stocks have continued to fall.

2. 勤奋、坚持不懈的人总会有成就；反之，怠惰、不求上进的人必然一事无成。
   Those who are diligent and persevering will succeed, whereas those who are lazy and do not strive to advance themselves are doomed to fail.

b. *反之 also indicates that if a situation is opposite to the aforementioned one, then a new situation could occur. 则 or 就 is usually used in the second clause of the compound sentence.*

1. 政治改革要循序渐进；反之，则会造成社会不稳定。
   Political reforms must proceed systematically; otherwise, there will be social unrest.

2. 公司需要不断开发新产品以满足客户的需要；反之，就会在竞争中被淘汰。
   Companies must develop new products continuously in order to satisfy customers' needs; otherwise, they will be eliminated from competition.

3. 传统文化需要不断跟上潮流才有价值；反之，则可能成为社会前进的包袱。
   Traditional cultures are only valuable if they have kept abreast of current trends; otherwise, they hinder societal advancement.

4. 财政手段运用得当，能起到促进经济的作用；反之，则会造成巨大的浪费。

Fiscal measures can boost the economy if used properly; otherwise, it could cause a huge waste.

# 4. 而（连）

*The properties and usages of 而 are numerous. The usages focused on in this lesson are as follows:*

a. *而, similar to 但是、然而, or 却, links two elements (words, phrases, or clauses) which are opposite in meaning.*

1. 这道菜浓而不腻。
   The flavor of this dish is strong but not overwhelming.

2. 这家酒店的装潢华丽而不俗。
   The interior decoration of this restaurant is magnificent but not gaudy.

3. 公司有规章制度而不执行，等于没有。
   It is useless to set up rules and regulations and not implement them.

4. 美国人的沟通方式是直言不讳，而中国人则比较含蓄。
   The American communication style is straightforward, whereas the Chinese style is more reserved.

5. 用降价来吸引顾客只是一时之计，而不断研发新产品，同时提高产品质量才是争取市场的最好方法。
   Attracting customers with discount prices is only a short-term strategy, while continuously developing new products and improving quality is the best way to gain market share.

b. *而, similar to 又 or 而且, combines elements which are complementary in meaning.*

1. 他的报告坚持精而简的原则。
   He insists on substance and conciseness when doing presentations.

2. 把钱存在银行是安全而可靠的储蓄方式之一。
One of the safest and most reliable ways of saving is to put money in the bank.

3. 向顾客提供价廉而物美的产品，一向是我们公司的宗旨。
Our company's primary mission has been to provide customers with high quality and inexpensive goods.

4. 利率和汇率是两个重要的经济指标，而这两者的变化又会对一国的经济产生重要的影响。
Interest rates and foreign exchange rates are two important economic indexes. Any change in these two indexes has a substantial influence on the economy of a country.

c. *而 can also link a disyllabic verb or adjective that indicates means or status and a monosyllabic verb which indicates action.*

1. 工资应因个人表现而异。
Wages should vary with each individual's performance.

2. 会议结束之后，他们两人相视而笑，表示对决策的满意。
After the meeting, the two of them exchanged a smile indicating their satisfaction with the decision.

3. 汽车顺着公路盘山而上，走了三个小时才到目的地。
The car followed the winding road up the mountain, and it took about three hours to reach the destination.

4. 随着国际互联网的发展，各种网络公司应运而生。
As the Internet developed, various dotcom companies emerged.

# 5. 之（代）

*之 is a classical Chinese word and is used in written form.*

*a. 之 is used as an object to substitute for a person or thing.*

1. 电影非常感人，许多观众为之流泪。
   Many in the audience cried because of the touching story of the movie.

2. 他对我们公司来讲是求之不得的人才。
   To our company, he is everything that we could wish for.

3. 打字机已经被电脑取而代之了。
   Typewriters have already been replaced by computers.

b. 之 *is the classical style of* 的, *and it is usually used in a fixed four-character pattern.*

1. 工作之余，他喜欢阅读有关政治和经济方面的书籍。
   In his spare time, he likes to read books related to politics and economics.

2. 博士毕业生在我们公司无用武之地。
   People with a Ph.D. are over-qualified for jobs in our company.

3. 这次上海之行的收获比上次的大。
   This time the trip to Shanghai was more fruitful than last time.

c. 之 *can also be used with localizers including:* 上、下、前、后、内、外、中、间、际. *The usage of* 之 *here is similar to* 以.

1. 改进促销手段之后，公司的销售额果然上升了许多。
   After improving the sales strategy, our company's sales greatly increased as expected.

2. 除了回扣之外，他的工资在一年内就升了百分之二十以上。
   Not including commissions, his salary has gone up by more than 20% within a year.

3. 他和几个同事之间的关系都很好。
   The relationship between him and his colleagues is very good.

4. 在此世纪交接之际，如何迈向未来是大家关注的问题。
   At the threshold of this new century, everyone is concerned about how to forge ahead into the future.

# 6. 在…上（介）"in the area of …"

*When 在 is accompanied with 上 to form a prepositional structure, it refers to a certain scope or aspect.*

1. 在卫星发射技术上，中国处于世界领先地位。
   Chinese technology for launching satellites has been in a position of leadership in the world.

2. 这两个财务分析师在公司是否应该向银行贷款的问题上有不同的看法。
   The two financial analysts had different opinions as to whether or not the company should get a bank loan.

3. 他们的研究在一定程度上已经取得了突破。
   Their research has made a breakthrough to some extent.

4. 在发展高科技上，中国每年都投入了大量的人力、物力和财力。
   China has invested tremendous human power, material resources, and capital in the area of high tech development.

5. 两家公司合并之后都在现有的基础上有了发展。
   Following their merger, both companies have developed from their original foundations.

# 7. 如何（代）"how"

*a. 如何 is a written form of 怎么.*

1. 如何合理调整利率是一个国家经济稳定发展的重要课题。
   How to reasonably adjust interest rates is the key to stable development of a country's economy.

2. 如何妥善处理银行坏帐是政府首先要研究的问题。
   The issue that the government should investigate first is how to properly tackle the banks' bad loans.

3. 以目前的进度看来，这个计划无论如何也无法按期完成。
   Judging from the present speed of progress, the project cannot be accomplished on schedule, no matter what happens.

b. 如何 is a written form of 怎么样.

1. 公司最近的财务状况如何？
   How is the company's financial situation lately?

2. 董事会还在进行中，结果如何现在很难预料。
   The board meeting is still in session, and it is hard to predict what the result will be.

 词语辨析

# 1. 变化　变动

变化（名、动）"change; to change"

*变化 refers to a change in quantity, form, content, condition, or structure. It is most frequently used as a noun, but can be used as an intransitive verb as well. Since the nature or form of the change described by 变化 is complex and enormous, 变化 is often used with adverbs such as 无常、多端, or 莫测 to intensify the expression.*

1. 改革开放以后，中国的经济领域和社会领域都发生了巨大的变化。
   After the "Reform and Open Door Policy," China has changed tremendously in both economic and social realms.

2. 市场行情变化莫测，所以要时刻观察，才能把握商机。
   Market situations are changing unpredictably and, therefore, one should observe them at all times in order to seize business opportunities.

3. 这里的天气变化多端，一会晴，一会雨。
   Weather changes dramatically here, so one moment it is sunny and the next it is raining.

变动（名、动）"change; to alter"

*变动 can be used as a noun or a verb. When used as a noun (as an object of a verb), it is usually used with verbs such as 发生 or 有.*

1. 最近国际局势没有什么变动。
   Recently, there has not been much change in the international situation.

2. 人事安排如果变动过快，在很大程度上会影响公司的正常运行。
   If personnel turnover is too fast, it will affect the company's normal operations to a great extent.

3. 如果文字能再作些变动，我们就可以签署这项协议书了。
   We are ready to sign the agreement if we can make some minor changes in wording.

*The main difference between 变动 and 变化 is that 变动 is usually used for social phenomena, whereas 变化 can be used for social or natural phenomena or people's feelings. Moreover, 变动 can have an object, but 变化 usually does not.*

# 2. 欲望　愿望

欲望（名）"desire; lust"

1. 人类无止境增长的欲望是促使经济发展的动力之一。
   Humanity's unlimited desire is one of the forces driving economic development.

2. 升官发财的欲望是导致腐败的原因之一。
   The desire to become powerful and rich is one of the reasons for corruption.

3. 大减价可以在短期内刺激人们的购物欲望。
   A big sale can temporarily stimulate people's desire to purchase things.

4. 随着教育设施的改善，学生的求知欲望越来越高。
   As the educational facilities have improved, the students' thirst for knowledge has increased.

愿望（名）"wish; aspiration"

1. 通过考试，他终于实现了出国留学的愿望。
   By passing the exam, he has finally realized his wish to go abroad to study.

2. 改善生活，提高生活水平是广大中国人民的愿望。
   The aspiration of the vast majority of Chinese people is to improve their living standards.

3. 和平共存是二十一世纪全世界人民的愿望。
   In the 21st century, peaceful coexistence is the aspiration of people around the world.

*Both* 欲望 *and* 愿望 *are used as nouns.* 欲望 *refers to human beings' needs, instincts, or desires, whereas* 愿望 *refers to an individual's hope or aspiration.*

# 3. 鼓励　勉励

鼓励（名、动）"encouragement; incentives; to encourage"

1. 新产品的试销成功，给了大家很大的鼓励。
   The success of the new product's trial sales was a great encouragement to everybody.

2. 物质鼓励和精神鼓励都很重要。
   Both material and moral incentives are important.

3. 总经理鼓励科技人员勇于创新，大胆开发。
   The general manager encouraged the technicians to be bold in innovation and development.

4. 在经济发展的不同阶段，政府或者是鼓励人们储蓄，或者是鼓励人们消费。
   During different stages of economic development, the government encouraged people either to save or to consume.

勉励（动）"to encourage"

1. 父母经常勉励子女认真学习。
   Parents often encourage their children to study diligently.

2. 学员们再三互相勉励，力求进步。
   The trainees repeatedly encouraged each other to strive to make progress.

3. 他经常以伟人成功的例子来勉励自己上进。
   He often motivates himself with examples of successful people.

*鼓励 is basically the same as 勉励. However, 鼓励 emphasizes the urging of people to take an active role or to act, whereas 勉励 stresses the advising of people to advance themselves. 鼓励 can be used both as a verb and as a noun, whereas, 勉励 can only be used as a verb. 勉励 can also be used for oneself, as well as people within one's group, such as 自勉 and 互勉, whereas 鼓励 can only be used for others.*

# 4.抑制　控制

抑制（动、名）"to suppress; to control; to inhibit; inhibition"

*抑制 usually pertains to organic things, such as the human body.*

1. 这种药物对癌症有较强的抑制作用。
   This kind of medicine has effectively controlled cancer.

2. 紧缩银根是抑制消费的有效手段。
   Tightening the moncy supply is an effective means of controlling consumption.

3. 当知道自己被录取时，他再也抑制不住内心的激动，放声欢呼起来。
   When he learned he was accepted, he could no longer suppress his emotions and started shouting for joy.

控制（动、名）"to control; to dominate; to keep something within limits"

*Nouns that can be used with 控制 are: 人、血压、情绪、感情、思想、生产、人口、交通、速度, etc.*

1. 总经理要求各个部门严格控制开支，以度过经济难关。
   The general manager demanded that each department control expenses in order to ride out the economic difficulties.

2. 石油价格完全控制在石油输出国组织的手中。
   OPEC has completely controlled oil prices.

3. 由于前方的汽车突然失去控制，造成了这场连环车祸。
   The car in front suddenly lost control, resulting in a multi-car accident.

*抑制 means to suppress something from happening or growing. 控制 means to control, to dominate, or to take some measure to keep something within certain limits. For example, 控制通货膨胀 means to control inflation when inflation has already happened. 抑制通货膨胀 means to suppress inflation when inflation has not happened yet. 控制 is used more widely than 抑制. When* applied to people, *抑制* is usually used for oneself, but *控制* can be used for oneself as well as for other people.

# 5.防止　避免

防止（动）"to keep something from occurring; to prevent"

1. 为了防止交通事故，高速公路设有时速限制。
   In order to prevent traffic accidents, there are speed limits on the highway.

2. 政府采取种种措施来防止贪污腐败现象的发生。
   The government has adopted various measures to prevent bribery and corruption.

3. 普及法律知识，可以起到防止犯罪的作用。
   Disseminating knowledge of laws may have an impact on preventing crimes.

避免（动）"to keep away from; to avoid"

1. 在签合同之前，公司应该深入调查对方，以避免受骗上当。
   Before signing contracts, companies should carry out due diligence in order to prevent fraud.

2. 中国人讲究以和为贵以避免冲突。
   Chinese people put a premium on harmony in order to avoid conflict.

3. 提高透明度，可以避免互相猜疑。
   A higher degree of transparency can eliminate suspicion.

*The main difference between these two verbs is that 防止 implies actively keeping something from occurring or existing; however, 避免 implies taking a precautionary act to keep away from or avoid something.*

# 6. 表示　表达　表明

表示（动、名）"to express; to show; to indicate; expression; indication; response"

*Nouns often used with* 表示 *are:* 关心、关怀、愤慨、同意、支持、赞同, *etc.*

1. 公司大楼的电灯还亮着，这表示还有人在加班工作。
   The building lights are still on, indicating that some people are still working overtime.

2. 纸箱上的玻璃杯标志表示"易碎物品"。
   The picture of a glass on a carton indicates "fragile."

3. 他口头上已经表示愿意跟我们合作。
   He has verbally indicated his willingness to cooperate with us.

4. 在商谈之前互赠小礼物是一种友好的表示。
   Exchanging small gifts before negotiations is an indication of friendliness.

5. 董事长亲自到现场对参加设备抢修的员工表示慰问。
   The chairman of the board personally went to the site to express his regards to the workers engaged in emergency repairs of the facilities.

6. 尽管公司去年上半年亏损严重，总经理明确表示不会因此而裁员。
   Even though the company had suffered a severe deficit in the first half of last year, the general manger firmly indicated that there would be no layoffs.

表达（动、名）"to express; expression"

1. 因为语言障碍，他的表达能力有一定的困难。
   Due to the language barrier, he has difficulty expressing his ideas.

2. 虽然他花了很多时间来说明这个问题，可惜还是没有把要点表达清楚。
Even though he spent a long time explaining this problem, he unfortunately failed to convey his key points clearly.

3. 主讲人在讨论会上表达了他对银行体系改革的看法。
At the conference, the keynote speaker expressed his views regarding the reform of the banking system.

表明（动）"to make clear; to make known; to state clearly"

1. 民意调查结果表明，大家对新上任的领导班子充满信心。
The survey revealed that people have confidence in the leadership team that just took office.

2. 这张图表表明我们公司的市场占有率在逐年上升。
This chart clearly indicates that our company's market share has increased each year.

3. 有迹象表明利率将会再次被调高。
There have been indications that interest rates will go up again.

4. 对这个提案，他到底是赞成还是反对，一直没有表明态度（表态）。
He has not expressed his position as to whether he will agree or disagree with this proposal.

5. 政府已经明确地表明了支持高科技产业发展的立场。
The government has explicitly made known its position in support of the development of high-tech industries.

*表示 means using language or action to demonstrate a person's emotion, thought, attitude, or determination. 表示 can also have an inanimate subject and means to make a concept or situation evident. 表达 is the expression of one's ideas or thoughts to others through language or action. The subject of 表示 can be a person as well as an animate or inanimate object, whereas the subject of 表达 is always person. The usage of 表明 is similar to 表示, except that 表明 is used to emphasize that something is being shown clearly.*

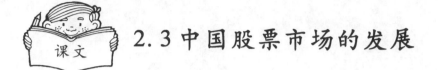

# 2.3 中国股票市场的发展

　　80年代中期，中国恢复了股票的发行和买卖，先后在上海和深圳成立了证券交易所。中国股票的发展与企业所有制改革有着密切的关系。通过改革，越来越多的公司从国有转向股份制，它们通过发行股票，在资本市场上筹集资金。

　　目前，按照股票上市地点和投资者的不同，中国企业的股票可分为A股、B股、H股和N股四种。A股是以人民币标明面值，供境内居民购买的股票；B股又叫人民币特种股票，是以人民币标明面值，以外币认购和买卖，供境外居民及机构购买的股票。2001年2月，B股市场已全面向境内投资者开放。A股和B股都有完全的投票权，与美国根据投票权不同而划分的普通股和优先股的概念不同。

　　此外，还有H股和N股。H股是中国企业在香港上市的股票。其中实力雄厚的中资企业在香港发行的股票一般叫作红筹股(Red Chips)，类似于美国的蓝筹股(Blue Chips)。N股是指中国企业在纽约上市的股票。

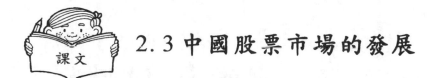

# 2.3 中國股票市場的發展

80年代中期，中國恢復了股票的發行和買賣，先後在上海和深圳成立了證券交易所。中國股票的發展與企業所有制改革有著密切的關係。通過改革，越來越多的公司從國有轉向股份制，它們通過發行股票，在資本市場上籌集資金。

目前，按照股票上市地點和投資者的不同，中國企業的股票可分為A股、B股、H股和N股四種。A股是以人民幣標明面值，供境內居民購買的股票；B股又叫人民幣特種股票，是以人民幣標明面值，以外幣認購和買賣，供境外居民及機構購買的股票。2001年2月，B股市場已全面向境內投資者開放。A股和B股都有完全的投票權，與美國根據投票權不同而劃分的普通股和優先股的概念不同。

此外，還有H股和N股。H股是中國企業在香港上市的股票。其中實力雄厚的中資企業在香港發行的股票一般叫作紅籌股(Red Chips)，類似於美國的藍籌股( Blue Chips)。N股是指中國企業在紐約上市的股票。

# 2.3 The Development of the Chinese Stock Market

In the mid 1980s, China resumed the issue and trade of stocks and set up stock exchanges in Shanghai and Shenzhen, successively. The development of the stock market in China is closely related to the enterprise ownership reforms that have been implemented in China. Under these reforms, more and more companies have transformed from state-owned enterprises into *joint-stock* companies, which raise funds from the capital market through issuing stocks.

Currently, there are four different types of stock: A-shares, B-shares, H-shares, and N-shares, which differ according to issuing place and investor. A-shares are denominated in *Renminbi* and are offered for purchase by Chinese citizens only. B-shares, also called special *Renminbi* stocks, are also denominated in *Renminbi*, but are purchased and traded with foreign currencies by offshore residents and organizations. In February 2001, the B share market was open to domestic investors as well. Owners of A-shares and B-shares have full voting rights. This is different than in the U.S., where the main difference between preferred and common stock is based on voting rights.

In addition, there are H-shares and N-shares. H-shares are stocks issued by Chinese companies in the Hong Kong stock market. These include so-called red chip stocks which are issued by powerful Chinese enterprises. Red chip stocks are analogous to blue chip stocks in the United States. N-shares are stocks issued by Chinese companies and are listed on the New York Stock Exchange.

**背景知识**

　　中国证券市场还处于发展阶段，相关的法律、法规和金融制度尚不健全，老百姓也缺乏投资知识和风险意识。为加强对金融体制的改革和对证券市场的监管，中国政府于1999年7月1日，正式颁布《证券法》，为促使中国股票市场走向规范、迅速而平稳的发展道路起了积极的推进作用。

**背景知識**

　　中國證券市場還處於發展階段，相關的法律、法規和金融制度尚不健全，老百姓也缺乏投資知識和風險意識。爲加強對金融體制的改革和對證券市場的監管，中國政府於1999年7月1日，正式頒布《證券法》，爲促使中國股票市場走向規範、迅速而平穩的發展道路起了積極的推進作用。

*Background Information*

China's stock markets are still in the developmental stage. Relevant laws, regulations, and financial systems are not yet perfected. Most people in China lack investment knowledge and risk awareness. In order to strengthen the financial system reform and enhance the supervision over the securities market, the Chinese government, on July 1, 1999, officially enacted the Securities Act, which plays an important role in promoting a standardized stock market and paving the way for the market to develop rapidly and steadily.

生词表

| 恢复 | 恢復 | huīfù | （动） | to resume; to recuperate; to return to |
| 发行 | 發行 | fāxíng | （名、动） | issuance; to issue |
| 证券交易所 | 證券交易所 | zhèngquàn jiāoyìsuǒ | （名） | stock exchange |
| 标明 | 標明 | biāomíng | （动） | to indicate; to mark |
| 面值 | 面值 | miànzhí | （名） | face value |
| 供 | 供 | gōng | （动） | to provide for |
| 认购 | 認購 | rèngòu | （动） | to offer to buy (stock) |
| 全面 | 全面 | quánmiàn | （形） | overall; comprehensive; all-around |
| 投票权 | 投票權 | tóupiàoquán | （名） | voting right |
| 划分 | 劃分 | huàfēn | （动） | to classify; to differentiate |
| 概念 | 概念 | gàiniàn | （名） | concept |
| 红筹股 | 紅籌股 | hóngchóugǔ | （名） | red chip stock |
| 类似 | 類似 | lèisì | （形） | similar to |

| 蓝筹股 | 藍籌股 | lánchóugǔ | （名） | blue chip stock |
|---|---|---|---|---|
| 处于 | 處於 | chǔyú | （动） | to be in a situation or position of ... |
| 阶段 | 階段 | jiēduàn | （名） | stage; period; phase |
| 相关 | 相關 | xiāngguān | （形） | related; relevant |
| 尚 | 尚 | shàng | （副） | still; yet |
| 健全 | 健全 | jiànquán | （形） | sound; perfect |
| 意识 | 意識 | yìshi | （名、动） | consciousness; to be aware of; to realize |
| 监管 | 監管 | jiānguǎn | （名、动） | supervision; regulation; to supervise; to regulate |
| 促使 | 促使 | cùshǐ | （动） | to spur; to promote |
| 规范 | 規範 | guīfàn | （形、名） | standard; normal; a standard |
| 道路 | 道路 | dàolù | （名） | path; way; road |

# 1. 恢复（动）

*The English equivalents of 恢复 vary depending on the context. They are organized as follows:*

*a.* "to resume, to return to, or begin again after an interruption"

1. 经过谈判，双方恢复了原来的合作关系。
   After the negotiations, both parties resumed the original cooperative relationship.

2. 问题澄清以后，他很快恢复了原来的职务。
After the problem was clarified, he quickly resumed his original post.

3. 自从两国恢复外交关系以来，双边贸易往来迅速增加。
Ever since the two countries resumed their diplomatic relationship, trade between them has increased rapidly.

b. "to recover; to recuperate; to regain strength"

1. 经过急救，病人已经慢慢开始恢复知觉了。
After receiving first aid, the patient slowly regained consciousness.

2. 经过短期疗养，他逐渐恢复了健康，气色也恢复过来了。
After a short rehabilitation, he regained his health, and his vitality has returned.

3. 我们公司在不断努力提高产品质量以后，又逐渐恢复了失去的市场份额。
After continuously making efforts to improve the product's quality, our company has regained lost market share.

c. "to restore, to reinstate"

1. 1997年，中国恢复了对香港行使主权。
In 1997, China reinstated its sovereignty over Hong Kong.

2. 大赦会使许多犯人恢复自由。
Amnesty would restore freedom to many criminals.

3. 社会秩序还没有恢复到原来的样子。
Social order has not yet been restored to its original state.

# 2. 通过（介、动）

通过 can be used as a preposition or as a verb.

*a.* （介）"through; by means of; via"

*When* 通过 *is used as a preposition, it indicates that an objective can be obtained through a certain means or method. The prepositional structure can be placed either before or after the subject.*

1. 即使在边远地区，通过卫星也可以收看到世界各地的电视节目。
   Even in remote areas, people can receive TV programs from all over the world via satellite.

2. 我们应该通过什么渠道才能采访到你们的首席代表？
   Which channels should we go through in order to interview your chief representative?

3. 通过人才流动，公司加强了市场营销的力度。
   By changing personnel, the company has increased its marketing strength.

*b.* （动）"to pass (a bill or an exam); to give approval"

1. 美国众议院通过了授予中国永久正常贸易关系的法案。
   The U.S. Senate passed the bill granting PNTR to China.

2. 这项新技术通过了国家技术鉴定，很快就可以运用到生产上了。
   The new technology has been tested and approved by the government; therefore, it can be used in production soon.

3. 在许多国家，有些职业（例如医生、律师）需要通过专业考试后，才能正式开业。
   In many countries, some professions such as doctors and lawyers need to pass special exams to be allowed to practice formally.

*c.* （动）"to go or make one's way through; to pass through"

1. 有些城市规定，下午6时以前，载货车辆不能通过市区。
   Some cities stipulate that trucks may not pass through the city before 6 p.m.

2. 旅客进入任何国家都要首先通过边防和海关检查。
   Travelers entering any country need to pass through immigration and customs first.

3. 主讲人通过贵宾接待室，走进了演讲厅。
   The guest speaker went into the auditorium through the VIP reception room.

## 3. ... 而 ... （连）

*Besides the usages that were explained in Lesson 2.2, Explanation of Terms, Section 4, 而 can link words which indicate an aim, reason, basis, means, or condition, to a verb indicating a causal relationship. This is often used in written Chinese.*

1. 产品的生产量需要根据供求关系而决定。
   Production volumes need to be determined on the basis of supply and demand.

2. 很多服装的款式都是根据欧洲流行的式样而制作的。
   Many clothing styles are made on the basis of European fashion.

3. 总裁的创业精神并没有因为年纪大而衰退，反而是越老越活跃。
   The President's entrepreneurial spirit has not declined due to his age. On the contrary, the older he gets, the more active he becomes.

4. 为了吸引顾客，百货公司的橱窗摆设经常因季节而改变。
   In order to attract customers, the department store's window decorations change with the seasons.

5. 这个项目因经费不足而被取消了。
The project has been cancelled due to a shortage of funds.

6. 因市场上个人电脑的需求降低而导致公司下半年的盈余将比去年同期减少。
Due to a decrease in demand for PCs in the market, this year's second quarter profits will be lower than the same period last year.

# 4. 指 ( 名、动 )

*Besides being used as a noun in combinations such as* 手指 *and* 指南, 指 *can also be used as a verb and has the following meanings:*

a. "to aim at; to be directed at; to refer to"

1. 大西部是指中国的哪些地区？
To which region in China does the term "The Great West" refer?

2. 他的这些意见都是指着你说的。
All his suggestions were directed at you.

3. "东方华尔街"是指上海的外滩。
"Wall Street of the East" refers to the Bund in Shanghai.

b. "to point at; to direct to; to indicate the position or direction by extending a finger"

1. 他指着电视屏幕，开始解说要点。
Pointing to the TV screen, he began to explain the main points.

2. "指南针"这个名称是由于那根针的一端总是指着南方。
The "South-pointing needle" is so called because one end of it is always pointing to the South.

3. 出租车司机朝着乘客指的方向开去。
The taxi driver drove in the direction that the passenger pointed.

 词语辨析

# 1.缺少　缺乏

缺少（动）"to lack; to be short of"

*缺少 is used to express that the number of people or things available is not enough to perform a task; the available resources could even be zero.*

1. 小时候缺少营养会影响一辈子的健康。
   Lack of nutrition in childhood can affect one's health later in life.

2. 改革开放以来，中国缺少高级管理人才的问题日益突出。
   Since the "Reform and Open Door Policy," the shortage of upper level managers has become more and more conspicuous.

3. 阳光和水分是人类生存所不可缺少的资源。
   Sun and water are indispensable resources for people to survive.

缺乏（动、形）"to lack; to be short of"

*缺乏 is used to express that there is a severe shortage of something which is absolutely needed or necessary. It is used more often in written form.*

1. 中国人一般都缺乏投资股票的经验和知识。
   In general, Chinese people lack experience and knowledge about investing in stocks.

2. 由于缺乏数据，这项计划暂时无法进行。
   Due to insufficient data, the project has been put on hold.

3. 很多非洲国家的医疗药品都非常缺乏。
   There is a dire shortage of medicine in many African countries.

4. 许多刚刚成立的网络公司因缺乏（缺少）资金而无法正常运
作。

Many newly established Internet companies cannot operate normally
because of insufficient capital.

*The differences between* 缺少 *and* 缺乏 *are both syntactic and semantic.
Although* 缺少 *and* 缺乏 *indicate that the amount of something is not enough or
is insufficient, the degree of insufficiency of* 缺乏 *is much stronger than* 缺少.
缺乏 *can be used as either an adjective or a verb, whereas* 缺少 *can only be
used as a verb.* 缺少 *does not use abstract nouns as its object, such as*
认识、了解、经验、研究、力量, *etc., but* 缺乏 *does.* 缺少 *can be used with*
不可、不能, *but* 缺乏 *cannot.*

# 2. 紧密　密切

紧密（形）"in numerous and rapid succession (closely connected in timing)"

紧密 *usually modify such nouns as* 团结、合作、相关、结合, *etc., but not*
来往.

1. 随着一阵紧密的锣声，演员就上场表演了。
After a rapid playing of gongs and drums, the actors went on stage to
perform.

2. 长期以来，英美两国一直保持紧密的政治、经济合作关系。
For a long time, the U.S. and Great Britain have maintained a close
cooperative relationship politically and economically.

3. 科学技术的发展与国家的经济建设紧密相联。
The development of scientific technology is inextricably related to the
economic development of a country.

密切（动、形、副）"to establish a close relationship; to be close; to be intimate; closely"

*密切 describes a close relationship between or among people, people and things, or things and things.*

1. 长期共同合作密切了他们的私人关系。
   Their relationship became closer after working together for a long time.

2. 政治和经济有密切的关系。
   Politics and economics are closely related.

3. 企业在制定市场策略时要密切注意竞争对手的情况。
   In making marketing strategies, companies need to pay close attention to their competitors' situations.

4. 市场部门需要与生产部门和技术开发部门密切配合，这样才能生产出顾客满意的产品。
   The marketing department needs to coordinate closely with the production and R&D departments, so that the company can produce products that satisfy customers.

*紧密 describes inseparable connections of multiple things, whereas 密切 describes a close or intimate relationship. 密切 can be used as an adverb meaning 仔细, whereas 紧密 cannot.*

# 3. 概念　观念

概念（名）"general concept; idea"

1. 经过他的讲解，我们对开放式基金有了清楚的概念。
   From his explanation, we have a general idea about open-ended funds.

2. 掌握语法概念有助于加快学习语言。
   Grasping general grammatical knowledge first would help speed up language acquisition.

3. 我对电脑程序只有一点模糊的概念 。
I only have a vague understanding of computer programs.

观念（名 ）"concept; idea"

1. 中国人的消费观念由于生活水平的提高而改变了。
Chinese concepts of consumption have changed because living standards have risen.

2. 陈旧的观念是改革的障碍。
Out-of-date concepts are a hindrance to reforms.

3. 受儒家思想影响的中国人道德观念比较强。
Chinese people who are influenced by Confucianism have a relatively higher concept of morality.

4. 缺乏时间观念的人，很难在事业上成功。
Persons with no concept of time have difficulty succeeding professionally.

*概 means "general; overall," and, therefore, 概念 is an overall or general rather than specific knowledge, idea, or notion about certain things. 观念 refers to a person's concept which is relative to a person's standpoint, attitude, or thoughts about something. The concept is usually deeply rooted and is not easily changed.*

# 4. 相关　有关

相关（动、形）"be interrelated with"

1. 进出口货物要按照相关法规办理海关手续。
Imports and exports need to be processed according to the relevant customs regulations.

2. 股票价值与一个国家的政治状况密切相关。
The value of stocks is closely related to a country's political situation.

3. 有人认为，地球变暖与大气中碳酸气的含量增加相关。
Some people believe that global warming is related to the increased
amount of carbon dioxide in the air.

有关（动、形）"to have something to do with; to relate to; regarding;
relevant"

1. 关于这项投资计划，有关部门还没有作正式报道。
Regarding this investment plan, the relevant department has not yet made a
formal announcement.

2. 中国企业在国外上市需要得到有关当局的许可。
To be listed in a foreign country, Chinese corporations must first obtain a
permit from the relevant authority.

3. 股票的价值差不多跟所有的社会现象有关。
Almost any social phenomenon can have an effect on the value of stocks.

4. 这个案子与他无关。
He had nothing to do with this case.

*相关 is an intransitive verb and is used to indicate a reciprocal relationship
between things. It can also be used as an adjective to modify nouns such as
部门、法规、事物、条件, etc. 有关 is also an intransitive verb, but the
relationship is not necessarily reciprocal. When used as a predicate, it must
take 和、跟、与, or 同 to introduce the relative things or people. 相关 is only
used in affirmative sentences; but 有关 can be used either in affirmative or
negative sentences, and the negative form is 无关.*

# 2.4 将上海建成国际金融贸易中心

上海不但是中国最大的城市，也是全国最重要的金融贸易中心。优越的地理条件，雄厚的工业基础、<u>繁荣</u>的商业经济、<u>优秀</u>的人口素质，以及充足的资金供应，都为上海成为中国，乃至世界金融贸易中心<u>奠定</u>了<u>坚实</u>的基础。

在改革开放的短短20年间，上海的金融业取得了<u>惊人</u>的发展。位于浦东陆家嘴的上海证券交易所是中国仅有的两家可以买卖上市股票的交易所之一。上海不但<u>云集</u>了国内金融公司，而且吸引了许多国际著名金融机构来<u>沪</u>发展业务，特别是<u>浦东</u>新区的建成，更为上海<u>博得</u>了"东方华尔街"的<u>美称</u>。

此外，上海的国际贸易也十分繁荣。上海港是中国进出口贸易的枢纽港口之一，也是世界十大港口之一。雄厚的传统工业基础，再加上近年来在浦东新区迅速发展起来的高新技术产业，为上海的对外贸易发展提供了有利的<u>保障</u>。

# 2.4 將上海建成國際金融貿易中心

課文

　　上海不但是中國最大的城市，也是全國最重要的金融貿易中心。優越的地理條件，雄厚的工業基礎、繁榮的商業經濟、優秀的人口素質，以及充足的資金供應，都為上海成為中國，乃至世界金融貿易中心奠定了堅實的基礎。

　　在改革開放的短短20年間，上海的金融業取得了驚人的發展。位于浦東陸家嘴的上海證券交易所是中國僅有的兩家可以買賣上市股票的交易所之一。上海不但雲集了國內金融公司，而且吸引了許多國際著名金融機構來滬發展業務，特別是浦東新區的建成，更為上海博得了"東方華爾街"的美稱。

　　此外，上海的國際貿易也十分繁榮。上海港是中國進出口貿易的樞紐港口之一，也是世界十大港口之一。雄厚的傳統工業基礎，再加上近年來在浦東新區迅速發展起來的高新技術產業，為上海的對外貿易發展提供了有利的保障。

**Text**

# 2.4 Turning Shanghai into an International Financial and Trade Center

Shanghai is not only China's largest city, but also the country's most important finance and trade center. It has favorable geographic conditions, a sound industry base, a prosperous commercial economy, a high caliber population, and a ready supply of capital. All of these constitute a solid base for Shanghai to develop into a financial and commercial center for China as well as the world.

In the two short decades since the "Reform and Open Door Policy," Shanghai's financial sector witnessed astounding development. The Shanghai Stock Exchange, located at Lujiazui in Pudong, is one of only two places where stocks can be traded in China. Many domestic financial companies converge in Shanghai. Moreover, many world famous international financial institutions have also been attracted to develop businesses in Shanghai. The development of the new Pudong region, in particular, has earned Shanghai the laudable title of "Wall Street of the East."

Furthermore, international trade is highly flourishing in Shanghai. Shanghai Harbor, one of China's main import/export hubs, is also one of the world's ten largest ports. The strong traditional industry base, together with the fast-developing high-tech industry in Pudong in recent years, ensures the development of Shanghai's international trade.

**背景知识**

　　陆家嘴金融贸易区是1990年宣布开发浦东后,在上海设立的中国唯一的国家级金融贸易开发区。区内建有高468米的东方明珠电视塔和世界第三高的金茂大厦。有83家中外金融机构在区内经营,其中外资金融机构42家。上海证券交易所、上海期货交易所等已迁入区内。近300家有影响的国内外大集团、大企业,如西门子、IBM、惠普、英特尔和宝钢等进驻陆家嘴。

**背景知識**

　　陸家嘴金融貿易區是1990年宣布開發浦東後,在上海設立的中國唯一的國家級金融貿易開發區。區內建有高468米的東方明珠電視塔和世界第三高的金茂大廈。有83家中外金融機構在區內經營,其中外資金融機構42家。上海證券交易所、上海期貨交易所等已遷入區內。近300家有影響的國內外大集團、大企業,如西門子、IBM、惠普、英特爾和寶鋼等進駐陸家嘴。

**Background Information**

After the 1990 announcement to develop the Pudong area in Shanghai, the Lujiazui Financial & Trade Zone was set up as the only national class financial trade zone in China. The 468-meter-high "Oriental Pearl" TV tower and the Jinmao Building – the third highest building in the world – were built in this zone. There are 83 financial institutions operating in the zone, among which, 42 are foreign institutions. The Shanghai Stock Exchange and the Shanghai Futures Exchange have already moved into the zone. Nearly 300 influential corporations, both domestic and international, such as Siemens, IBM, HP, Intel, and Bao Steel, have also entered the zone.

生词表

| 繁荣 | 繁榮 | fánróng | （形） | prosperous; flourishing |
|---|---|---|---|---|
| 优秀 | 優秀 | yōuxiù | （形） | outstanding; excellent; splendid |
| 奠定 | 奠定 | diàndìng | （动） | to establish; to settle |
| 坚实 | 堅實 | jiānshí | （形） | solid; strong; substantial; firm |
| 惊人 | 驚人 | jīngrén | （形） | astonishing; amazing |
| 云集 | 雲集 | yúnjí | （动） | to gather |
| 沪 | 滬 | hù | （专） | an abbreviated name for Shanghai |
| 浦东 | 浦東 | Pǔdōng | （专） | Pudong |
| 博得 | 博得 | bódé | （动） | to win; to gain; to earn |
| 美称 | 美稱 | měichēng | （名） | good name; laudable title |
| 保障 | 保障 | bǎozhàng | （名、动） | guaranty; to guarantee |

# 1. 乃至（连） "and even"

*乃至 has the same meaning and usage as* 甚至 *(see Lesson 1.2, Explanation of Terms, Section 4). It is placed at the end of multiple items to intensify the expression. It is mostly used in written form and can take the alternative form* 乃至于.

1. 长城在中国乃至全世界都是有名的旅游景点。
   The Great Wall is well known in China, and throughout the world, as a tourist attraction.

2. 他的管理模式在整个行业乃至于全国都享有盛名。
   His management model is highly reputed throughout the entire industry and even across the whole country.

3. "三角债"会影响企业正常运作，使资金周转不灵，乃至于破产。
   "Triangle Debt" will affect normal operations and cash flow, and can even lead to bankruptcy.

# 2. 取得（动） "to gain; to obtain"

*取得 must have an object that has a positive connotation such as* 成绩、成果、经验、协助、联系、胜利, *etc. Please refer to the comparison with* 获得 *in Lesson 3.3, Distinguishing Synonyms, Section 4.*

1. 中国的经济改革取得了举世瞩目的成绩。
   China's economic reforms have obtained results that have astounded the world.

2. 近几年来，共同基金的投资者都取得了超出预期的高回报。
   In the last few years, mutual fund investors have been able to obtain returns that have been higher than expected.

3. 我们公司取得了数家跨国公司在华的独家代理权。
   Our company has obtained the sole representation rights from many MNCs.

# 3. 规模（名）"scale; scope"

规模 *usually refers to the scale or the capacity of a project, activity, business facility, organization, etc. When used with* 大 *or* 小*, it can be used as an adverb.*

1. 由于资金不足，公司被迫缩小投资规模。
   Due to insufficient capital, the company was forced to reduce the scale of its investment.

2. 历史上从未有过规模这么大的工程。
   Throughout history there has never been a project of this scale.

3. 三峡水坝的建筑工程已初具规模了。
   The Three Gorges Dam project has already begun to take shape.

4. 九十年代之后，中国政府正式大规模发展浦东。
   In the '90s, China formally began to develop Pudong on a large scale.

 词语辨析

# 1. 此外　另外

此外（连）"besides; in addition; as well as; aside from"

*此外 can be followed by either an affirmative expression or a negative expression. If it is followed by a negative expression, in addition to its normal conjunction role, it emphasizes that there are no additional options to those previously mentioned.*

1. 公司上市可以筹集资金，此外，还可以建立知名度。
   Listing a company allows the company to raise capital. In addition, the company can also increase its name recognition.

2. 今天的议程包括选举董事会成员，此外还要讨论一下各成员的分工问题。
   Today's agenda includes election of the board members. In addition, there will be a discussion of each member's responsibilities.

3. 为了度过这次难关，公司只好裁员、精减机构，此外，别无办法。
   In order to overcome the difficulties this time, the company had no choice but to lay off employees and trim operations.

另外（形、副、连）"other; another; in addition; moreover; besides"

*When 另外 is used as an adjective, 的 is needed before the noun; however 的 is optional before a number. When 另外 is used as an adverb, it is often coupled with another adverb such as 还、又, or 再, which can be placed before or after 另外. Note: 另 is the abbreviated form of 另外. It is used only with monosyllabic verbs, and is not coupled with 还、又, or 再.*

1. 今天只讨论人事安排，另外的问题改天讨论。
   Today we will only discuss the personnel issue. Other issues will be discussed another day.

2. 我们公司已经拥有四个专利，另外（的）三个还在申请中。
   Our company already owns four patents, and three more are in the application process.

3. 我们公司为新成立的合资企业提供资金和技术培训，另外还提供经营管理和业务发展方面的资讯。
   In addition to management and business development information, our company also provides capital and training to newly formed joint venture companies.

4. 投产的事改天另议。
   We will hold a meeting to discuss the issue of production some other day.

5. 他大量投资股票，另外，还投资房地产。
   In addition to real estate, he has invested a great deal in stocks.

*Both 此外 and 另外 function as conjunctions before additional remarks or information. However, 另外 can also be used as an adjective or an adverb. Another difference is that 此外 is used mostly in written Chinese, while 另外 is used mostly in spoken Chinese.*

## 2. 注目　瞩目

注目（动）"to stare; to fix one's eyes on"

1. 比尔·盖茨是世界注目的人物。
   Bill Gates is a person who draws the world's attention.

2. 他以引人注目的设计赢得最佳服装设计大奖。
   He won the best fashion design award with an eye-catching design.

3. 选手们进入会场，引起全场观众的注目。

When the athletes entered the stadium, they caught everyone's attention.

瞩目（动）"to draw or bring attention to (from a group, society, etc)"

1. 浦东新区的发展引起了世界的广泛瞩目。

The development of Pudong brought worldwide attention.

2. 近年来，电子商务的发展特别令人瞩目。

E-commerce has caught everyone's attention in recent years.

3. 中国的经济建设已经取得了令人瞩目的成就。

The development of the Chinese economy has attained noteworthy achievements.

*注目 means "staring at or focusing attention towards something or someone." The emphasis is on visually looking at a target. 瞩目 means "to draw the attention of a group of people, such as a society or nation to something or someone." An additional difference is that 注目 can have an object, whereas 瞩目 cannot. Both 注目 and 瞩目 are used in written form only and have a narrow range of use. They are most often used in idiomatic expressions such as 引人注目 and 令人瞩目.*

# 3. 焦点　热点

焦点（名）"focal point; focus; central issue"

1. 拍照片时，镜头要对准焦点。

The lens needs to be focused on the subject when taking pictures.

2. 信息技术是当今世界经济发展的焦点之一。

Information Technology (IT) is one of the main focuses of today's economic development around the world.

3. 两国谈判的焦点是平等互惠的双边贸易问题。

Equal and mutually-beneficial bilateral trade is the focal point of the two countries' negotiations.

热点 "hot point; hot spot"

1. 每四年举行一次的奥运会是各大媒体报道的热点。
   The Olympic Games, which are held once every four years, are the focus of major media reports.

2. 黄山是中国著名的旅游热点。
   Huangshan is a famous tourist spot in China.

*Both* 焦点 *and* 热点 *refer to a focal point or something that is drawing attention.* 焦点, *however, means drawing attention because it is important or crucial, whereas* 热点 *means drawing attention because it is popular or a fad.*

# 4. 保证　保障

保证（动、名）"to guarantee; to assure; to pledge; guarantee"

1. 我厂的产品全部都有书面质量保证。
   Our factory's products all come with written quality warranties.

2. 金钱可以带来物质享受，但不能保证幸福。
   Money can bring material enjoyment, but cannot guarantee happiness.

3. 中国政府从开始拥有核武器时，就向世界保证不首先使用核武器。
   The Chinese government assured the world that they would not be the first to use nuclear weapons ever since it possessed them.

保障（动、名）"to guarantee; to secure; to ensure; to safeguard"

1. 退休金是老年人的生活保障。
   Pensions are a security for senior citizens' livelihood.

2. 宪法有条款规定，保障人民的言论和信仰自由。
   The constitution has articles that guarantee people's freedom of speech and religion.

3. 卫星导航技术为现代航海、航空事业提供了安全保障。
   Satellite guidance technology provides safeguards for ocean and air
   navigation in modern times.

*保证 and 保障 can be used interchangeably when they are used as nouns
meaning "guarantee." For example, 知识是不断进步的保障（保证）.
But, when they are used as verbs, 保障 stresses the point of protecting or
safeguarding, whereas 保证 ensures that one will carry out a promise.*

# 第三章

# 市场营销

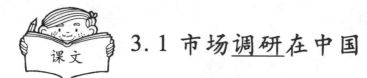

# 3.1 市场调研在中国

在优胜劣汰的市场竞争中，及时把握信息并迅速作出准确的市场预测是企业经营成败的关键。随着中国经济市场化程度的加深，越来越多的企业开始认识到市场调研的重要性，对信息的需求量及依赖性也不断增加。

市场调研的内容十分广泛，它主要包括对消费者的调查、对商品的调查和对促销手段的调查。对消费者的调查主要是收集消费者的生活习惯、收入水平、家庭结构、教育程度、年龄差异以及职业性质等数据，以了解消费者的需求和购买动机。对商品的调查则要求掌握在特定时期、特定市场中商品的来源、数量、价格等情报，以获取商品供求关系的最新信息。对促销手段的调查主要包括广告、人员推销和公共关系等方面，其中广告最受关注。要制定出有效的营销策略，就必须正确地对广告的信息传递效果和销售效果进行评估。

随着社会各方面对市场调研作用的逐渐认识，专门从事市场调研的公司（包括合资公司）也从80年代初的零家迅速增长到目前的数千家左右。尽管如此，在中国市场上

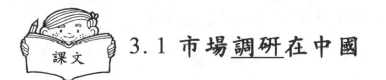

# 3.1 市場調研在中國

在優勝劣汰的市場競爭中，及時把握信息並迅速作出準確的市場預測是企業經營成敗的關鍵。隨著中國經濟市場化程度的加深，越來越多的企業開始認識到市場調研的重要性，對信息的需求量及依賴性也不斷增加。

市場調研的内容十分廣泛，它主要包括對消費者的調查、對商品的調查和對促銷手段的調查。對消費者的調查主要是收集消費者的生活習慣、收入水平、家庭結構、教育程度、年齡差異以及職業性質等數據，以了解消費者的需求和購買動機。對商品的調查則要求掌握在特定時期、特定市場中商品的來源、數量、價格等情報，以獲取商品供求關係的最新信息。對促銷手段的調查主要包括廣告、人員推銷和公共關係等方面，其中廣告最受關注。要制定出有效的營銷策略，就必須正確地對廣告的信息傳遞效果和銷售效果進行評估。

隨著社會各方面對市場調研作用的逐漸認識，專門從事市場調研的公司（包括合資公司）也從80年代初的零家迅速增長到目前的數千家左右。儘管如此，在中國市場上调研工作<u>仍然</u>面临着很多困难。<u>辽阔</u>的国土、不完善的通讯及运输系统、消费行为的地区<u>差异</u>，以及专业调研人员的缺乏等因素，都在一定程度上影响了市场调研工作的质量。

調研工作<u>仍然</u>面臨著很多困難。<u>遼闊</u>的國土、不完善的通訊及運輸系統、消費行爲的地區<u>差異</u>，以及專業調研人員的缺乏等因素，都在一定程度上影響了市場調研工作的質量。

# 3.1 Market Research in China

In a marketplace governed by the principle of survival of the fittest, it is crucial for the success of any business to get a hold of timely information and make predictions quickly and accurately. As China intensifies its market economy, more and more businesses are beginning to recognize the importance of market research, and their demand for and reliance on market research has continuously increased.

Market research is a very extensive field. It involves researching market variables associated with consumers, products, and promotional methods. Consumer-oriented market research involves collecting information about consumer lifestyle, income, family structure, educational level, age distribution, and professional classification. The purpose of collecting such information is to gain an understanding of consumer needs and spending motivation. Product market research involves obtaining information about certain products in specific markets at specific times. Information such as the source of the product, its quantity, and its price are all gathered in order to determine the most current relationship between supply and demand. Market research of promotional methods involves investigating the efficacy of various kinds of promotions--including advertisements, direct marketing, and public relations. Among these, advertisement receives the most scrutiny. If a company is to formulate an efficient marketing strategy, then it must accurately assess the efficacy of its advertisement in terms of information transmission and sales.

As the importance of market research has gradually gained recognition in China, the number of market research companies (including joint ventures) has rapidly increased from zero in the early '80s to thousands today. Even so, market research in China still faces formidable difficulties. The country's vast size, its often-imperfect communication and transportation systems, significant regional differences in consumption patterns, and the shortage of professional researchers are all factors that, to a certain extent, detract from the quality of market research currently being conducted in China.

在中国，市场调研还应包括对投资环境的调查。中国领土辽阔，各地的投资环境、政策和文化都不同。外资公司进入中国市场时，应在对当地的<u>风土人情</u>、交通运输状况及政策方针等方面有了初步了解之后，再对人口<u>分布</u>、购买者的消费水平、<u>竞争对手</u>的实力等情况进行调研。这样，才有可能对将要面临的商业环境有一个<u>公正</u>而全面的了解。可口可乐公司能在中国取得成功的主要原因是在进入中国之前就对投资环境进行了充分的调查。

背景知識

在中國，市場調研還應包括對投資環境的調查。中國領土遼闊，各地的投資環境、政策和文化都不同。外資公司進入中國市場時，應在對當地的<u>風土人情</u>、交通運輸狀況及政策方針等方面有了初步了解之後，再對人口<u>分布</u>、購買者的消費水平、<u>競爭對手</u>的實力等情況進行調研。這樣，才有可能對將要面臨的商業環境有一個<u>公正</u>而全面的了解。可口可樂公司能在中國取得成功的主要原因是在進入中國之前就對投資環境進行了充分的調查。

**Background Information**

In China, market research must also take the investment climate into consideration. China is a massive country, and the investment environment, policies, and cultures in different regions vary considerably. When foreign companies enter the Chinese market, they should first become acquainted with the local customs and conditions and familiarize themselves with transportation, communication, and policy issues. Then they should proceed to research population distribution, consumer purchasing power, and the strength of competitors. Only after all these aspects have been researched can a company be said to have a comprehensive and impartial understanding of the market environment that it is about to enter. The main reason that Coca-Cola has been able to penetrate China so successfully is that they conducted full-scale research of the Chinese investment market beforehand.

生词表

| 调研 | 調研 | diàoyán | （名） | investigation and research |
|------|------|---------|--------|----------------------------|
| 优胜劣汰 | 優勝劣汰 | yōushèng liètài | （成） | survival of the fittest |
| 信息 | 信息 | xìnxī | （名） | information |
| 准确 | 準確 | zhǔnquè | （形） | accurate |
| 预测 | 預測 | yùcè | （名、动） | prediction; to predict; to forecast |
| 依赖 | 依賴 | yīlài | （名、动） | reliance; to rely on; to depend on |
| 广泛 | 廣泛 | guǎngfàn | （形） | broad; extensive; wide-ranging; widespread |
| 促销 | 促銷 | cùxiāo | （名、动） | promotion; to promote sales |

| 结构 | 結構 | jiégòu | （名） | structure; construction; setup; organization |
|------|------|--------|--------|----------------------------------------------|
| 教育 | 教育 | jiàoyù | （名、动） | education; to educate |
| 年龄 | 年齡 | niánlíng | （名） | age |
| 动机 | 動機 | dòngjī | （名） | motive; intention |
| 特定 | 特定 | tèdìng | （形） | certain; specific; special |
| 来源 | 來源 | láiyuán | （名） | source |
| 获取 | 獲取 | huòqǔ | （动） | to procure; to obtain |
| 供求 | 供求 | gōngqiú | （名） | supply and demand |
| 推销 | 推銷 | tuīxiāo | （动） | to sell; to market |
| 传递 | 傳遞 | chuándì | （名、动） | transmission; to transmit; to deliver |
| 尽管 | 儘管 | jǐnguǎn | （副） | even though; in spite of |
| 如此 | 如此 | rúcǐ | （代） | so; such; in this way |
| 仍然 | 仍然 | réngrán | （副） | still; yet |
| 辽阔 | 遼闊 | liáokuò | （形） | vast; broad; boundless; wide (usually in reference to places) |
| 差异 | 差異 | chāyì | （名） | difference; divergence; discrepancy; diversity |
| 风土人情 | 風土人情 | fēngtǔ rénqíng | （成） | local customs and practices |
| 分布 | 分布 | fēnbù | （名、动） | distribution; to be scattered (in a certain area); to be distributed; to be dispersed |
| 竞争对手 | 競爭對手 | jìngzhēng duìshǒu | （名） | competitor |
| 公正 | 公正 | gōngzhèng | （形） | fair; just; impartial |

# 1. 及时（形、副）

*及时 indicates that an action takes place or something happens at the proper time. It can be used as an adjective or as an adverb. Unlike 立刻 and 马上, 及时 is not accompanied by 就 when used as an adverb.*

a.（副）"immediately; right away; without delay"

1. 遇到问题应该及时解决。
   When encountering problems one should solve them right away.

2. 伤亡相当严重的原因是救护人员无法及时赶到现场抢救。
   Serious casualties resulted from the fact that rescue workers could not arrive immediately.

3. 我们在测试过程中所发现的技术问题都及时向质量管理部门汇报。
   Technical problems discovered during the test were reported immediately to the quality management department.

b.（形、副）"timely; at the proper time"

1. 一场及时雨，下得正是时候。
   The rain fell at the proper time.

2. 幸亏有一些库存卖得及时，否则公司的亏损将会更大。
   Fortunately, some inventory was sold at the right time; otherwise the company would have suffered even greater losses.

# 2. 关键（名、形）"key (point); crux; critical; important issues or points in time"

1. 谈判成功的关键在于双方是否都抱有诚意。
   The key to success in negotiations depends on whether the two parties are sincere or not.

2. 市场调研的关键首先在于对自己生产的产品，或者提供的服务进行市场定位。
   The key to market research is to correctly position your product or service in the market place.

3. 产品质量的优劣是决定市场占有率的关键问题。
   Product quality is the critical issue that determines market share.

4. 能在关键的时刻保持沉着冷静，是企业家成功的必备条件之一。
   One of the qualities a successful entrepreneur must have is the ability to remain calm at critical moments.

# 3. 手段（名）

手段 *is the means or method used to reach a person's desired goal. It can have either positive or negative connotations.*

*a.* "means; method"

手段 *is used in the following examples to show a positive or commendable means for achieving a desired end or goal.*

1. 营销部经理在促销方面很有手段。
   The marketing and sales manager is very skillful at promoting sales.

2. 张技术员手段高明，任何电脑方面的问题他都能解决。
   Technician Zhang is so skillful that he can solve any computer related problem.

3. 除了刑事诉讼，政府还采用宣传手段，以防止青少年吸毒现象的蔓延。

   In addition to criminal litigation, the government has also adopted propaganda measures to prevent the spread of drug abuse among teenagers.

*b.* "trick; deception; artifice"

*手段 is used in the following examples to show a negative or inappropriate means for achieving a desired end or goal.*

1. 商场如战场，竞争对手有时可能会使用各种手段以达到赚钱的目的。

   Business is like a battlefield; competitors might use all kinds of tactics in order to earn profits.

2. 公司里人际关系复杂，有些人喜欢耍手段、搞阴谋。

   Interpersonal relationships in the office are complicated; some people like to play tricks and engage in conspiracies.

3. 为了想当市场战略部的部长，他不择手段。

   He used every trick possible in order to become the head of the marketing strategy division.

# 4. 受（动）

*The meaning of 受 is close to 接受 or 遭受 depending on the situation. It requires a noun as its object to complete its meaning or intention.*

*a.* "to receive; to accept; to obtain"

1. 美国的快餐连锁店在中国很受欢迎。

   American fast food chains are popular in China.

2. 尽管前来应聘工作的人很多，可是受过教育和训练的人并不多。
   Although many candidates applied for the job, there were not many who were well-educated or had received training.

3. 他的销售业绩特别好，所以经常受到表扬。
   He often receives praise because his sales record is exceptional.

*b.* "to suffer; to sustain; to be subjected to"

*The verb's object (noun) usually has a negative connotation.*

1. 他是因为受朋友的影响而犯罪的。
   He committed a crime because he came under the bad influence of a friend.

2. 靠关系做生意，能避免受骗。
   Doing business through "guanxi" can prevent being cheated.

3. 任何员工都不能受歧视、受委屈。
   No employee should be subjected to discrimination or misjudgment.

# 5. 尽管 "in spite of; despite; although; though; even though"

*a.* （连）

尽管 *has the same meaning as* 虽然 *which also means "in spite of the fact that." When used as a conjunction, it is placed in the first clause and is often used with adverbs such as* 还是、但是、可是、仍然、然而, *or* 却 *in the second clause.*

1. 尽管市场变化莫测，市场调研所反映的情况大体上还是可以信赖的。
   In spite of market fluctuations, the situation reflected by the market research is, on the whole, still trustworthy.

2. 尽管海外投资有各种风险，为了扩大市场、追求利润，跨国公司还是积极展开全球化战略。

Even though investing overseas entails various risks, MNCs are still actively implementing their global strategy to expand their markets and pursue profits.

3. 尽管公司受到起诉，可是产品销售量并没有受到影响。

The sales volume of the products was not affected in spite of the fact that the company was being sued.

b. 尽管 *can also be used in the second clause with the same usage that was illustrated in part a; however, no adverb is needed in this case.* 尽管如此 *is used to emphasize or reinforce what has previously been stated. The above examples can be rewritten as follows:*

1. 市场变化莫测，尽管如此，市场调研所反映的情况大体上还是可以信赖的。

The situation reflected by the market research is, on the whole, still trustworthy, despite market fluctuations.

2. 海外投资会有各种风险，尽管如此，为了扩大市场、追求利润，跨国公司仍然积极展开全球化战略。

MNCs are still actively implementing their global strategy to expand their markets and pursue profits, even though investing overseas entails various risks.

c. （副）

尽管 *can be used as an adverb meaning "feel free (to do something); do not hesitate (to do something); to keep on (doing something); by all means."*

1. 只要是有利于工作的意见，大家尽管说。

Please feel free to bring up any opinion, as long as it is beneficial to our work.

2. 别老尽管抱怨、批评，多提些有建设性、对实际工作比较有用的建议。

Don't just keep on complaining and criticizing; give more constructive suggestions that are more useful for the actual work.

3. 工作由我们承担，你尽管放心吧。

By all means, rest assured that we will take full responsibility for the job.

 词语辨析

# 1. 把握　掌握

把握（名、动）"confidence; assurance; certainty; to grasp; to steer"

1. 你有没有把握办好这件事？
   Do you have confidence that you will do this well?

2. 虽然作了广泛的市场调研，但大家对新产品的销售仍然没把握。
   Though we have done extensive market research, we still have no confidence in the sales of the new product.

3. 当领导的一定要把握好公司的方向。
   Leaders must have a firm grip on the direction of the company.

掌握（动）"to know well; to grasp; to master"

1. 一个好的销售人员不但要对自己的产品十分熟悉，而且要掌握销售技巧。
   A good salesman not only needs to be familiar with the product he sells, but also needs to have a good grasp of salesmanship as well.

2. 命运其实是掌握在自己手中的。
Your fate is actually in your own hands.

3. 由于掌握了现代技术以及正确的操作方法，那家公司的产品质量大大提高了。
Due to mastering modern technology and correct operational methods, the quality of products of that company has been improved a great deal.

*把握 can be used as a verb or a noun, but it is most often used as a noun. When used as a noun, it means having confidence in or being certain about a particular event or matter. As a verb, it must have an accompanying noun. The choice of nouns is limited to abstract nouns such as* 机会、时机、商机、要领, *or* 本质 *and non-abstract noun such as* 方向盘. 掌握 *means to grasp an idea, principle, skill, or knowledge, but not an opportunity. It is usually used with abstract nouns such as* 理论、原则、技术、方法, *etc.*

## 2. 依赖　依靠　靠

依赖（动、名）"to depend on; to be dependent on others"

1. 在因特网普及之前，信息来源主要依赖于媒体报道。
Prior to the ubiquity of the Internet, information sources depended mainly on media reports.

2. 很多发达国家的生产原材料在很大程度上依赖于从第三世界国家的进口。
Many developed countries rely to a great extent on imports of raw materials from third world countries.

3. 依赖性太强的人，比较不容易培养独立自主的能力。
People accustomed to being dependent (on others) have difficulties developing an ability to stand on their own feet.

依靠（动、名）"to rely on; to depend on; a support; something to fall back on"

1. 依靠大家的力量，我们公司才能提前完成今年的出口目标。
   Our company must depend on everybody's efforts to reach this year's export target ahead of schedule.

2. 失业后，他只好依靠政府的救济生活。
   After he lost his job, he had no other choice but to depend on government subsidies for a living.

3. 他失去双亲后，顿时失去了生活的依靠。
   After he lost both of his parents, he suddenly lost all support for his livelihood.

靠（动）"to rely on; to depend on; to lean against; to be close to"

1. 靠并购整合而继续生存下去的公司越来越多。
   More and more companies depend on mergers and acquisitions to continue to survive.

2. 他靠在沙发上睡着了。
   He fell asleep leaning back on the couch.

3. 依山靠海的别墅价格最高。
   Houses close to a mountain or an ocean are the most expensive.

*依赖 implies that people or things are dependent on something. 依赖 usually has a negative connotation in that the dependence is too strong or too heavily relied upon (i.e. without this support, someone or something cannot function or exist). 依靠 also suggests that one has the aid or support of something or someone. However, in contrast, this support is neither too strong nor too heavily relied upon. The connotation is neutral. 靠 is similar to 依靠 in the sense of aid or support with a neutral connotation. However, 靠 also means to physically be close to or to lean against something.*

# 3. 广泛　广大

广泛（形、副）"extensive; comprehensive; widespread; extensively"

1. 这本杂志因涉及的题材广泛而受到广大群众的欢迎。
   Due to the extensive variety of its content, the magazine is well received by a great number of readers.

2. 网络的普及对现代人的生活有着广泛的影响。
   The ubiquitous use of the Internet has an extensive impact on people's lifestyles nowadays.

3. 为了广泛征求顾客的意见，以提高服务质量，饭店及宾馆一般都设有意见箱。
   Hotels and restaurants usually set up a "suggestion box" to extensively solicit opinions from customers in order to improve service quality.

广大（形）"numerous; vast; wide; expansive"

1. 人一旦成名，一举一动都会受到广大群众的瞩目。
   Once someone becomes famous, his/her every move receives a great amount of attention from the public at large.

2. 中国人口众多，任何产品都可能有广大的消费群体。
   The population in China is huge and, therefore, any product could enjoy a vast market.

3. 为了减少环境污染、防止水土流失，中国政府在全国掀起了广大的植树造林运动。
   In order to reduce environmental pollution and prevent erosion, the Chinese government started a vast campaign for planting trees and reforestation.

*Both 广泛 and 广大 have the meaning of "big and vast." However, 广泛 refers to a widespread or extensive scope or range, especially with regards to different types or genres. It is often used to describe abstract things. 广大 refers to the magnitude or dimension to which something covers or extends, emphasizing the actual number or size rather than the variety. It can be used to describe both abstract and concrete nouns.* 广泛 *can be used as an adjective or an adverb; but* 广大 *can only be used as an adjective.*

# 4. 关注　关心

关注（动、名）"to pay attention to; concern"

1. 证券交易所大厅内每天都聚集着很多关注股市行情的股民。
   Many individual investors who are concerned about the stock market gather in the hall of the stock exchange everyday.

2. 国际刑警组织已经开始关注跨国贩卖人口案件。
   International police organizations have begun to pay attention to incidents of cross-border kidnapping.

3. 总裁表达了对此事的关注（关心）。
   The president expressed his concern over the matter.

关心（动、名）"to care for; to be concerned about"

1. 关心员工的福利是加强员工对公司的忠诚度、提高生产率的有效手段。
   Caring about employee welfare issues is an effective way to strengthen employee loyalty and increase productivity.

2. 教育改革问题是全世界每个国家都普遍关心的问题。
   Countries all over the world are concerned about reforms in the education system.

3. 开发电子商务的企业，关心的不只是技术，而且还包括如何树立名牌、打开市场等问题。
   When developing e-commerce, companies are concerned not only about technology, but also about establishing brand equity and opening new markets.

*Both* 关注 *and* 关心 *mean to show one's concerns about something. The main difference between* 关注 *and* 关心 *is that* 关注 *is stronger in magnitude and attaches greater importance to that matter; it is also used for matters that are more serious, formal, or professional. Another difference is that 关注 can be used to show concern only for non-living objects or matters, whereas 关心 can also be used to show concern for people.*

# 5. 面临　面对

面临（动）"to be faced with; to be facing; to be up against"

1. 尽管面临重重困难，公司还是以员工的利益为重。
   Although facing many difficulties, the company still regards employee benefits as its primary responsibility.

2. 面临压力的时候，尤其需要仔细考虑、冷静处理，才能避免失误。
   When facing pressure, one needs to think carefully, remain calm, and only then can he/she avoid mistakes.

3. 目前网络公司都面临着激烈的竞争，建立公司品牌是公司生存下去的关键。
   Dotcom companies are all facing fierce competition, so establishing a brand name is the key to survival.

面对（动）

a. "to be facing something or someone; to be across from"

1. 这是他首次面对董事会提出下季度的生产计划。
   This was the first time he presented the next quarter's production plan in front of the board.

2. 海关大楼和工商银行大厦都面对着外滩。
   The Customs Building and the Commercial Bank Building are both across from the Bund.

*b.* "to face; to confront"

1. 除非公司面对现实，关闭亏损工厂，否则经营状况不可能改变。
   Unless the company faces reality and shuts down its unprofitable factories, the business situation cannot possibly improve.

2. 在市场供求不断变化的情况下，任何国家随时都有可能面对货币贬值的压力。
   Under conditions of continuous changes in market supply and demand, any country could face the pressure of currency devaluation at any time.

3. 面对着火山爆发的威胁，地质学家仍然深入现场收集第一手资料。
   Although facing the threat of a volcanic eruption, the geologists still went deep into the site to gather firsthand data.

*Both 面临 and 面对 are used with concrete and abstract objects meaning "facing a certain situation or condition." The main difference between the two is the proximity of the situation. 面临 emphasizes a situation that is less imminent, whereas 面对 stresses a situation that is very imminent. 面对 can also be used for situations with people such as a presentation, but 面临 cannot.*

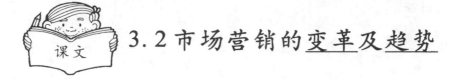

# 3.2 市场营销的变革及趋势

好产品并不<u>等于</u>好商品，好产品在没有获得好的市场份额之前不能称为好商品。而市场营销是一个产品或一个<u>品牌</u>通向市场、成为商品的<u>桥梁</u>。近几年，中国企业已经逐渐认识到市场营销的重要性，开始采用现代营销方式。

"现代营销方式"<u>面向</u>市场，完全以消费者需求为<u>导向</u>，它是产品、价格、<u>分销</u>、促销等<u>环节</u>的<u>组合</u>。西方的市场学又称 4P (Product, Price, Placement, & Promotion)。多数从事市场营销的人士都按4P来<u>策划</u>自己的市场营销策略。

通过多年<u>实践</u>，中国企业在营销策略中的促销方面进步很大。目前，中国企业已经普遍采用广告和优惠券（如降价、<u>折扣券</u>）等现代促销手段来达到薄利多销、扩大市场占有率的目的。随着科技的发展，近几年又出现了电视购物、<u>网络</u>购物等新一代的营销方式。营销方式的发展进一步推动了企业营销意识的转变。中国企业正在逐步建立起以消费者需求为中心、以市场为导向的现代营销体系。

# 3.2 市場營銷的<u>變革</u>及<u>趨勢</u>

課文

　　好產品並不<u>等於</u>好商品，好產品在沒有獲得好的市場份額之前不能稱爲好商品。而市場營銷是一個產品或一個<u>品牌</u>通向市場、成爲商品的<u>橋梁</u>。近幾年，中國企業已經逐漸認識到市場營銷的重要性，開始採用現代營銷方式。

　　"現代營銷方式"<u>面向</u>市場，完全以消費者需求爲<u>導向</u>，它是產品、價格、<u>分銷</u>、促銷等<u>環節</u>的<u>組合</u>。西方的市場學又稱 4P (Product, Price, Placement, & Promotion)。多數從事市場營銷的人士都按4P來<u>策劃</u>自己的市場營銷策略。

　　<u>通過多年實踐</u>，中國企業在營銷策略中的促銷方面進步很大。目前，中國企業已經普遍採用廣告和優惠券（如降價、<u>折扣券</u>）等現代促銷手段來達到薄利多銷、擴大市場佔有率的目的。隨著科技的發展，近幾年又出現了電視購物、<u>網絡</u>購物等新一代的營銷方式。營銷方式的發展進一步推動了企業營銷意識的轉變。中國企業正在逐步建立起以消費者需求爲中心、以市場爲導向的現代營銷體系。

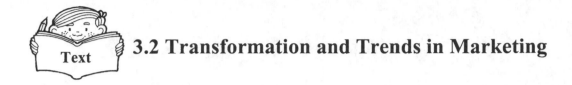

# 3.2 Transformation and Trends in Marketing

A good product isn't necessarily a successful product. A good product cannot be called a commercial success until it gains market share. Marketing is the bridge for a product or a brand to get into the market and to become merchandise. Chinese enterprises have gradually come to recognize the importance of marketing over the past several years and have begun adopting modern marketing methods.

Modern marketing is driven by the market and totally directed by consumer demands. It emphasizes the integration of product, price, placement, and promotion, known in Western marketing parlance as the 4 Ps. Most marketers plan their marketing strategies according to the 4 Ps.

With the benefit of several years of practical experience, Chinese businesses have improved markedly in the promotional aspect of marketing strategy. Marketing tools such as advertisements and price incentives (such as offering discounts or providing coupons) have been widely adopted in China in order to attain greater profit through low-margin, high-volume sales and to expand market share. Following on the heels of recent technological developments, the latest generation of marketing methods such as television and Internet shopping are being utilized as well. New developments in marketing methods are transforming the way businesses approach marketing. Chinese businesses are gradually building a modern marketing system centered on consumer demands and directed by the market.

**背景知识**

在改革开放以前，中国市场上消费品普遍<u>紧缺</u>，是一个<u>典型</u>的卖方市场，许多企业的产品是"<u>皇帝的女儿不愁嫁</u>"。随着改革开放的实施和深化，国外消费品，如家用电器等，纷纷涌入中国市场，对国产商品造成了<u>强烈的冲击</u>，促使卖方市场向买方市场转变，<u>迫使</u>中国企业采取现代营销策略4P来推销自己的产品，<u>占据</u>市场。

**背景知識**

在改革開放以前，中國市場上消費品普遍<u>緊缺</u>，是一個<u>典型</u>的賣方市場，許多企業的產品是"<u>皇帝的女兒不愁嫁</u>"。隨著改革開放的實施和深化，國外消費品，如家用電器等，紛紛涌入中國市場，對國產商品造成了<u>強烈的冲擊</u>，促使賣方市場向買方市場轉變，<u>迫使</u>中國企業采取現代營銷策略4P來推銷自己的產品，<u>佔據</u>市場。

**Background Information**

Before economic reforms were implemented in China, consumer goods were in short supply, and a typical seller's market was in place, so most products were in no danger of having no takers. After reforms were implemented and began to take effect, foreign consumer products such as household appliances began to pour into the Chinese market. They had a formidable impact on domestic products, and transformed the seller's market into a buyer's market. Chinese companies were forced to adopt modernized marketing techniques, primarily the 4Ps model, to promote their own products and retain their market share.

# 生词表

| | | | | |
|---|---|---|---|---|
| 变革 | 變革 | biàngé | （名、动） | transformation; to transform; change |
| 趋势 | 趨勢 | qūshì | （名） | trend; tendency |
| 等于 | 等於 | děngyú | （动） | to equal; to be equivalent to |
| 品牌 | 品牌 | pǐnpái | （名） | brand |
| 桥梁 | 橋梁 | qiáoliáng | （名） | bridge |
| 面向 | 面向 | miànxiàng | （动） | to face; to turn one's face to; to turn in the direction of |
| 导向 | 導向 | dǎoxiàng | （名、动） | direction; to direct towards; to guide |
| 分销 | 分銷 | fēnxiāo | （名、动） | distribution (of products); to distribute (products) |
| 环节 | 環節 | huánjié | （名） | link (in a chain); part; element |
| 组合 | 組合 | zǔhé | （名、动） | combination; to compose; to constitute (a whole) |
| 策划 | 策劃 | cèhuà | （动） | to plan; to hatch (a plot) |

| 实践 | 實踐 | shíjiàn | （名、动） | practical experience; to put into practice |
| 折扣券 | 折扣券 | zhékòu quàn | （名） | discount coupon |
| 网络 | 網絡 | wǎngluò | （名） | network |
| 紧缺 | 緊缺 | jǐnquē | （形） | to be short (in supply) |
| 典型 | 典型 | diǎnxíng | （形、名） | typical; classic case |
| 皇帝的女儿不愁嫁 | 皇帝的女兒不愁嫁 | huángdì de nǚér bùchóu jià | （口） | "The emperor's daughter is not worried about not being able to get married," which means being free of worry about having no takers. |
| 强烈 | 強烈 | qiángliè | （形） | strong; intense |
| 冲击 | 沖擊 | chōngjī | （名、动） | impact; to pound; to lash |
| 迫使 | 迫使 | pòshǐ | （动） | to force; to compel |
| 占据 | 佔據 | zhànjù | （动） | to occupy; to hold in one's possession |

# 1. 以 ... 为 ...

*以 ... 为 ..., a prepositional phrase, is a written form of 把 ... 当作 ... or
认为 ... 是 ... meaning to "regard ... as ..." or "consider ... as ..." or "take ...
as ..."*

1. 我们公司这个月销售业绩又是以他为最高。
   Once again, his sales performance this month is regarded as the highest in
   our company.

2. 商业在发展的初期是以等价交换为标准的。
   Commerce in its earliest developmental stage used equal value bartering as
   a standard.

3. 日本员工对公司特别忠心，总是以公司为家。
   Japanese employees are quite loyal to their companies; they always regard
   the company as family.

4. 找实习工作时，应该以获得工作经验为主，以报酬为辅。
   When looking for internship opportunities, one should consider gaining
   work experience as the primary goal, and getting paid as secondary.

 词语辨析

# 1.逐渐　逐步

逐渐（副）"gradually"

1. 五点钟后，天色逐渐暗了下来。
   It gradually gets dark after five o'clock.

2. 服用中药以后，他的身体逐渐康复了。
   He gradually recovered after taking the Chinese medicine.

3. 随着年龄的增长和生活经验的积累，人们对事物的认识会逐渐（逐步）加深，为人处世也会更加稳重。
   As one grows older and accumulates more life experience, his/her understanding of things will gradually deepen and his/her conduct towards life and human interaction will also become more composed.

逐步（副）"step by step; progressively"

1. 自从实行对内改革、对外开放的政策以来，中国的经济逐步好转，人民生活水平也有了明显提高。
   Since the implementation of the "Reform and Open Door Policy," the Chinese economy has improved step by step, and the people's living standards have also visibly risen.

2. 通过引进、消化和开发，中国逐步缩小了在制造业方面同先进国家之间的差距。
   Through the introduction, incorporation, and development (of technology), China is progressively narrowing its gap with developed countries in manufacturing industries.

3. 彼此信赖、互相尊重是逐步建立起良好合作关系的基础。
   Having mutual trust and respect is the foundation for gradually establishing a good collaborative relationship.

*Both 逐渐 and 逐步 are used to describe a situation, condition, or behavior that is changing slowly and gradually. However, if the progress is unconscious and occurs little by little, then 逐渐 is used. 逐步 is used if the change is conscious, occurs step by step, and is usually in line with a certain path, order, or sequence.*

# 2. 采用　采取

采用（动）"to use; to employ; to adopt"

1. 他的营销方案因为没有结合当地的特殊情况而未能被公司采用。
   His marketing plan was not accepted by the company due to insufficient incorporation of local conditions.

2. 采用电脑多媒体的方式做工作报告，既简洁又明了。
   Making presentations using computer-based multi-media is more clear and concise.

3. 中国企业广泛采用资源系统管理的模式。
   The Enterprise Resource Planning (ERP) system has been extensively adopted by Chinese enterprises.

采取（动）"to adopt; to take (a policy, measure, method, means, attitude, etc.); to employ"

1. 零售商店通常采取降价措施，以处理滞销的库存商品。
   Retail stores usually use price reduction to get rid of old, slow-moving inventories.

2. 人事部门必须采取公正的立场来考核每位员工。
   HR departments must take an impartial attitude when evaluating each employee.

3. 解决问题应该采取实事求是的态度。
   When solving problems, one should have a realistic and truth-seeking mindset.

*采用 means to adopt or employ something and utilize it, with an emphasis on utilization. Whereas 采取 means to choose one particular option out of many to be utilized or implemented, with an emphasis on choosing. Note that there are some overlapping circumstances with these verbs. However, in many cases, the accompanying object dictates which verb will be used. For example, 采取 is usually used with nouns such as 办法、步骤、措施、方针、方法、手段、态度、行动、形式、政策、策略, etc. 采用 is usually accompanied by nouns such as 工具、方案、方法、方式、技术、设备、文字、语言, etc.*

# 3. 实践　实行　实现

实践（名、动）"practical experience; to put into practice"

1. 通过实践总结经验，可以改进工作方法。
   Accumulating experience by carrying out various activities can improve work methods.

2. 书本上的理论常常会与生活实践有出入，这就需要靠丰富的生活经验来补偿。
   Theories that one learns from books are often different from what one experiences in real life. Therefore, book knowledge needs to be complemented with an abundance of real life experiences.

3. 一旦答应，他一定会实践（实现）自己的承诺。
   Once he promises something, he will definitely keep his word.

实行（动）"to carry out; to put into practice; to implement"

*The usage of 实行 was explained in Lesson 1.1, Distinguishing Synonyms, Section 3. For the comparison purposes with 实践 and 实现, here are a few more examples:*

1. 公司决定实行薄利多销的营销策略来打开市场。
   The company decided to use a low price and high sales volume strategy to enter the market.

---

2. 实行"产销一条龙"的管理模式，能使公司根据市场的需求迅速调整产品结构，从而减少库存积压的风险。
The integrated management model of merging production and sales enables companies to be responsive to market needs and to adjust their product portfolios in a timely manner, thereby minimizing inventory risks.

实现（动）"to realize; to fulfil; to bring about; to come true"

1. 只有通过努力，才能实现白己的理想。
Only through hard work can one realize his/her dreams.

2. 公司通过选举，产生了新的总经理，实现了领导班子更新换代。
By electing a new general manager, the company brought in a new generation of leadership.

*实践 refers to actually carrying out or performing some activities. It can be used either as a noun or a verb. Some fixed expressions are: 通过实践 and 实践诺言. 实行 means to carry out or implement a policy or plan through action. It is only used as a verb. 实现 means to make something positive into a reality. It usually has disyllabic nouns as its object. Neither 实践 nor 实行 has the meaning of making something become a reality.*

# 4. 策略　战略

策略（名）"tactics; strategy"

1. 公司应该根据市场变化时刻调整营销策略。
The company should continuously adjust its marketing and sales strategy in accordance with changes in the market.

2. 跨国公司都设有计划策略部门，负责为不同的地区及领域制定不同的管理、销售目标。
MNCs have strategy planning divisions to set management and sales goals for different regions.

3. 他因缺乏策略而竞选失败。
He was defeated due to his lack of tactics.

战略（名）"strategy"

1. 不断更新市场战略是公司在竞争中取得胜利的关键。
Continuously renewing marketing strategy is the key to success in competition.

2. 在中国投资设厂是我们公司的长期发展战略。
Investing and building factorics in China is our company's long-term strategy.

3. 为了应付突发事件，各个国家都拥有或多或少的石油战略储备。
In order to deal with emergencies, every country has a certain number of strategic oil reserves.

*策略 refers to a tactic or method. 战略 refers to an overall plan, policy, guiding principle, or strategy to realize a goal. 战略 originally was a military term, but now it is also used in other areas such as business and sports.*

# 5. 建立　树立

建立（动）"to build up; to establish"

*建立 was compared with 成立 and 设立 in Lesson 1.3, Distinguishing Synonyms, Section 5. For the purpose of comparing with 树立, here are a few more examples:*

1. 二次大战后，美国依靠其雄厚的经济及军事实力，建立起以美元为中心的世界经济新秩序。
After WWII, based on its solid economic and military strength, the U.S established a new world economic order centered on the U.S. dollar.

2. 我们公司在中国大陆已经建立了生产基地，下一步是寻找更有效的国内销售渠道。

Our company has already established a manufacturing base in China, and the next step will be to search for effective domestic distribution channels.

3. 顾客的正面反馈使我们建立起了对这种产品的信心。

Positive feedback from customers helped us build confidence in the product.

树立（动） "to cultivate; to foster; to establish"

1. 中国产品要走向世界，就必需在国际市场上树立高质量、高标准的形象。

To successfully enter the global market, Chinese products must establish an image of high quality and high standards.

2. 总裁在全公司树立了很高的个人威望。

The CEO has established a prestigious personal image in the company.

3. 俗语说"上梁不正下梁歪"，领导人自己首先要树立良好的榜样。

There is a Chinese saying, "If the upper beam is not straight, the lower beams will go askew." This implies that leaders should set good examples.

*建立 is used with abstract or concrete nouns, whereas 树立 is usually used with abstract and positively connotated nouns. The main difference is that 建立 emphasizes that something is established through hard work or perseverance, whereas 树立 emphasizes that things are built up by means of cultivation and fostering.*

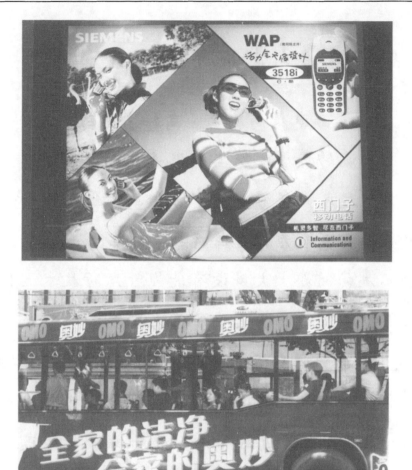

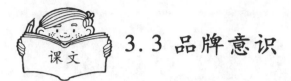

# 3.3 品牌意识

所谓名牌产品就是高质量、高知名度的产品。只有一流的技术、一流的管理才能生产出真正的名牌产品。国际上一般认为，技术开发资金至少占企业销售总额5%的企业才能开发出具有竞争力的名牌产品。过去，中国企业普遍存在资金不足的问题，大多没有能力开发新技术，因此中国几乎没有能在国际市场上竞争的名牌产品。

随着中国消费者生活水平和购买能力的普遍提高，人们的消费观念转变了，逐步建立起品牌意识，愿意以较高的价格购买名牌商品。近20年来，国外知名品牌的专卖店纷纷进入中国，并获得了很大的成功，如皮尔·卡丹在10年前便进入中国并占稳了市场。

目前，中国市场上的名牌多数属于高档高价的外国产品，由于中国不同地区的消费者收入水平相差很大，整体购买力不均衡，因此高档产品的市场有限。相比之下，开发适合中、低消费档次的名牌产品在中国市场上会具有更大的潜力。因此，中国企业在开发名牌产品、增强市场竞

# 3.3 品牌意識

所謂名牌產品就是高質量、高知名度的產品。只有一流的技術、一流的管理才能生產出真正的名牌產品。國際上一般認為，技術開發資金至少佔企業銷售總額5%的企業才能開發出具有競爭力的名牌產品。過去，中國企業普遍存在資金不足的問題，大多沒有能力開發新技術，因此中國幾乎沒有能在國際市場上競爭的名牌產品。

隨著中國消費者生活水平和購買能力的普遍提高，人們的消費觀念轉變了，逐步建立起品牌意識，願意以較高的價格購買名牌商品。近20年來，國外知名品牌的專賣店紛紛進入中國，并獲得了很大的成功，如皮爾·卡登在10年前便進入中國並佔穩了市場。

目前，中國市場上的名牌多數屬於高檔高價的外國產品，由於中國不同地區的消費者收入水平相差很大，整體購買力不均衡，因此高檔產品的市場有限。相比之下，開發適合中、低消費檔次的名牌產品在中國市場上會具有更大的潛力。因此，中國企業在開發名牌產品、增強市場競争力的同时，还应该多<u>档次</u>化。换句话说，不但要生产高档名牌产品，也要生产中、低档名牌产品。

爭力的同時，還應該多<u>檔次</u>化。換句話説，不但要生產高檔名牌產品，也要生產中、低檔名牌產品。

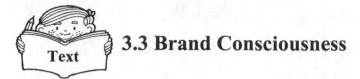

# 3.3 Brand Consciousness

A so-called "brand name" product is a high quality product with strong name recognition. Only businesses with top-notch technology and management can expect to produce genuine brand-name products. Internationally, it is generally thought that research and development should be at least 5% of a company's gross revenue in order for the company to develop a competitive brand. In the past, Chinese companies commonly faced capital shortages, so most of them couldn't develop new technology. Therefore, there were practically no competitive Chinese brands in the international market.

As the standard of living and purchasing power among Chinese consumers increased, consumers' notions changed. Gradually, they began to form a sense of brand consciousness and became more willing to spend more for brand-name products. Over the past 20 years, specialty shops selling foreign name brands have entered China one after another and have become extremely successful. Pierre Cardin, for instance, entered the Chinese market ten years ago and has established a stable market position.

Currently, most well-known brands in the Chinese market are high-quality, expensive foreign goods. There are wide differences in income levels among the various regions in China and purchasing power is highly uneven throughout the country, so the market for superior products is limited. In contrast, developing brands that are suitable for middle- and low-income consumers have a much greater potential in China's domestic market. Consequently, as Chinese businesses develop brand-name products and attempt to enhance their competitiveness, they should at the same time also pay attention to market segmentation. In other words, they should produce not only high-end brands, but also mid- and low-end brands.

中国人崇尚名牌的消费观念主要基于两个原因：一方面，消费者普遍认为"一分钱，一分货"。名牌商品虽然价格偏高，但是既有可靠的质量保证，又有完善的售后服务，物有所值。另一方面，名牌是身份和地位的象征。很多人购买商品不仅是为了满足温饱，而且也是为了获得社会的认知，提高自己的身价。

中國人崇尚名牌的消費觀念主要基於兩個原因：一方面，消費者普遍認為"一分錢，一分貨"。名牌商品雖然價格偏高，但是既有可靠的質量保證，又有完善的售後服務，物有所值。另一方面，名牌是身份和地位的象徵。很多人購買商品不僅是為了滿足溫飽，而且也是為了獲得社會的認知，提高自己的身價。

**Background Information**

There are two main reasons why Chinese people adore brand names. First, consumers generally subscribe to the notion that "you get what you pay for." Although brand-name products are higher priced, they come with reliable warranties and good after-sales service, so the goods are worth the price. Second, brand name products are symbolic of personal status. Many people purchase products not only out of necessity, but also out of a desire to obtain societal recognition and as a way of elevating their status.

生词表

| 所谓 | 所謂 | suǒwèi | （形） | so called; what is called |
|------|------|--------|--------|---------------------------|
| 知名度 | 知名度 | zhīmíngdù | （名） | degree of renown or celebrity |
| 一流 | 一流 | yīliú | （名） | first class; first rate; top-notch |
| 至少 | 至少 | zhìshǎo | （副） | at least |
| 属于 | 屬於 | shǔyú | （动） | to belong to; to be part of |
| 高档 | 高檔 | gāodàng | （名） | high/top grade; superior quality |
| 均衡 | 均衡 | jūnhéng | （名） | balance; equilibrium; parity |
| 相比 | 相比 | xiāngbǐ | （动） | to compare |
| 相比之下 | 相比之下 | xiāngbǐ zhīxià | （词组） | by comparison |
| 档次 | 檔次 | dàngcì | （名） | grade of products or goods |
| 崇尚 | 崇尚 | chóngshàng | （动） | to adore |
| 基于 | 基於 | jīyú | （介） | because of; owing to |
| 一分钱 一分货 | 一分錢 一分貨 | yìfēn qián yìfēn huò | （成） | the higher the price, the better the quality |
| 偏高 | 偏高 | piāngāo | （形） | slightly high |
| 售后服务 | 售後服務 | shòuhòu fúwù | （名） | after-sale service |
| 物有所值 | 物有所值 | wùyǒu suǒzhí | （成） | goods have their value; worthy; worthwhile |
| 身份 | 身份 | shēnfen | （名） | status; identity |
| 象征 | 象徵 | xiàngzhēng | （名、动） | symbol; to stand for; to symbolize |

| 温饱 | 溫飽 | wēnbǎo | （名） | adequate food and clothing; basic necessities of life |
| 认知 | 認知 | rènzhī | （名） | recognition; cognition |
| 身价 | 身價 | shēnjià | （名） | social status |

# 1. 所谓 "so-called; what is called"

1. 所谓的洋货就是指从国外进口的商品。
   So-called "foreign goods" refers to imported commodities.

2. 所谓 "以价取胜" 就是以低于对手的价格来夺取市场。
   The so-called "win with price" refers to capturing market share using prices lower than the competitors'.

3. 在种植过程中不施用任何化学农药的食品就是所谓的 "有机食品"。
   What we call "organic food" refers to food to which no chemical fertilizers or pesticides were administered during its growing period.

# 2. 只有 ... 才 ... "only; only if ... would ..."

只有 is used as a conjunction indicating that whatever follows it is a necessary condition for something to materialize. It is then followed by 才, which indicates the result. Together they complete a conditional pattern.

1. 只有总经理才有权签署贷款合同。
   Only the general manager can sign the loan contract.

2. 只有名牌产品才能以高于市场平均价格的价格出售。
Only brand-name products can be sold at a premium price.

3. 海外投资有很多风险，只有充分考虑各种因素，才能避免损失。
Overseas investments are risky, and only by carefully considering all factors can one prevent losses.

4. 只有靠并购整合，才能使没有实力的公司生存下去。
Only through merger and acquisition can a weak company survive.

# 3. 一般（形、副）

*a.* "general; ordinary; usually"

1. 这种产品从制造到发货一般需要一个月的时间。
This kind of product usually takes one month from manufacturing to delivery.

2. 为了避免市中心的各种社会问题，美国人一般不住在城里。
In order to avoid various social problems in the inner cities, most Americans usually do not live in the downtown area.

3. 他们不是一般的雇佣关系，而是有很深的交情。
Their relationship is not an ordinary employer-employee relationship, but rather a deep friendship.

4. 一般来说，价格更高的商品质量更好。
Generally speaking, the higher the price, the better the quality.

*b.* "the same as; just like"

*一般 can be used to modify a monosyllabic adjective without 的 meaning 一样. 象 ... 一般 or 如同 ... 一般 is a pattern used either as an adjective or an adverb to modify a noun or a verb. 一 can be omitted if words in the pattern contain more than two syllables.*

1. 中国有一句俗话 " 五个手指都不一般齐 " ，这句话的意思是说每个人都有各自的特点。

   There is a saying in Chinese, "Five fingers are not of the same length," which means each person is unique in his/her own way.

2. 虽然我们公司的资本和竞争对手一般多，但是我们的新技术产品在市场上更受欢迎。
   Although our company has the same amount of capital as our competitors, our new high tech products are better received in the market.

3. 现在的孩子营养好，身体如同牛一般壮。
   Nowadays children have good nutrition; therefore, they are as strong as bulls.

4. 进口限制一解除，各国品牌产品就象 " 雨后春笋 " 般出现在中国市场上。
   When import restrictions were lifted, brand name products from all over the world sprouted in the market like "bamboo shoots after the rain."

c. "average; common; ordinary"

1. 最近他在公司的表现一般。
   His recent performance in the company was average.

2. 这部电影的题材一般。
   The theme of the movie was ordinary.

# 4. 便

便 is the written form of 就, and 便 can always be replaced by 就. The uses focused on in this lesson are as follows:

a.（副）便 is used before a verb indicating that an action has happened earlier than expected.

1. 他大学没有毕业便已成为百万富翁了。
   He became a millionaire before graduating from college.

2. 电影还没有正式上映，媒体便已大肆宣传了。
   The media gave enormous publicity to the movie even before it was officially shown in theatres.

3. 他出差一回来，便马上投入了工作。
   As soon as he came back from the business trip, he plunged into work.

4. 产品一上市，便销售一空。
   As soon as the product reached the market, it was sold out.

b. （连）When used as a conjunction, 便 is placed in the second clause to indicate that the first clause is a precondition of the second clause. 只要 or 如果 can be used in the first clause indicating a hypothetical situation.

1. 没有大家的协助，便无法完成这个项目。
   Without everybody's joint effort, the project could never have been completed.

2. 只要筹足资金，便可以按时完成这项工程。
   As long as we can raise sufficient capital, the project can be finished on time.

3. 只要大家齐心协力，便能克服困难。
   As long as we work together, we can conquer all difficulties.

# 5. 在 ... 同时 "while; at the same time; simultaneously"

1. 政府在大力发展经济的同时，也要注重人文教育。
   While promoting economic development, the government should also pay attention to humanities education.

2. 在公司业务突飞猛进的同时，难免出现这样或那样的问题。
   At the same time that the company's business grew by leaps and bounds, it was inevitable that all kinds of problems would emerge.

3. 在发展高档产品的同时，也要注重开发中、低档的产品，这样才能满足广大消费者的需求。
   While developing high end products, the company should simultaneously emphasize the development of mid- and low- end products, thereby satisfying the demands of a wide range of customers.

 词语辨析

# 1. 意识　认识

意识（名、动）"consciousness; to be aware of; to realize"

*意识 indicates either one's state of mind or one's awareness of an object, state, value, or fact. When used as a noun, it is preceded by the verb 有. When used as a verb, it is often followed by 到.*

1. 投资股票的人要有风险意识。
   People who invest in stocks need to be conscious of the risk.

2. 运动员一般都有很强的竞争意识。
   Athletes are generally very conscious of competition.

3. 他无意识地把电脑关上后，才发觉忘了存盘。
   He unconsciously turned off the computer and then realized that he forgot to save his work.

4. 中国企业家在八十年代后才意识到市场调研的重要性。
It was only after the 1980s that Chinese entrepreneurs became aware of the importance of market research.

认识（动、名）"to understand; to know; to recognize; recognition; understanding"

*认识 means not only to be aware of, but also to have a certain amount of knowledge or understanding about something or someone. It can be used as a noun or a verb.*

1. 通过新闻报道，人们终于认识了事件的真相。
Through news reports, people finally learned the truth.

2. 通过比赛，我才认识到我们的网球水平还很低。
Not until we participated in the competition did I realize that our skill level in tennis was still quite low.

3. 他终于认识到，由于自己的工作失误，给公司造成了很大的经济损失。
He finally realized that, due to his mistakes, the company had suffered a great financial loss.

4. 很多年轻人对国际事物缺乏认识，也不了解经济全球化的意义。
Many younger people lack understanding of international affairs, nor do they understand the significance of economic globalization.

*意识 places more emphasis on the internal state of mind or awareness of something. Whereas 认识 indicates awareness, but emphasizes that there is additional understanding or knowledge.*

# 2. 普遍 普及 遍及

普遍（形）"general; widespread"

*普遍 is used to express that the nature of something is widespread or universally accepted.*

1. 中国的工艺品在世界各国普遍受到欢迎。
   Chinese arts and crafts are very popular throughout the world.

2. 在职教育能够普遍提高职员素质。
   On-the-job training programs could generally improve employee quality.

3. 在不久的将来，使用移动电话会比固定电话更普遍。
   In the near future, mobile phones will be more popular than fixed line telephones.

普及（动）"to popularize; to make universal; to spread"

*普及 is used as a verb, meaning to popularize knowledge, education, technology, etc.*

1. 普及职业道德教育可以减少不法现象。
   Popularizing occupational ethics education can diminish violation of the law.

2. 美国是世界上电脑普及程度最高的国家。
   Usage of computers is more widespread in the U.S. than any other country in the world.

3. 随着社会逐渐老龄化，敬老院也开始在中国普及起来了。
   Retirement homes are starting to spread throughout China as the population grows older.

遍及（动）"to reach everywhere; to extend or spread all over"

1. 美国大选所产生的影响遍及全球。
   The impact of the U.S. presidential election reaches all over the world.

2. 考察团的足迹遍及南极大陆。
   The expedition team left their footprints all over the Antarctic.

*Both* 普及 *and* 遍及 *are used as verbs.* 普及 *means to make something become more common.* 遍及 *stresses that footprints or an influence reach all over, and it usually has a locational word as its object.*

# 3. 转变　转化

转变（动、名）"to change; to transform; transformation; transition"

转变 *is usually used in a situation where the transformation or change is for the better.*

1. 把计划经济体制转变为具有中国特色的市场经济体制是中国经济改革的一大尝试。
   To switch from a planned economy to a market economy with Chinese characteristics is a big attempt at economic reform in China.

2. 他习惯于大锅饭制度，对合同制的转变一时还接受不了。
   He was accustomed to the "big common pot" system, so he could not adjust to the contract employment system in a short time.

3. 经过这次教训后，他一向自负的态度有了很大的转变。
   After the recent hard lesson, he underwent a major change in his arrogant attitude.

转化（动）"to change; to transform; to turn into"

转化 *means to transform into the reverse or opposite of a previous state.*

1. 他把悲痛转化为力量，准备东山再起。
   He turned his sorrow into strength and prepared to try all over again.

2. 公司只有采取有效战略，才能将劣势转化为优势。
   Only by adopting effective strategies can the company turn its disadvantages into advantages.

3. 在市场经济下，供求关系发生了转化：以前是供不应求，没有选择；现在是供过于求，选择太多。

Under the market economy, the relationship between supply and demand
has transformed: In the past, demand surpassed supply and customers had
no choice; now, supply surpasses demand and customers have too much
choice.

*转变 refers to changing one's viewpoint, attitude, or behavior and it also refers
to changing something's situation, condition, direction, or orientation. It is used
to express that the change is for the better. 转化 refers to changing the
characteristics of something into an opposite condition. The change or
transformation can be either for the better or for the worse.*

# 4.获得　取得

获得（动）"to obtain; to win; to reap"

1. 贸易洽谈会是供需双方互相交流，获得信息的绝佳场所。
   Tradeshows are the best kinds of places for suppliers and buyers to
   exchange ideas and acquire information.

2. 中间商从这笔交易中获得了巨额的利润。
   The intermediary made a huge profit from this deal.

3. 董事会决定从上半年度获得的利润中取出三分之一向希望工
   程捐款，以回报社会。
   The board decided to take one third of the profit obtained from the first
   half of the year and donate it to the "Hope Project" as recompense to
   society.

4. 上网注册可以获得本公司为客户提供的免费服务。
   By registering online, customers can get free services provided by the
   company.

取得(动) "to gain; to acquire; to obtain"

*取得 was explained in Lesson 2.4, Explanation of Terms, Section 2. Here are a
few more examples to be compared with 获得.*

1. 在同事的鼓励下，他的实验工作取得了很大进展。
   With the encouragement of colleagues, he made great progress in his experiment.

2. 管理人员可以通过高级经理培训班取得工商管理硕士学位。
   Through executive training classes, managers can get MBA degrees.

3. 降低价格并不能保证在竞争中取得优势。
   Lowering prices does not guarantee success against the competition.

*Both 获得 and 取得 are used with abstract and positive nouns. The magnitude and tone of 获得 is stronger than 取得.*

# 5. 均衡　平衡

均衡（形）"balanced; even"

1. 政治、社会和地理环境的不同造成了各地区经济发展的不均衡。
   Political, social, and geographic differences resulted in unevenness in economic development among various regions.

2. 中国人口的不均衡分布给市场调研工作带来了很大困难。
   In China, uneven population distribution causes difficulties in market research.

3. 总公司希望各地分公司的实力保持均衡。
   The headquarters hopes that the strength of all the subsidiaries can be kept in balance.

平衡（形、名、动）"balanced; equilibrium; to balance; to maintain equilibrium"

1. 奖罚不明会造成员工心理不平衡。
   Fuzzy reward and penalty policies could result in psychological imbalance among employees.

2. 杂技演员在走钢丝时要始终保持身体平衡。

Acrobatic performers need to keep their balance while walking on the high wire.

3. 产销一旦失去平衡就需要马上采取措施加以调整。

As soon as production and sales are out of equilibrium, we will need to adopt measures to adjust the situation at once.

4. 两队的实力需要平衡一下。

The strengths of the two teams need to be evened out a bit.

*Both 均衡 and 平衡 mean a state of being balanced or having equilibrium. However, 均衡 is used for a state which involves more than two elements, whereas 平衡 can be used for only two elements.*

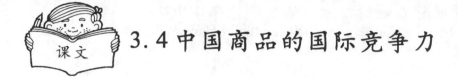

# 3.4 中国商品的国际竞争力

改革开放后，中国利用人口<u>众多</u>、<u>劳动力</u>成本低的<u>优势</u>，大力发展劳动<u>密集</u>型产业，向国际市场出口了大量商品。在短短几年间，中国就取代了台湾和韩国，成为<u>纺织品</u>、服装和玩具的出口大国。

然而，中国"<u>以价取胜</u>"的竞争优势正面临着<u>严峻</u>的<u>挑战</u>，因为劳动力成本只是影响价格的<u>因素</u>之一，除此之外，汇率、质量、<u>包装</u>和品牌等<u>诸多</u>因素也在很大程度上影响商品的价格。

东南亚国家货币的汇率在90年代<u>末</u>大<u>幅度</u>下降，而这些国家的出口商品结构与中国十分相似，因此对中国的出口贸易<u>形成</u>了巨大的<u>威胁</u>。而中国的<u>某</u>些企业只注重短期利益，出口<u>假冒伪劣</u>产品，<u>严重损害</u>了中国商品在国际市场上的形象。近年来，中国企业虽然对商品包装与广告宣传等推销手段有了进一步的重视，但与发达国家相比，尚存在着很大差距。

# 3.4 中國商品的國際競爭力

改革開放後，中國利用人口眾多、勞動力成本低的優勢，大力發展勞動密集型產業，向國際市場出口了大量商品。在短短幾年間，中國就取代了臺灣和韓國，成為紡織品、服裝和玩具的出口大國。

然而，中國"以價取勝"的競爭優勢正面臨著嚴峻的挑戰，因為勞動力成本只是影響價格的因素之一，除此之外，匯率、質量、包裝和品牌等諸多因素也在很大程度上影響商品的價格。

東南亞國家貨幣的匯率在90年代末大幅度下降，而這些國家的出口商品結構與中國十分相似，因此對中國的出口貿易形成了巨大的威脅。而中國的某些企業只注重短期利益，出口假冒偽劣產品，嚴重損害了中國商品在國際市場上的形象。近年來，中國企業雖然對商品包裝與廣告宣傳等推銷手段有了進一步的重視，但與發達國家相比，尚存在著很大差距。

不过，中国社会安定，经济增长迅速，通胀率低，汇率稳定，而且拥有<u>广阔</u>的市场，这些都为进一步提高中国商品的国际竞争力提供了有力的保障。

　　不過，中國社會安定，經濟增長迅速，通脹率低，匯率穩定，而且擁有<u>廣闊</u>的市場，這些都爲進一步提高中國商品的國際競爭力提供了有力的保障。

# 3.4 International Competitiveness of Chinese Products

After economic reforms were implemented in China, the country was able to take advantage of its large population and low labor costs to rapidly develop labor-intensive industry and export a huge volume of products. In only a few years, China effectively replaced Taiwan and Korea as the world's dominant exporter of textiles, clothing, and toys.

However, China's low-price competitive advantage is now being seriously challenged, because labor cost is only one of the factors in determining the price of goods. Foreign exchange rates, quality, packaging, branding, and numerous other factors also influence the price of merchandise to a great extent.

Given the similarities in the structure of export commodities between China and Southeast Asian countries, the drastic depreciation of Southeast Asia currencies in the 1990s constituted a significant threat to Chinese trade dominance. Furthermore, some Chinese businesses, caring only about short-term profits, export fake or inferior goods, which damages the overall image of Chinese merchandise on the international market. Even though Chinese businesses have taken further steps over the past several years to stress promotional strategies, such as packaging and advertising, there is still a big gap when China is compared to developed nations in this regard.

Nevertheless, Chinese society is relatively stable. The country maintains rapid economic growth, low inflation, and a stable foreign exchange rate. Moreover, China has a massive market. Taken together, these factors provide the necessary conditions for Chinese products to improve in international competitiveness.

中国产品的竞争优势主要是价格低。这有两个原因：首先，中国的劳动力成本低，因此产品价格低。如中国的制鞋成本只有美国的三分之一，意大利的二分之一。其次，部分中国企业故意压低出口价格，以换取外汇。中国政府已经制定政策，扶持高<u>附加值</u>产品的出口，并严禁企业压价出口。

中國產品的競爭優勢主要是價格低。這有兩個原因：首先，中國的勞動力成本低，因此產品價格低。如中國的製鞋成本只有美國的三分之一，意大利的二分之一。其次，部分中國企業故意壓底出口價格，以換取外匯。中國政府已經制定政策，扶持高<u>附加值</u>產品的出口，並嚴禁企業壓價出口。

**Background Information**

The competitive advantage for Chinese merchandise is low price. There are two reasons for this: First, labor costs in China are low, which gives a price advantage to goods made there. For example, the cost of shoe manufacturing in China is only one-third that of the U.S., and half that of Italy. Secondly, some Chinese businesses deliberately reduce export prices in order to get foreign currency.

The Chinese government has already set policies to support the export of value-added products and to prohibit the export of products with artificially low prices.

 生词表

| 众多 | 眾多 | zhòngduō | （形） | numerous |
| 劳动力 | 勞動力 | láodònglì | （名） | labor force |
| 优势 | 優勢 | yōushì | （名） | superiority; advantage; dominant position |
| 密集 | 密集 | mìjí | （形） | intensive; dense |
| 型 | 型 | xíng | （名） | model; type; pattern |
| 纺织品 | 紡織品 | fǎngzhī pǐn | （名） | textile products |
| 以价取胜 | 以價取勝 | yǐjià qǔshèng | （成） | to win with low prices |
| 严峻 | 嚴峻 | yánjùn | （形） | severe; serious |
| 挑战 | 挑戰 | tiǎozhàn | （名、动） | challenge; to challenge |
| 因素 | 因素 | yīnsù | （名） | factor; element |
| 包装 | 包裝 | bāozhuāng | （名、动） | packaging; to pack |
| 诸多 | 諸多 | zhūduō | （形） | a lot of |
| …末 | …末 | …mò | （名） | at the end of ... |
| 幅度 | 幅度 | fúdù | （名） | range; scope; extent |
| 形成 | 形成 | xíngchéng | （动） | to form; to shape |
| 威胁 | 威脅 | wēixié | （名、动） | threat; to threaten; to endanger; to menace |
| 某 | 某 | mǒu | （代） | certain (person or thing) |
| 假冒 | 假冒 | jiǎmào | （形、动） | forged; to forge; to pass oneself off as; to palm off |
| 伪 | 僞 | wěi | （形） | fake; bogus |

| 劣 | 劣 | liè | （形） | inferior; bad; low quality |
| 损害 | 損害 | sǔnhài | （动、名） | to harm; to damage; to injure; harm; damage; injury |
| 广阔 | 廣闊 | guǎngkuò | （形） | vast; broad |
| 附加值 | 附加值 | fùjiāzhí | （名） | added value |

# 1. 大力（副） "energetically; vigorously"

*大力 is used to modify a disyllabic word and means to energetically put the utmost effort in carrying out something.*

1. 为了解决经济发展不均衡的问题，中国政府正在大力推动西部大开发。
   To solve the uneven economic development problem, the Chinese government is strongly pushing the "great development of the West" movement.

2. 我们公司所进行的这项研究项目得到了政府的大力支持。
   Our company's research project received vigorous government support.

3. 各大电讯公司都在大力发展一种能把网络、电脑、电视和电话等通讯工具都集中于一体的新技术。
   All major telecommunication companies are devoting major efforts to developing a new technology that can integrate the Internet, computer, TV, and telephone into one single unit.

4. 在大力发展经济的同时，也要避免环境污染。
While developing the economy, we must simultaneously make a great effort to avoid environmental pollution.

## 2. 取代（动） "to replace; to substitute for; to take over; to supersede"

1. 进口商品由于价廉物美，逐渐取代了国内产品。
Because imported goods are good and inexpensive, they are gradually replacing domestic goods.

2. 通过大选，现任政权被反对党取代了。
Through the election, the administration in power was superseded by the opposition party.

3. 尽管生产已经实现完全自动化了，但是机器始终取代不了人的作用。
Although the manufacturing process has been totally automated, machines still cannot replace the role of humans.

## 3. 影响

*a.*（动）"to affect; to influence"

1. 摄取过多咖啡因会影响睡眠。
Ingesting too much caffeine will affect one's sleep.

2. 臭氧层的变化正在逐渐地影响生态平衡。
The change in the ozone layer is gradually affecting the ecological equilibrium.

3. 公司将大幅降低工资的谣言居然影响不了员工的情绪。
The rumor of massive salary cuts surprisingly did not influence employee morale.

4. 除了价格以外，影响产品竞争的因素还很多，例如质量和包装。

Besides price, there are many factors that influence product competitiveness such as quality and packaging.

b. （名） "influence; effect; impact"

*Patterns used most often are:* 对 ... 产生影响, 受 ... 影响, *and* 在 ... 影响下.

1. 九十年代末在东南亚发生的金融风暴对全球经济产生了巨大的影响。

The Asian financial crisis in the late 90s had a strong impact on the world economy.

2. 由于受汇率上升的影响，公司的出口订单大幅度下降。

Due to the effect of rising exchange rates, the company's export orders declined sharply.

3. 在中国经济飞速发展的影响下，很多国家在国际市场上失去了竞争优势。

Many countries have lost their competitive advantage (in the international market) due to the impact of rapid economic development in China.

# 4. 某（代） "certain (person, thing, etc.)"

*某 is used to indicate a certain person or thing that is already known so it is not necessary to point it out. It is also used when someone does not want to identify a certain person or thing. If 某 is used in reference to yourself, it either shows modesty or self-assurance. If it is used after someone else's last name, it sometimes carries a negative connotation.*

1. 由于某种原因，公司的产品不能按时在市场上行销。

For certain reasons, the company could not get the product to the market on time.

2. 这幢大楼曾经在某年某月某日发生过抢劫案。
Once upon a time (lit. on a certain day in a certain month of a certain year), a robbery happened in this building.

3. 在试验中，如果发生某种现象，就马上把发动机关上。
If something happens during the course of testing, turn off the motor immediately.

4. 公司财务人员张某因为挪用公款而被开除。
Accountant Zhang so-and-so was fired for embezzlement of company funds.

5. 您对我的帮助，我李某永远铭记在心。
I, Li so-and-so, will always remember the assistance you have extended to me.

 词语辨析

# 1. 严峻　严肃　严重

严峻（形）"severe; serious"

1. 加入WTO后，中国国有企业将面临更严峻的考验。
China's state-owned companies will face even more severe tests after China enters the WTO.

2. 核武器的出现，使现代战争的形势变得非常严峻。
The emergence of nuclear weapons has made the nature of modern warfare extremely severe.

3. 迫于火山爆发的严峻威胁，岛上的居民已经全部迁移到安全地带了。
The island residents were evacuated to safe areas under the severe threat of a volcanic eruption.

4. 他严峻的眼色（神情）使人畏惧。
The stern expression in his eyes makes people fear him.

严肃（形、动）"serious; solemn; earnest; to be serious"

1. 他的表情和态度都严肃得令人不敢亲近。
His expression and demeanor are so serious that they make people afraid to approach him.

2. 法庭里有一种不寻常的严肃气氛。
The courtroom has an unusually solemn atmosphere.

3. 任何违反纪律的行为都应该严肃认真地加以处理。
Any behavior that defies discipline should be seriously and conscientiously dealt with.

4. 只有严肃公司纪律，才能维持良好的工作秩序。
Only by strictly enforcing company regulations and discipline can good working order be maintained.

严重（形）"serious"

1. 他的病情恶化了，情况越来越严重。
His illness has been deteriorating and the situation has become increasingly serious.

2. 合资双方在如何分配利润上存在着严重分歧。
The joint venture partners have serious disputes over profit sharing.

3. 擅自挪用公款是严重的犯罪行为。
Embezzlement of company funds is a serious crime.

4. 化工厂的工业废水严重污染了周围的环境。
Industrial waste from the chemical plant seriously contaminated the surrounding environment.

*严峻 is used to describe a situation, condition, or a certain test which is severe or serious. It can also be used to describe a person's expression, particularly of the eyes. It is not commonly used but, when it is used, it usually modifies such nouns as:* 考验、挑战、形势、眼色、神情, *etc.* 严肃 *is used to describe a person's serious and earnest attitude or demeanor, or the solemnity or sedateness of the atmosphere of a place or a ceremony.* 严肃 *may be used as a verb, adjective, or adverb.* 严峻 *is used as an adjective only.* 严重 *is used to describe a serious situation or undesirable condition that would result or does result in great danger or has an enormous impact.*

# 2. 形成  成形

形成（动）"to form; to take form; to take shape, to become"

1. 上网聊天在年轻人中已经形成了一种风气。
   Online chatting has become a trend among young people.

2. 进口产品与国内产品在包装上形成了鲜明对比。
   In terms of packaging, imported and domestic goods form a sharp contrast.

3. 由于合作双方在投资比例上不能达成一致，谈判形成僵局。
   The joint venture partners could not reach agreement on the investment ratio, so the negotiation has reached a deadlock.

成形（动）"to physically become a form; to physically take form"

1. 一种产品的开发，从概念到成形，大约要花数年时间。
   The development of a new product from concept to reality probably takes several years.

2. 总的来说，男孩子体格成形得比女孩子晚。
   It takes longer for boys to grow up (lit. to take form) than for girls.

3. 这个雕像还没成形。
   The sculpture has not yet taken shape.

成形 *is only used in reference to something physically taking form.* 形成 *usually refers to things that are more abstract. One use of* 形成 *is (writing or artistic) styles, habits, or fads of a person or group of persons slowly taking shape over a period of time. Another use is the forming of a contrast, resolution, or deadlock.*

# 3. 注重　注意　重视

注重（动）"to pay attention to; to emphasize; to stress; to attach importance to"

1. 现代公司都很注重培养自己公司的企业文化。
   Modern companies emphasize creating their own company culture.

2. 制定市场竞争策略首先要注重了解顾客需要，其次是分析竞争对手的实力。
   To form a competitive marketing strategy, first a company should pay attention to understanding customers' needs, and then analyze its competitors' capabilities.

3. 中国除了发展劳动密集型行业之外，还必须注重开发知识密集形产业。
   In addition to developing labor-intensive industries, China also needs to stress the importance of developing knowledge-intensive industries.

注意（动、名）"to pay attention to; to be attentive to; attention"

1. 接受面试的时候要注意穿着与谈吐。
   During an interview, the interviewee should pay attention to his/her attire and speech.

2. 孩子在成长阶段要注意增加营养。
   One should pay attention to children's nutrition during their growth period.

3. 财务部长的突然辞职引起了公众的注意。
   The sudden resignation of the finance minister caught people's attention.

4. 他不能集中注意力的原因在于还不能适应新的工作环境。
The reason that he is unable to focus his attention is that he has not yet adjusted to the new working environment.

重视（动） "to attach importance to; to take something seriously; to think highly of; to esteem"

1. 有创意的年轻人在广告公司倍受重视。
Young people with innovative ideas are highly esteemed in advertising companics.

2. 各跨国公司都很重视本土化的市场营销方式。
All MNCs give importance to their localized marketing strategies.

3. 与其他行业相比，制药公司尤其重视产品的研发。
Compared to other industries, pharmaceutical companies attach greater importance to R&D.

*注意 means to apply one's mind and pay attention to a particular thing or person. It can be used as a verb or as a noun. Similar to 注意, the compound 注重 has another meaning, which is to additionally stress the importance of the thing or person to which attention is being paid. It is used as a verb only. 重视 has a meaning very close to 注重. However, 重视 means to regard someone or something as valuable and to deal with him/her or it seriously.*

# 4. 损害　伤害　危害　损坏

损害（动） "to harm; to damage; to injure"

*损害 means to lose or harm as a result of some circumstance or instance. It is commonly used with nouns such as 健康、事业、利益、名誉、权利, etc.*

1. 长期操作电脑会损害视力。
Working long hours with computers will damage one's eyesight.

2. 让不合格商品流入市场，会损害公司的信誉。
   Letting substandard products get into the market will damage a company's reputation.

3. 每个员工都不应该做任何损害公司利益的事情。
   No employee should do anything that would damage the interests of the company.

伤害（动） "to injure; to harm; to hurt"

伤害 *refers to physical or mental damage of someone or some animal.*

1. 熬夜、酗酒和抽烟都会伤害身体。
   Staying up all night, excessive drinking, and smoking will ruin one's health.

2. 保护动物权益者认为用动物当实验品，是伤害动物的行为。
   Animal rights protectionists believe that using animals in laboratory tests violates animals' rights.

3. 当众批评一个人会伤害他的自尊心。
   Criticizing someone publicly will hurt his/her self-esteem.

危害（动、名） "to harm; to jeopardize; to endanger; harm; danger; jeopardy"

危害 *refers to bringing damage to such things as* 健康、生命安全、和平、秩序、社会治安、利益, *etc.*

1. 过度劳累或运动不足都会危害身体健康。
   Excessive exertion or insufficient exercise will harm one's health.

2. 战争无论大小都会严重危害人民的生命财产。
   War, whether big or small, will cause great harm to people's lives and property.

3. 每年的洪水泛滥给居民带来的危害是难以估计的。
The damage caused by the flood each year is hard to estimate.

4. 官僚作风、贪污腐败严重危害社会秩序。
Bureaucracy and corruption severely jeopardizes social order.

*In addition to having different nouns as their objects as shown above, the main difference among these three words is the magnitude or degree of the damage. The degree of damage caused by* 损害 *is light and partial; the degree of the damage with* 伤害 *can be either light or severe; and the damage caused by* 危害 *is quite serious. These three words can be used interchangeably when the object refers to things associated with people such as health, eyesight, etc. The main difference is the degree of harm.*

损坏（动）"to damage; to break"

损坏 *means that a certain tangible thing has been damaged and has lost its original usefulness and efficacy.* 损坏 *is not interchangeable with the previous three verbs.*

1. 在运输途中受到损坏的物品都会得到全额补偿。
All goods that are damaged during transportation will be fully compensated for.

2. 保险公司在赔款以前，先要对损坏的汽车进行评估。
Before the insurance company pays the claim, it will first conduct an appraisal of the damaged vehicle.

3. 文化大革命期间许多宝贵的文化遗产遭到了损坏。
During the Cultural Revolution, many precious cultural artifacts were damaged.

索引

# 词汇索引

| chǎnyè | 产业 | 產業 | （名） | industry | 1.1 |
|---|---|---|---|---|---|
| chāyì | 差异 | 差異 | （名） | difference; divergence; discrepancy; diversity | 3.1 |
| chéngbāo | 承包 | 承包 | （动） | to contract | 1.2 |
| chéngdān | 承担 | 承擔 | （动） | to undertake; to bear; to assume | 1.4 |
| chéngwéi | 成为 | 成爲 | （动） | to become | 1.1 |
| chōngjī | 冲击 | 衝擊 | （名、动） | impact; to pound; to lash | 3.2 |
| chóngshàng | 崇尚 | 崇尚 | （动） | to adore | 3.3 |
| chuándì | 传递 | 傳遞 | （名、动） | transmission; to transmit; to deliver | 3.1 |
| chǔyú | 处于 | 處於 | （动） | to be in a situation or position of | 2.3 |
| cǐwài | 此外 | 此外 | （连） | in addition; besides; moreover | 1.1 |
| cóng'ér | 从而 | 從而 | （连） | thus; thereby | 1.1 |
| cóngshì | 从事 | 從事 | （动） | to go into (a profession or business); to be engaged in | 1.2 |
| cùjìn | 促进 | 促進 | （动） | to promote; to advance; to accelerate | 1.1 |
| cùshǐ | 促使 | 促使 | （动） | to spur; to promote | 2.3 |
| cùxiāo | 促销 | 促銷 | （名、动） | promotion; to promote sales | 3.1 |

# D

| dāng ... shí | 当...时 | 當...時 | （介） | when; while | 2.2 |
|---|---|---|---|---|---|
| dàngcì | 档次 | 檔次 | （名） | grade of products or goods | 3.3 |
| dàolù | 道路 | 道路 | （名） | path; way; road | 2.3 |
| dǎoxiàng | 导向 | 導向 | （名、动） | direction; to direct towards; to guide | 3.2 |
| děngyú | 等于 | 等於 | （动） | to equal; to be equivalent to | 3.2 |
| diàndìng | 奠定 | 奠定 | （动） | to establish; to settle | 2.4 |
| diǎnxíng | 典型 | 典型 | （形、名） | typical; classic case | 3.2 |
| diàowǎng | 调往 | 調往 | （动） | to transfer to; to shift to | 2.2 |

| diàoyán | 调研 | 調研 | （名） | investigation and research | 3.1 |
|---|---|---|---|---|---|
| dòngjī | 动机 | 動機 | （名） | motive; intention | 3.1 |
| dúzī | 独资 | 獨資 | （名） | wholly owned (foreign enterprise) | 1.4 |

# E

| é | 额 | 額 | （名） | a specified quantity | 1.4 |
|---|---|---|---|---|---|

# F

| fǎguī | 法规 | 法規 | （名） | laws and regulations | 1.2 |
|---|---|---|---|---|---|
| fāhuī | 发挥 | 發揮 | （动） | to bring into play; to give free rein to | 2.1 |
| fáng | 坊 | 坊 | （名） | handicraftsman's workplace; workshop | 1.2 |
| fángzhǐ | 防止 | 防止 | （动） | to prevent; to keep something from occurring | 2.2 |
| fǎngzhī pǐn | 纺织品 | 紡織品 | （名） | textile products | 3.4 |
| fánróng | 繁荣 | 繁榮 | （形） | prosperous; flourishing | 2.4 |
| fǎnzhī | 反之 | 反之 | （连） | conversely; whereas; on the other hand; on the contrary | 2.2 |
| fāxíng | 发行 | 發行 | （名、动） | issuance; to issue | 2.3 |
| fēnbù | 分布 | 分布 | （名、动） | distribution; to be scattered (in a certain area); to be distributed; to be dispersed | 3.1 |
| fēndān | 分担 | 分擔 | （动） | to share (burden / responsibility) | 1.4 |
| fēngtǔ rénqíng | 风土人情 | 風土人情 | （成） | local customs and practices | 3.1 |
| fēngxiǎn | 风险 | 風險 | （名） | risk; hazard | 1.4 |
| fēnlí | 分离 | 分離 | （动） | to separate | 2.1 |
| fēnpèi | 分配 | 分配 | （动） | to distribute; to allocate; to assign | 1.1 |

| fēnxiǎng | 分享 | 分享 | （动） | to share (joy, rights, etc.) | 1.4 |
|---|---|---|---|---|---|
| fēnxiāo | 分销 | 分銷 | （名、动） | distribution (of products); to distribute (products) | 3.2 |
| fúchí | 扶持 | 扶持 | （动） | to support | 2.1 |
| fúdù | 幅度 | 幅度 | （名） | range; scope; extent | 3.4 |
| fùjiāzhí | 附加值 | 附加值 | （名） | added value | 3.4 |
| fúzhí | 扶植 | 扶植 | （动） | to foster; to support | 1.3 |

# G

| gāi | 该 | 該 | （代） | the aforementioned | 2.2 |
|---|---|---|---|---|---|
| gǎigé | 改革 | 改革 | （名、动） | reform; to reform | 1.1 |
| gàiniàn | 概念 | 概念 | （名） | concept | 2.3 |
| gǎizǔ | 改组 | 改組 | （动、名） | to reorganize; reorganization | 1.2 |
| gāodǎng | 高档 | 高檔 | （名） | high/top grade; superior quality | 3.3 |
| gètǐ | 个体 | 個體 | （名、形） | sole proprietorship; individual (enterprise) | 1.2 |
| gōng | 供 | 供 | （动） | to provide for | 2.3 |
| gōngchéng | 工程 | 工程 | （名） | project; engineering | 1.1 |
| gōngqiú | 供求 | 供求 | （名） | supply and demand | 3.1 |
| gōngyìng | 供应 | 供應 | （名、动） | supply; to supply | 1.1 |
| gōngzhèng | 公正 | 公正 | （形） | fair; just; impartial | 3.1 |
| guānbì | 关闭 | 關閉 | （动） | to close; to shut down | 1.1 |
| guǎngfàn | 广泛 | 廣泛 | （形） | broad; extensive; wide-ranging; widespread | 3.1 |
| guǎngkuò | 广阔 | 廣闊 | （形） | vast; broad | 3.4 |
| guānjiàn | 关键 | 關鍵 | （名、形） | key (point or issue); crux; crucial; critical | 2.2 |
| guǎnlǐjú | 管理局 | 管理局 | （名） | administrative / management bureau | 2.2 |
| gǔfèn | 股份 | 股份 | （名） | share; stock | 1.4 |
| guī ... suǒyǒu | 归 ...所有 | 歸 ...所有 | （动） | to belong to… | 1.4 |

| guīfàn | 规范 | 規範 | （形、名） | standard; normal; a standard | 2.3 |
|--------|------|------|------------|------------------------------|-----|
| gǔlì | 鼓励 | 鼓勵 | （动、名） | to encourage; encouragement | 2.2 |
| guówùyuàn | 国务院 | 國務院 | （名） | the State Council (of China) | 2.1 |

# H

| héhuǒ | 合伙 | 合夥 | （动） | to form a partnership | 1.2 |
|-------|------|------|--------|-----------------------|-----|
| hézuò | 合作 | 合作 | （名、动） | cooperative (enterprises); to cooperate | 1.4 |
| hóngchóugǔ | 红筹股 | 紅籌股 | （名） | red chip stock | 2.3 |
| hù | 沪 | 滬 | （专） | an abbreviated name for Shanghai (used in written form) | 2.4 |
| huàfēn | 划分 | 劃分 | （动） | to classify; to differentiate | 2.3 |
| huángdì de nǚér bù chóu jià | 皇帝的女儿不愁嫁 | 皇帝的女兒不愁嫁 | （口） | "The emperor's daughter is not worried about not being able to get married," which means being free of worry about having no takers | 3.2 |
| huánjié | 环节 | 環節 | （名） | link (in a chain); part; element | 3.2 |
| huíbào | 回报 | 回報 | （名、动） | return (on an investment); to repay; to reciprocate | 2.2 |
| huīfù | 恢复 | 恢復 | （动） | to resume; to recuperate; to return to | 2.3 |
| huò | 获 | 獲 | （动） | to gain; to obtain; to achieve | 1.4 |
| huǒbàn | 伙伴 | 夥伴 | （名） | partner; companion | 1.4 |
| huòbì | 货币 | 貨幣 | （名） | currency | 2.2 |
| huòdé | 获得 | 獲得 | （动） | to obtain; to gain | 2.2 |
| huólì | 活力 | 活力 | （名） | vitality; vigor; strength | 1.1 |
| huòqǔ | 获取 | 獲取 | （动） | to procure; to obtain | 3.1 |
| huòzhǔn | 获准 | 獲准 | （动） | to be permitted; to be allowed | 2.1 |

# J

| | | | | | |
|---|---|---|---|---|---|
| jiājǐn | 加紧 | 加緊 | （动） | to intensify; to step up; to speed up | 1.1 |
| jiǎmào | 假冒 | 假冒 | （形、动） | forged; to forge; to pass oneself off as | 3.4 |
| jiānbìng | 兼并 | 兼併 | （动、名） | to merge; to annex (territories); merger | 1.2 |
| jiāndū | 监督 | 監督 | （动） | to supervise; to control | 2.1 |
| jiānguǎn | 监管 | 監管 | （名、动） | supervision; regulation; to supervise; to regulate | 2.3 |
| jiànlì | 建立 | 建立 | （动） | to build; to establish; to set up; to found | 1.1 |
| jiànquán | 健全 | 健全 | （形） | sound; perfect | 2.3 |
| jiànshè | 建设 | 建設 | （动） | to build; to construct | 1.3 |
| jiānshí | 坚实 | 堅實 | （形） | solid; strong; substantial; firm | 2.4 |
| jiàoyù | 教育 | 教育 | （名、动） | education; to educate | 3.1 |
| jiàzhí | 价值 | 價值 | （名） | value | 2.2 |
| jīchǔ shèshī | 基础设施 | 基礎設施 | （名） | Infrastructure | 1.3 |
| jiēduàn | 阶段 | 階段 | （名） | stage; period; phase | 2.3 |
| jiégòu | 结构 | 結構 | （名） | structure; construction; setup; organization | 3.1 |
| jièrù | 介入 | 介入 | （动） | to intervene; to interpose | 1.2 |
| jìngnèi | 境内 | 境內 | （名） | location within the borders of a country | 1.4 |
| jīngrén | 惊人 | 驚人 | （形） | astonishing; amazing | 2.4 |
| jǐnguǎn | 尽管 | 儘管 | （副） | even though; in spite of | 3.1 |
| jìngzhēng duìshǒu | 竞争对手 | 競爭對手 | （名） | competitor | 3.1 |
| jǐnquē | 紧缺 | 緊缺 | （形） | to be short (in supply) | 3.2 |
| jǐnsuō | 紧缩 | 緊縮 | （动） | to tighten; to reduce | 2.2 |
| jítuán | 集团 | 集團 | （名） | conglomerate; a number of subsidiary companies | 1.2 |
| jiùyè | 就业 | 就業 | （动） | to obtain employment | 1.1 |
| jīyú | 基于 | 基於 | （介） | because of; owing to | 3.3 |

| | | | | | |
|---|---|---|---|---|---|
| jīzhì | 机制 | 機制 | （名） | mechanism | 1.4 |
| jù | 具 | 具 | （动） | to have; to possess | 1.3 |
| jūmín | 居民 | 居民 | （名） | resident | 2.2 |
| jūnhéng | 均衡 | 均衡 | （名） | balance; equilibrium; parity | 3.3 |
| jùyǒu | 具有 | 具有 | （动） | to have; to possess | 1.1 |

## K

| | | | | | |
|---|---|---|---|---|---|
| kāizhǎn | 开展 | 開展 | （动） | to develop; to launch | 1.4 |
| kànhǎo | 看好 | 看好 | （动） | to seem good; to look promising | 1.1 |
| kèfú | 克服 | 克服 | （动） | to overcome; to conquer | 1.1 |
| kòngzhì | 控制 | 控制 | （动） | to control; to dominate | 2.2 |
| kuīsǔn | 亏损 | 虧損 | （名、动） | financial loss; deficit; to suffer a loss | 1.1 |

## L

| | | | | | |
|---|---|---|---|---|---|
| láiyuán | 来源 | 來源 | （名） | source | 3.1 |
| lánchóugǔ | 蓝筹股 | 藍籌股 | （名） | blue chip stock | 2.3 |
| láodònglì | 劳动力 | 勞動力 | （名） | labor force | 3.4 |
| lèisì | 类似 | 類似 | （形） | similar to | 2.3 |
| lěngquè | 冷却 | 冷卻 | （动） | to cool down | 2.2 |
| liáokuò | 辽阔 | 遼闊 | （形） | vast; broad; boundless; wide (usually in reference to places) | 3.1 |
| liè | 列 | 列 | （动） | to list; to categorize | 1.3 |
| liè | 劣 | 劣 | （形） | inferior; bad; low quality | 3.4 |
| lìfǎ | 立法 | 立法 | （名、动、形） | legislation; to legislate; legislative | 1.1 |
| lǐngyù | 领域 | 領域 | （名） | domain; field; territory | 1.2 |
| lìng | 令 | 令 | （动） | to cause; to make | 1.2 |
| lìrùn | 利润 | 利潤 | （名） | profit | 1.4 |
| liúdòng | 流动 | 流動 | （名、动、形） | flow; circulation; to flow; to circulate; to be on the | 2.2 |

|          |        |        |         | move; mobile; fluid |     |
|----------|--------|--------|---------|---------------------|-----|
| liúrù    | 流入   | 流入   | （动）  | to flow into | 1.1 |
| lǒngduàn | 垄断   | 壟斷   | （动、名） | to monopolize; monopoly | 1.2 |
| lùxù     | 陆续   | 陸續   | （副）  | one after another; in succession | 1.3 |

# M

|           |        |        |         |                          |     |
|-----------|--------|--------|---------|--------------------------|-----|
| měichēng  | 美称   | 美稱   | （名）  | good name; laudable title | 2.4 |
| miànxiàng | 面向   | 面向   | （动）  | to face; to turn one's face to; to turn in the direction of | 3.2 |
| miànzhí   | 面值   | 面值   | （名）  | face value | 2.3 |
| mìjí      | 密集   | 密集   | （形）  | intensive; dense | 3.4 |
| mò        | …末    | …末    | （名）  | at the end of | 3.4 |
| mǒu       | 某     | 某     | （代）  | certain (person or thing) | 3.4 |

# N

|           |        |        |         |                       |     |
|-----------|--------|--------|---------|-----------------------|-----|
| nèilù     | 内陆   | 內陸   | （名）  | inland; interior | 1.3 |
| néngyuán  | 能源   | 能源   | （名）  | energy sources | 1.3 |
| niánlíng  | 年龄   | 年齡   | （名）  | age | 3.1 |
| nóngyè    | 农业   | 農業   | （名）  | agriculture; farming | 2.1 |

# P

|           |        |        |           |                              |     |
|-----------|--------|--------|-----------|------------------------------|-----|
| pī        | 批     | 批     | （量）    | batch; group of (goods or people) | 1.1 |
| piāngāo   | 偏高   | 偏高   | （形）    | slightly high | 3.3 |
| pǐnpái    | 品牌   | 品牌   | （名）    | brand | 3.2 |
| pīzhǔn    | 批准   | 批准   | （名、动） | approval; to approve; to ratify | 2.2 |
| pòshǐ     | 迫使   | 迫使   | （动）    | to force; to compel | 3.2 |
| Pǔdōng    | 浦东   | 浦東   | （专）    | Pudong | 2.4 |

# Q

|           |        |        |         |                  |     |
|-----------|--------|--------|---------|------------------|-----|
| qiángliè  | 强烈   | 強烈   | （形）  | strong; intense | 3.2 |

| qiáoliáng | 桥梁 | 橋梁 | （名） | bridge | 3.2 |
|---|---|---|---|---|---|
| qícì | 其次 | 其次 | （连） | next; secondly; then | 2.2 |
| qìyuē | 契约 | 契約 | （名） | contract | 1.4 |
| quánmiàn | 全面 | 全面 | （形） | overall; comprehensive; all-around | 2.3 |
| quánqiú | 全球 | 全球 | （形、名） | global; the whole world | 1.4 |
| qǔdài | 取代 | 取代 | （动） | to replace; to substitute | 1.4 |
| qǔdé | 取得 | 取得 | （动） | to obtain; to gain | 1.2 |
| quèdìng | 确定 | 確定 | （动、形） | to determine; to decide; to confirm; definite; fixed | 2.1 |
| quēfá | 缺乏 | 缺乏 | （动） | to lack; to be short of | 1.1 |
| qūshì | 趋势 | 趨勢 | （名） | trend; tendency | 3.2 |

# R

| rèngòu | 认购 | 認購 | （动） | to offer to buy (stock) | 2.3 |
|---|---|---|---|---|---|
| réngrán | 仍然 | 仍然 | （副） | still; yet | 3.1 |
| rènkě | 认可 | 認可 | （动、名） | to approve; to accept; to recognize; approval; acceptance | 1.2 |
| rènwù | 任务 | 任務 | （名） | mission; assignment; task; job | 2.1 |
| rènzhī | 认知 | 認知 | （名） | recognition; cognition | 3.3 |
| róngzī | 融资 | 融資 | （名） | financing; a loan | 2.1 |
| rúcǐ | 如此 | 如此 | （代） | so; such; in this way | 3.1 |

# S

| shàng | 尚 | 尚 | （副） | still; yet | 2.3 |
|---|---|---|---|---|---|
| shèjí | 涉及 | 涉及 | （动） | to involve; to be related to | 1.2 |
| shèlì | 设立 | 設立 | （动） | to establish; to set up | 1.3 |
| shēnfen | 身份 | 身份 | （名） | status; identity | 3.3 |
| shèngyú | 剩余 | 剩餘 | （名、动） | surplus; remainder; to have a surplus | 1.4 |
| shēngzhí | 升值 | 升值 | （动、名） | to appreciate; appreciation | 2.2 |

| tuīxíng | 推行 | 推行 | （动） | to carry out; to implement; to put into practice | 1.1 |

## W

| wǎngluò | 网络 | 網絡 | （名） | network | 3.2 |
| wánshàn | 完善 | 完善 | （动） | to perfect; to improve | 1.1 |
| wěi | 伪 | 偽 | （形） | fake; bogus | 3.4 |
| wéichí | 维持 | 維持 | （动） | to maintain; to keep; to preserve | 1.1 |
| wèizhi | 位置 | 位置 | （名） | (geographical) location; place; position | 1.3 |
| wēixié | 威胁 | 威脅 | （名、动） | threat; to threaten; to endanger; to menace | 3.4 |
| wēnbǎo | 温饱 | 溫飽 | （名） | adequate food and clothing; basic necessities of life | 3.3 |
| wěndìng | 稳定 | 穩定 | （形、动） | stable; steady; to stabilize | 1.1 |
| wùyǒu suǒzhí | 物有所值 | 物有所值 | （成） | goods have their value; worthy; worthwhile | 3.3 |

## X

| xiāngbǐ | 相比 | 相比 | （动） | to compare | 3.3 |
| xiāngbǐ zhīxià | 相比之下 | 相比之下 | （词组） | by comparison | 3.3 |
| xiāngguān | 相关 | 相關 | （形） | related | 2.3 |
| xiàngmù | 项目 | 項目 | （名） | project; item | 2.1 |
| xiàngzhēng | 象征 | 象徵 | （名、动） | symbol; to stand for; to symbolize | 3.3 |
| xiānhòu | 先后 | 先後 | （副、名） | one after another; successively; being early or late; priority | 1.3 |
| xiāofèipǐn | 消费品 | 消費品 | （名） | consumer goods | 1.3 |
| xiāotiáo | 萧条 | 蕭條 | （名） | depression | 2.2 |
| xiézhù | 协助 | 協助 | （动、名） | to assist; to help; assistance | 1.4 |

| | | | | thing, organization, etc.) | |
|---|---|---|---|---|---|
| zhìshǎo | 至少 | 至少 | （副） | at least | 3.3 |
| zhíxíng | 执行 | 執行 | （动） | to implement; to carry out | 2.1 |
| zhìyào | 制药 | 製藥 | （名） | pharmaceutical (industry) | 1.3 |
| zhīyī | 之一 | 之一 | （代） | one of ... | 1.1 |
| zhìyuē | 制约 | 制約 | （动） | to restrict; to constrain | 1.1 |
| zhìzào | 制造 | 製造 | （动） | to make; to manufacture | 1.3 |
| zhòngduō | 众多 | 眾多 | （形） | numerous | 3.4 |
| zhōngyāng | 中央 | 中央 | （名、形） | center; central | 1.1 |
| zhōngzhǐ | 终止 | 終止 | （名、动） | termination; to terminate | 1.4 |
| zhuǎnbiàn | 转变 | 轉變 | （动、名） | to change; transformation | 1.1 |
| zhuǎnhuàn | 转换 | 轉換 | （动） | to change; to transform | 1.4 |
| zhùcè | 注册 | 注册 | （动、名） | to register; registration | 1.2 |
| zhǔdǎo | 主导 | 主導 | （形、名） | leading; dominant; guiding principle | 1.2 |
| zhūduō | 诸多 | 諸多 | （形） | a lot of | 3.4 |
| zhǔmù | 瞩目 | 矚目 | （动） | to fix one's eye on; to focus one's attention on | 1.2 |
| zhǔnquè | 准确 | 準確 | （形） | accurate | 3.1 |
| zìfù yíngkuī | 自负盈亏 | 自負盈虧 | （词组） | to assume sole responsibility for profit or loss | 2.1 |
| zǔchéng | 组成 | 組成 | （动） | to form; to make up; to compose | 2.1 |
| zǔhé | 组合 | 組合 | （名、动） | combination; to compose; to constitute (a whole) | 3.2 |
| zǔjiàn | 组建 | 組建 | （动） | to put together (a group); to organize | 1.2 |
| zūlìn | 租赁 | 租賃 | （动、名） | to rent; to lease; lease | 1.2 |

# 词语例释索引

## M-R

| měidāng | 每当 | 每當 | 2.2(2) |
|---|---|---|---|
| mǒu | 某 | 某 | 3.4(4) |
| nǎizhì | 乃至 | 乃至 | 2.4(1) |
| qí | 其 | 其 | 1.4(9) |
| qǐ | …起 | …起 | 1.3(1) |
| qǐ | 起 | 起 | 2.1(3) |
| qǐ | 起（补） | 起（補） | 1.3(4) |
| qǔdài | 取代 | 取代 | 3.4(2) |
| qǔdé | 取得 | 取得 | 2.4(2) |
| rúhé | 如何 | 如何 | 2.2(7) |

## S-X

| shènzhì | 甚至 | 甚至 | 1.2(4) |
|---|---|---|---|
| shǐ | 使 | 使 | 2.1(4) |
| shòu | 受 | 受 | 3.1(4) |
| shǒuduàn | 手段 | 手段 | 3.1(3) |
| suízhe | 随着 | 隨著 | 2.1(5) |
| suǒ | 所＋V＋的 | 所＋V＋的 | 1.4(5) |
| suǒwèi | 所谓 | 所謂 | 3.3(1) |
| tōngguò | 通过 | 通過 | 2.3(2) |
| wèi | 为（介） | 爲（介） | 1.3(5) |
| wèi | 为（动） | 爲（動） | 1.4(1) |
| wèile | 为了（介） | 爲了（介） | 1.1(3) |
| xiānhòu | 先后 | 先後 | 1.3(2) |

# Y

| | | | |
|---|---|---|---|
| yǐ | 以（介） | 以（介） | 1.2(5) |
| yǐ | 以（连） | 以（連） | 1.3(6) |
| yǐ...wéi | 以...为... | 以...爲... | 3.2(1) |
| yībān | 一般 | 一般 | 3.3(3) |
| yǐlái | ...以来 | ...以來 | 1.2(1) |
| yǐngxiǎng | 影响 | 影響 | 3.4(3) |
| yǐshàng | 以上 | 以上 | 1.3(3) |
| yóu | 由 | 由 | 1.1(1) |
| yuèlái yuèduō | 越来越多 | 越來越多 | 1.1(7) |

# Z

| | | | |
|---|---|---|---|
| zài...shàng | 在...上 | 在...上 | 2.2(6) |
| zài...tóngshí | 在...同时 | 在...同時 | 3.3(5) |
| zài...xià | 在...下 | 在...下 | 1.1(2) |
| zài...zhōng | 在...中 | 在...中 | 2.1(2) |
| zé | 则 | 則 | 1.4(8) |
| zhī | 之 | 之 | 2.2(5) |
| zhǐ | 指 | 指 | 2.3(4) |
| zhídào | 直到 | 直到 | 1.2(2) |
| zhǐyǒu...cái | 只有...才... | 只有...才... | 3.3(2) |
| zhuǎnbiàn | 转变 | 轉變 | 1.1(4) |

# 词语辨析索引

## B

| | | | 章节 | 同义词 |
|---|---|---|---|---|
| bānbù | 颁布 | 頒布 | 1.2(3) | 公布 |
| bǎozhàng | 保障 | 保障 | 2.4(4) | 保证 |
| bǎozhèng | 保证 | 保證 | 2.4(4) | 保障 |
| bǎwò | 把握 | 把握 | 3.1(1) | 掌握 |
| biàndòng | 变动 | 變動 | 2.2(1) | 变化 |
| biànhuà | 变化 | 變化 | 2.2(1) | 变动 |
| biànjí | 遍及 | 遍及 | 3.3(2) | 普遍、普及 |
| biànwéi | 变为 | 變爲 | 1.1(3) | 成为 |
| biǎodá | 表达 | 表達 | 2.2(6) | 表示、表明 |
| biǎomíng | 表明 | 表明 | 2.2(6) | 表示、表达 |
| biǎoshì | 表示 | 表示 | 2.2(6) | 表达、表明 |
| bìmiǎn | 避免 | 避免 | 2.2(5) | 防止 |

## C

| | | | | |
|---|---|---|---|---|
| cǎiqǔ | 采取 | 採取 | 3.2(2) | 采用 |
| cǎiyòng | 采用 | 採用 | 3.2(2) | 采取 |
| cèluè | 策略 | 策略 | 3.2(4) | 战略 |
| chénglì | 成立 | 成立 | 1.3(2) | 建立、设立 |
| chéngxíng | 成形 | 成形 | 3.4(2) | 形成 |
| cǐwài | 此外 | 此外 | 2.4(1) | 另外 |

## D

| | | | | |
|---|---|---|---|---|
| duì | 对 | 對 | 1.4(3) | 对于 |
| duìyú | 对于 | 對於 | 1.4(3) | 对 |

# F

| fāngfǎ | 方法 | 方法 | 1.2(5) | 方式 |
|--------|------|------|--------|------|
| fāngshì | 方式 | 方式 | 1.2(5) | 方法 |
| fángzhǐ | 防止 | 防止 | 2.2(5) | 避免 |
| fāzhǎn | 发展 | 發展 | 2.1(2) | 展开、开展 |
| fēndān | 分担 | 分擔 | 1.4(2) | 分享 |
| fēnxiǎng | 分享 | 分享 | 1.4(2) | 分担 |

# G

| gàiniàn | 概念 | 概念 | 2.3(3) | 观念 |
|---------|------|------|--------|------|
| gōngbù | 公布 | 公布 | 1.2(3) | 颁布 |
| guǎngdà | 广大 | 廣大 | 3.1(3) | 广泛 |
| guǎngfàn | 广泛 | 廣泛 | 3.1(3) | 广大 |
| guānniàn | 观念 | 觀念 | 2.3(3) | 概念 |
| guānxīn | 关心 | 關心 | 3.1(4) | 关注 |
| guānzhù | 关注 | 關注 | 3.1(4) | 关心 |
| gǔlì | 鼓励 | 鼓勵 | 2.2(3) | 勉励 |

# H

| huòdé | 获得 | 獲得 | 3.3(4) | 取得 |
|-------|------|------|--------|------|

# J

| jí | 及 | 及 | 2.1(1) | 以及 |
|----|---|---|--------|------|
| jiànlì | 建立 | 建立 | 1.3(2) | 成立、设立 |
| jiànlì | 建立 | 建立 | 3.2(5) | 树立 |
| jiāodiǎn | 焦点 | 焦點 | 2.4(3) | 热点 |
| jǐnmì | 紧密 | 緊密 | 2.3(2) | 密切 |
| jūnhéng | 均衡 | 均衡 | 3.3(5) | 平衡 |

# K

| kāizhǎn | 开展 | 開展 | 2.1(2) | 展开、发展 |
|---|---|---|---|---|
| kào | 靠 | 靠 | 3.1(2) | 依赖、依靠 |
| kòngzhì | 控制 | 控制 | 2.2(4) | 抑制 |
| kuòchōng | 扩充 | 擴充 | 1.2(4) | 扩大 |
| kuòdà | 扩大 | 擴大 | 1.2(4) | 扩充 |

# L

| liánxù | 连续 | 連續 | 1.3(1) | 陆续 |
|---|---|---|---|---|
| lǐngtǔ | 领土 | 領土 | 1.2(2) | 领域 |
| lìngwài | 另外 | 另外 | 2.4(1) | 此外 |
| lǐngyù | 领域 | 領域 | 1.2(2) | 领土 |
| lùxù | 陆续 | 陸續 | 1.3(1) | 连续 |

# M

| miànduì | 面对 | 面對 | 3.1(5) | 面临 |
|---|---|---|---|---|
| miǎnlì | 勉励 | 勉勵 | 2.2(3) | 鼓励 |
| miànlín | 面临 | 面臨 | 3.1(5) | 面对 |
| mìqiè | 密切 | 密切 | 2.3(2) | 紧密 |

# P

| pínghéng | 平衡 | 平衡 | 3.3(5) | 均衡 |
|---|---|---|---|---|
| pǔbiàn | 普遍 | 普遍 | 3.3(2) | 普及 |
| pǔjí | 普及 | 普及 | 3.3(2) | 普遍 |

# Q

| | | | | |
|---|---|---|---|---|
| qǔdé | 取得 | 取得 | 3.3(4) | 获得 |
| quēfá | 缺乏 | 缺乏 | 2.3(1) | 缺少 |
| quēshǎo | 缺少 | 缺少 | 2.3(1) | 缺乏 |

# R

| | | | | |
|---|---|---|---|---|
| rèdiǎn | 热点 | 熱點 | 2.4(3) | 焦点 |
| rènkě | 认可 | 認可 | 1.2(1) | 许可、允许 |
| rènshi | 认识 | 認識 | 3.3(1) | 意识 |

# S

| | | | | |
|---|---|---|---|---|
| shānghài | 伤害 | 傷害 | 3.4(4) | 损害、危害、损坏 |
| shíjiàn | 实践 | 實踐 | 3.2(3) | 实行、实现 |
| shíxiàn | 实现 | 實現 | 3.2(3) | 实践、实行 |
| shíxíng | 实行 | 實行 | 1.1(2) | 推行 |
| | | | 3.2(3) | 实践、实现 |
| shèlì | 设立 | 設立 | 1.3(2) | 成立、建立 |
| shùlì | 树立 | 樹立 | 3.2(6) | 建立 |
| sǔnhài | 损害 | 損害 | 3.4(4) | 伤害、危害、损坏 |
| sǔnhuài | 损坏 | 損壞 | 3.4(4) | 损害、伤害、危害 |

# T

| | | | | |
|---|---|---|---|---|
| tǐzhì | 体制 | 體制 | 1.1(1) | 制度 |
| tuīxíng | 推行 | 推行 | 1.1(2) | 实行 |

# W

| wēihài | 危害 | 危害 | 3.4(4) | 损害、伤害、损坏 |
|--------|------|------|--------|-----------------|

# X

| xiāngguān | 相关 | 相關 | 2.3(4) | 有关 |
|-----------|------|------|--------|------|
| xíngchéng | 形成 | 形成 | 3.4(2) | 成形 |
| xíngshì | 形式 | 形式 | 1.4(1) | 形状 |
| xíngzhuàng | 形状 | 形狀 | 1.4(1) | 形式 |
| xǔkě | 许可 | 許可 | 1.2(1) | 认可、允许 |

# Y

| yánjùn | 严峻 | 嚴峻 | 3.4(1) | 严肃、严重 |
|--------|------|------|--------|-----------|
| yánsù | 严肃 | 嚴肅 | 3.4(1) | 严峻、严重 |
| yánzhòng | 严重 | 嚴重 | 3.4(1) | 严峻、严肃 |
| yǐjí | 以及 | 以及 | 2.1(1) | 以 |
| yīkào | 依靠 | 依靠 | 3.1(2) | 依赖、靠 |
| yīlài | 依赖 | 依賴 | 3.1(2) | 依靠、靠 |
| yìshi | 意识 | 意識 | 3.3(1) | 认识 |
| yìzhì | 抑制 | 抑制 | 2.2(4) | 控制 |
| yǒuguān | 有关 | 有關 | 2.3(4) | 相关 |
| yuànwàng | 愿望 | 願望 | 2.2(2) | 欲望 |
| yǔnxǔ | 允许 | 允許 | 1.2(1) | 认可、许可 |
| yùwàng | 欲望 | 欲望 | 2.2(2) | 愿望 |

# Z

| zhǎngwò | 掌握 | 掌握 | 3.1(1) | 把握 |
| zhǎnkāi | 展开 | 展開 | 2.1(2) | 开展、发展 |
| zhànlüè | 战略 | 戰略 | 3.2(4) | 策略 |
| zhìdù | 制度 | 制度 | 1.1(1) | 体制 |
| zhòngshì | 重视 | 重视 | 3.4(3) | 注重、注意 |
| zhuǎnbiàn | 转变 | 轉變 | 3.3(3) | 转化 |
| zhuǎnhuà | 转化 | 轉化 | 3.3(3) | 转变 |
| zhúbù | 逐步 | 逐步 | 3.2(1) | 逐渐 |
| zhújiàn | 逐渐 | 逐渐 | 3.2(1) | 逐步 |
| zhǔmù | 瞩目 | 瞩目 | 2.4(2) | 注目 |
| zhùmù | 注目 | 注目 | 2.4(2) | 瞩目 |
| zhùyì | 注意 | 注意 | 3.4(3) | 注重、重视 |
| zhùzhòng | 注重 | 注重 | 3.4(3) | 注意、重视 |

练习

## Introduction

This Exercise Book contains practice exercises corresponding to each lesson found in Volume One of the textbook entitled *Open for Business: Lessons in Chinese Commerce for the New Millennium.* These exercises are designed to challenge students and improve their ability to use Chinese business lexicon correctly. Particular emphasis is placed on sentence structure and reading comprehension. The "Questions and Exploration" section is also included with each set of exercises to encourage students to use their newly acquired skills outside of the classroom, to perform further research on the Internet, and to present such information either orally or in writing for further classroom discussion.

There are two sections in this Exercise Book. The first section contains exercises in simplified Chinese while the second section contains the same exercises in traditional Chinese. The pages of this book are conveniently perforated so that students can remove and submit completed assignments for correction and review by instructors. Solutions to selected exercises from each lesson can be found in the "Exercise Answers" section at the end of the book in both simplified and traditional Chinese. However, solutions to sentence construction, translation, and open-ended reading comprehension are purposely not provided so as to stimulate individual thought and to help generate meaningful discussions in the classroom.

# Table of Contents

(continued on the next page)

# Table of Contents, continued

# 练习

# 1.1 练习

## 1. 选择适当的动词填空：
Fill in each blank with the most appropriate verb:

促进　吸引　建立　成立　克服

实行　看好　鼓励　分配　充满

a. (　　　　　)困难　　　　f. (　　　　　)公司

b. (　　　　　)发展　　　　g. (　　　　　)资源

c. (　　　　　)外资　　　　h. (　　　　　)市场

d. (　　　　　)信心　　　　i. (　　　　　)生产

e. (　　　　　)体制　　　　j. (　　　　　)改革

## 2. 选词填空：
Fill in each blank with the most appropriate word:

a. 中国有可能＿＿＿＿经济大国吗？

　　1) 成为　　　2) 变为　　　3) 转为

b. 因为长期亏损，我们只好把公司＿＿＿＿了。

　　1) 倒闭　　　2) 关闭　　　3) 关门

c. 改革的步伐应该再＿＿＿＿一点儿。

　　1) 加快　　　2) 加速　　　3) 加强

d. 政府应该赶快_____下岗职工再就业。

    1）指导       2）领导       3）引导

e. 目前哪一个国家的失业问题最_____呢？

    1）严重       2）严厉       3）严格

f. 中国从1979年开始_____经济体制改革，刚开始____的时候，遇到很多困难。

    1）推行       2）实行       3）实施

g. 你们公司的管理_____很现代化吗？

    1）体制       2）制度       3）体系

h. 我们要把不利的条件_____有利的条件。

    1）变为       2）成为       3）转变为

## 3. 完成句子并翻译：
Complete the following sentences and translate the sentences into English:

a. 在领导的鼓励下，_____

    翻译：_____

b. 为了降低失业率，_____

    翻译：_____

c. 公司分了两个月的奖金，此外，_____

    翻译：_____

d.　中国实行计划经济政策是为了＿＿＿＿＿＿＿＿＿＿＿＿＿＿＿＿

　　翻译：＿＿＿＿＿＿＿＿＿＿＿＿＿＿＿＿＿＿＿＿＿＿＿＿


e.　为了公平起见，＿＿＿＿＿＿＿＿＿＿＿＿＿＿＿＿＿＿＿＿＿

　　翻译：＿＿＿＿＿＿＿＿＿＿＿＿＿＿＿＿＿＿＿＿＿＿＿＿＿


f.　＿＿＿＿＿＿＿，从而促使美国公司进一步扩大在中国的投资。

　　翻译：＿＿＿＿＿＿＿＿＿＿＿＿＿＿＿＿＿＿＿＿＿＿＿＿＿


g.　越来越多的＿＿＿＿＿＿＿＿＿＿＿＿＿＿＿＿＿＿＿＿＿＿＿

　　翻译：＿＿＿＿＿＿＿＿＿＿＿＿＿＿＿＿＿＿＿＿＿＿＿＿＿


h.　经过多年的努力，他已经成为＿＿＿＿＿＿＿＿＿＿＿＿＿＿＿

　　翻译：＿＿＿＿＿＿＿＿＿＿＿＿＿＿＿＿＿＿＿＿＿＿＿＿＿


## 4. 翻译：
Translate into Chinese/English:

a.　Besides Taiwanese and Hong Kong business people, there are also business people coming from all over the world to invest in China.

_____


b.　Under the planned economic system, productivity is very low.

_____

c.　The members of the delegation were selected by the Ministry of Foreign Affairs.

_____

d.　More and more privately-owned enterprises have purchased state-owned enterprises.

_____

e.　Which company will become the world's largest manufacturer of laptops?

_____

f.　Before Nixon visited China, the diplomatic relationship between the U.S. and China had not been officially formed.

_____

g.　He still can not change his opinion.

_____

h.　所有的员工都由此进出。

_____

i.　国有企业的经营方式正在转变。

_____

j.　这家软件公司在世界各地都建立了子公司。

_____

## 5. 问题与探讨：
Questions and Exploration:

a. 外国投资者可不可以收购中国的国有企业？

b. 处理国有企业资产的主要困难是什么？

c. 多数下岗职工的再就业有什么问题？

d. 中国政府怎样解决失业问题？

# 1.2 练习

**1.** 选择适当的动词填空：
Fill in each blank with the most appropriate verb:

涉及　扩大　公布　得到

从事　允许　取得　颁布

a. (　　　　)成绩　　　　e. (　　　　)名单

b. (　　　　)领域　　　　f. (　　　　)规模

c. (　　　　)法规　　　　g. (　　　　)认可

d. (　　　　)活动　　　　h. (　　　　)改革

**2.** 解释以下句子中"以"的用法并翻译：
Explain the different meanings of "以" in the following sentences and translate the sentences into English:

a. 公司应以公平的原则对待员工。

解释：＿＿＿＿＿＿＿＿＿＿＿＿＿＿＿＿＿＿＿＿＿＿

翻译：＿＿＿＿＿＿＿＿＿＿＿＿＿＿＿＿＿＿＿＿＿＿

b. 以你现在的健康状况来说，不适合长途旅行。

解释：＿＿＿＿＿＿＿＿＿＿＿＿＿＿＿＿＿＿＿＿＿＿

翻译：＿＿＿＿＿＿＿＿＿＿＿＿＿＿＿＿＿＿＿＿＿＿

c. 私有经济在沿海地区发展迅速，<u>以深圳来说</u>，多数企业都是
私有企业。

解释：＿＿＿＿＿＿＿＿＿＿＿＿＿＿＿＿＿＿＿＿

翻译：＿＿＿＿＿＿＿＿＿＿＿＿＿＿＿＿＿＿＿＿

d. <u>以人口来说</u>，中国是世界上第一大国。

解释：＿＿＿＿＿＿＿＿＿＿＿＿＿＿＿＿＿＿＿＿

翻译：＿＿＿＿＿＿＿＿＿＿＿＿＿＿＿＿＿＿＿＿

# 3. 用"甚至"改写下列句子：
Rewrite the following sentences with "甚至"：

a. 国企被私有企业并购后，有些减少了亏损，有些还有盈利。

＿＿＿＿＿＿＿＿＿＿＿＿＿＿＿＿＿＿＿＿＿＿＿

b. 有些私有企业规模不断扩大，不但在国内拥有子公司，而且
在国外成立办事处或分支公司。

＿＿＿＿＿＿＿＿＿＿＿＿＿＿＿＿＿＿＿＿＿＿＿

c. 他工作很忙，忘了吃饭。

＿＿＿＿＿＿＿＿＿＿＿＿＿＿＿＿＿＿＿＿＿＿＿

d. 在中国的计划经济体制下，中央政府统一分配资源，统一组
织生产，还统一销售。

＿＿＿＿＿＿＿＿＿＿＿＿＿＿＿＿＿＿＿＿＿＿＿

e. 现在不仅年轻人和中年人用电脑，老年人也用。

_____

## 4. 用"不仅"改写下列句子：
Rewrite the following sentences with "不仅"：

a. 这次会议没有解决问题，却加深了矛盾。

_____

b. 近年来，中国的私有企业数量增多，规模扩大。

_____

c. 中国加入WTO以后，国有企业要和国内其它企业竞争，也要和外国的企业竞争。

_____

d. 中国政府改革了税收和金融体制，也改革了外贸体制。

_____

## 5. 选词填空：
Fill in each blank with the most appropriate word:

a. 认可　许可　允许

　1)企业要得到对外经济贸易合作部的正式_____才能从事进出口业务。

　2)中国政府_____一部分人先富起来的政策促进了中国的私有经济。

3) 这项计划已经得到生产部门的＿＿＿＿了。

4) 很多国际航班都不＿＿＿＿乘客吸烟。

b. 领域　领土

1) 过了这条河，就是另一个国家的＿＿＿＿了。

2) 私有经济已经进军高科技＿＿＿＿了。

3) 这个公司的经营范围很广，已经在房地产、金融和贸易等多个＿＿＿＿进行投资。

4) 现在香港是中国的＿＿＿＿了。

c. 颁布　公布

1) 下个月将正式＿＿＿＿得奖名单。

2) 自从政府＿＿＿＿新的投资法以来，到这里来投资的外商越来越多。

3) 比赛的结果还没＿＿＿＿。

4) 总统＿＿＿＿禁严令，宣布整个城市进入紧急战争状态。

d. 扩大　扩充

1) 经过几年的发展，私有企业逐步＿＿＿＿了经营范围。

2) 在这个行业，目前每个公司都在努力＿＿＿＿研发实力。

3) 我们公司不仅要＿＿＿＿规模，而且要＿＿＿＿设备。

e. 方式　方法

1) 承包是国有企业改革中经常采用的＿＿＿＿之一。

2) 他们夫妻俩的生活＿＿＿＿不一样。

3）在生活中，我们要用科学的＿＿＿解决问题。

4）他用各种＿＿＿算这道题，几个小时过后仍然找不到答案。

## 6. 用括号里的词语完成句子并翻译：
Complete the following sentences with the words given in parentheses and translate the sentences into English:

a. ＿＿＿＿＿＿＿＿＿＿＿＿＿，这里的气温就一直很高。（以来）

翻译：＿＿＿＿＿＿＿＿＿＿＿＿＿＿＿＿＿＿＿＿＿

b. ＿＿＿＿＿＿＿＿＿＿＿＿＿＿＿，他才到会场。（直到）

翻译：＿＿＿＿＿＿＿＿＿＿＿＿＿＿＿＿＿＿＿＿＿

c. 公司上半年的业绩，＿＿＿＿＿＿＿＿＿＿＿。（令）

翻译：＿＿＿＿＿＿＿＿＿＿＿＿＿＿＿＿＿＿＿＿＿

d. 私有企业的规模不断扩大，＿＿＿＿＿＿＿＿。（甚至）

翻译：＿＿＿＿＿＿＿＿＿＿＿＿＿＿＿＿＿＿＿＿＿

e. 他＿＿＿＿＿＿＿＿＿＿＿＿＿参加了这次会议。（以）

翻译：＿＿＿＿＿＿＿＿＿＿＿＿＿＿＿＿＿＿＿＿＿

f. 他的销售额总是第一，实在＿＿＿＿＿＿＿＿＿。（令）

翻译：＿＿＿＿＿＿＿＿＿＿＿＿＿＿＿＿＿＿＿＿＿

**7. 翻译：**

Translate the following sentences into English:

a. 自从引进先进的技术以来，工厂的效益就不断提高。

_____

b. 私有企业在中国存在的时间不长，但已取得了令人瞩目的成就。

_____

c. 这个项目要是经理不认可，就无法进行。

_____

d. 政府垄断的行业不允许私有企业介入。

_____

e. 中国鼓励发展多种经济形式，以私有经济来说，就有个体、合伙及有限责任公司等多种形式。

_____

**8. 问题与探讨：**

Questions and Exploration:

a. 私有企业对中国经济发展有什么作用？

b. 中国哪一省的私有企业最多？它们多半从事什么行业？

c. 中国将来是否有可能允许私有企业经营银行业？

# 1.3 练习

## 1. 选择适当的动词填空：
Fill in each blank with the most appropriate verb:

建立　　制造　　扶植　　提高

给予　　吸引　　提供　　推动

a. (　　　　)投资　　　　　d. (　　　　)资金

b. (　　　　)优惠　　　　　e. (　　　　)特区

c. (　　　　)企业　　　　　f. (　　　　)飞机


## 2. 选词填空：
Fill in each blank with the most appropriate word:

a. 会议开始十分钟后还有代表＿＿＿入场。

　　1)连续　　　　2)陆续　　　　3)继续


b. 公司已经＿＿＿亏损三年了。

　　1)连续　　　　2)陆续　　　　3)继续


c. 中国广阔的市场＿＿＿了越来越多的外国投资者。

　　1)吸引　　　　2)吸收　　　　3)吸取


d. 很多发达国家政府向本国企业＿＿＿出口信贷，鼓励出口。

　　1)提供　　　　2)供给　　　　3)供应

e. 国家＿＿＿＿＿了专门基金，解决贫困地区的教育问题。

　　1)建立　　　2)设立　　　3)成立

f. 你认为这个理论能＿＿＿＿＿吗？

　　1)建立　　　2)设立　　　3)成立

g. 中国与世界上大多数国家都＿＿＿＿＿了正式的外交关系。

　　1)建立　　　2)设立　　　3)成立

## 3. 将指定的词语插入适当的位置并翻译：

Indicate where each designated word belongs in the sentence and translate the sentences into English:

a. 起

1)公司从下半年开始实行新的奖惩制度。

　　翻译：＿＿＿＿＿＿＿＿＿＿＿＿＿＿＿＿＿＿＿＿＿＿＿＿

2)长城自山海关一直延续了几个省份。

　　翻译：＿＿＿＿＿＿＿＿＿＿＿＿＿＿＿＿＿＿＿＿＿＿＿＿

b. 以　　以便

1)希望消费者多提意见，我们改进产品质量。

　　翻译：＿＿＿＿＿＿＿＿＿＿＿＿＿＿＿＿＿＿＿＿＿＿＿＿

2)政府制定了许多优惠政策，吸引外资。

　　翻译：＿＿＿＿＿＿＿＿＿＿＿＿＿＿＿＿＿＿＿＿＿＿＿＿

3) 公司设有食堂，方便员工用餐。

翻译：_____

c. 纷纷

1) 几家公司看好他的设计，找他合作。

翻译：_____

d. 先后

1) 考察团参观了几个工厂。

翻译：_____

2) 请大家按顺序进入会场。

翻译：_____

e. 以上

1) 我想对发言作个总结。

翻译：_____

2) 我列出了投资环境比较好的几个城市。

翻译：_____

# 4. 解释划线词语的意思并翻译：
Explain the underlined words or phrases and translate the sentence into English:

a. <u>为了</u>吸引外资，中国政府<u>为</u>外国投资者提供了理想的投资环境。

解释：_____

翻译：＿＿＿＿＿＿＿＿＿＿＿＿＿＿＿＿＿＿＿＿＿＿＿

b. 对这项改革方案，大家意见<u>纷纷</u>。

解释：＿＿＿＿＿＿＿＿＿＿＿＿＿＿＿＿＿＿＿＿＿

翻译：＿＿＿＿＿＿＿＿＿＿＿＿＿＿＿＿＿＿＿＿＿

c. 公司降低工资以减少生产成本。

解释：＿＿＿＿＿＿＿＿＿＿＿＿＿＿＿＿＿＿＿＿＿

翻译：＿＿＿＿＿＿＿＿＿＿＿＿＿＿＿＿＿＿＿＿＿

d. 中国从1979年<u>起</u>实行市场经济政策。

解释：＿＿＿＿＿＿＿＿＿＿＿＿＿＿＿＿＿＿＿＿＿

翻译：＿＿＿＿＿＿＿＿＿＿＿＿＿＿＿＿＿＿＿＿＿

e. 大学毕业生找工作<u>以</u>计算机专业最吃香。

解释：＿＿＿＿＿＿＿＿＿＿＿＿＿＿＿＿＿＿＿＿＿

翻译：＿＿＿＿＿＿＿＿＿＿＿＿＿＿＿＿＿＿＿＿＿

## 5. 用括号里的词语完成句子并翻译：
Complete the following sentences with the words given in parentheses and translate the sentences into English:

a. 为了引进先进技术，中国企业＿＿＿＿＿＿＿＿＿＿＿。（纷纷）

翻译：＿＿＿＿＿＿＿＿＿＿＿＿＿＿＿＿＿＿＿＿＿

b. 人们对政府降息的计划，_____。（纷纷）

翻译：_____

c. _____，中国政府降低外商所得税税率。（为了）

翻译：_____

d. 中国政府_____开始推行经济体制改革。（从...起）

翻译：_____

# 6. 问题与探讨：
Questions and Exploration:

a. 经济特区的主要特点和作用。

b. 经济特区吸引外资是否主要靠优惠政策？

c. 中国最大的经济技术开发区在哪个城市？

d. 为什么中国政府将在政策上侧重开发大西部？具体措施有哪些？探讨目前中国西北部开发区的发展状况。

# 1.4 练习

## 1. 选择适当的动词填空：
Fill in each blank with the most appropriate verb:

制定　分享　协助　承担　转换

获得　分配　分担　取代　加速

a. (　　　　　)利润　　　　　e. (　　　　　)改革

b. (　　　　　)伙伴　　　　　f. (　　　　　)机制

c. (　　　　　)风险　　　　　g. (　　　　　)责任

d. (　　　　　)经验　　　　　h. (　　　　　)政策


## 2. 选词填空：
Fill in each blank with the most appropriate word:

a. 形式　形状

　1)这个工厂生产各种_____的钟表。

　2)在政府的鼓励下，投资_____多样化。

　3)那朵云的_____象只狗。

　4)这两个方案_____不同，但内容是一样的。


b. 对　对于

　1)公司_____项目的回报率要求很高。

　2)开发新产品_____一个企业非常重要。

3)＿＿＿＿中方来说，引进资金才是他们建立合资企业的真正目的。

4)年终决算时各个部门需要与财务部门＿＿＿＿帐。

c. 分享　分担

1)科研小组共同＿＿＿＿研究成果。

2)这次旅行的费用，我们彼此＿＿＿＿。

3)总公司同意＿＿＿＿这项投资的损失。

4)全体员工都能＿＿＿＿公司所得。

## 3. 用"则"把A、B中合适的部分搭配起来：

Match the phrases in column A with the corresponding phrases in column B and indicate where "则" belongs in the sentence:

| A | B |
|---|---|
| 如果资金短缺 | 内地发展缓慢 |
| 计划经济不改革 | 人们的生活水平无法提高 |
| 中国人想到外国去做生意 | 这个项目无法完成 |
| 沿海城市经济发展迅速 | 外国人想到中国投资 |

## 4. 用"来"把A、B中合适的部分搭配起来：

Match the phrases in column A with the corresponding phrases in column B and indicate where "来" belongs in the sentence:

| A | B |
|---|---|
| 外商采用与中方合资的方式 | 庆祝公司周年庆 |
| 公司引进先进技术 | 分配利润 |
| 你们用什么方式 | 提高竞争力 |
| 合资公司一般按投资比例 | 进入中国市场 |

## 5. 用"～化"填空：

Use "～化" to fill in the blanks:

a. 为了提高生产效率，生产流程应该_____。

b. 上海已成为_____的城市。

c. 我们应该不断_____改革。

d. 我们要_____环境，_____城市。

## 6. 在以下含有"～则"的句子中填空：

Fill in the blanks in the following sentences containing "～则":

a. 如果投资失败，轻则_____，重则_____。

b. 合作期限一般不会太长，少则_____，多则_____。

## 7. 解释划线词语的意思并翻译：

Explain the underlined words or phrases and translate the sentences into English:

a. 香港被称<u>为</u>"东方之珠"。

解释： _____

翻译： _____


b. 年轻人都要有所作<u>为</u>。

解释： _____

翻译： _____


c. 经营企业不应该仅以赚钱<u>为</u>目的。

解释： _____

翻译： _____


d. 这里保姆的工资是<u>按</u>月计算的。

解释： _____

翻译： _____


e. 如果政府早一点实行改革开放政策，<u>或者</u>中国的经济会更加强大。

解释： _____

翻译： _____


f. 特区里不论软环境<u>或者</u>硬环境都已达到国际标准。

解释： _____

翻译： _____


g. 过去我们对他一直不太了解，只是从最近的报道中才知道<u>其</u>人<u>其</u>事。

解释：_____

翻译：_____

h. 为了让大家了解这个项目的重要性，他不厌<u>其</u>烦地作解释。

解释：_____

翻译：_____

## 8. 用括号里的词语完成句子：
Complete the following sentences by using the words given in parentheses:

a. _____，这个项目太难了。（对于…而言）

b. 到中国开办网络公司是_____。（为）

c. 在美国，距离是_____。（按）

d. 如果中国不设立经济特区，_____。（则）

e. 我们可以到中国投资建厂，_____。（或者）

## 9. 翻译：
Translate the following sentences into English/Chinese:

a. 你所建议的投资计划已被董事会批准。

_____

b. 他们所关心的问题是提高生产力。

_____

c. As far as investors are concerned, financial return is the most important issue.

_____

d. Whether you approve or disapprove, you must make your decision.

_____

e. We are not in charge of the foreign investment. Perhaps MOFTEC can help.

_____


**10.  问题与探讨：**
Questions and Exploration:

a. 中国政府为何会允许外商在中国设立独资企业？独资企业对中国的发展有何作用？

b. 中国为保护国内企业，是否会对外商采取一些限制性措施？

# 2.1练习

## 1. 选择适当的动词填空：
Fill in each blank with the most appropriate verb:

垄断 分离 获准 承担 自负

执行 发挥 确定 扶持 自主

a. (　　　　　)作用　　　　f. (　　　　　)市场

b. (　　　　　)利率　　　　g. (　　　　　)任务

c. (　　　　　)营业　　　　h. (　　　　　)盈亏

d. (　　　　　)职能　　　　i. (　　　　　)责任

e. (　　　　　)政策　　　　j. (　　　　　)经营

## 2. 根据课文内容填入正确的词语：
Fill in each blank with the most appropriate word according to the text reading for this lesson:

a. 银行与保险公司都属于＿＿＿＿机构。

b. 子公司成立后将自主＿＿＿＿，＿＿＿＿盈亏。

c. 银行在中国经济发展中发挥的＿＿＿＿越来越大。

d. 银行业是金融体系中重要的＿＿＿＿部分。

e. 中国银行体制的改革重点是分离银行的＿＿＿＿和＿＿＿＿职能。

f. 花旗银行是最早进入中国市场的＿＿＿＿银行之一。

## 3. 解释划线词语的意思：
Explain the underlined words or phrases:

a. 他随着参观者进入了会场。

解释：＿＿＿＿＿＿＿＿＿＿＿＿＿＿＿＿＿＿

b. 他的强硬态度使人难以接受。

解释：＿＿＿＿＿＿＿＿＿＿＿＿＿＿＿＿＿＿

c. 这起车祸使他不得不住院三个月。

解释：＿＿＿＿＿＿＿＿＿＿＿＿＿＿＿＿＿＿

d. 改革开放以后，中国的经济起了很大的变化。

解释：＿＿＿＿＿＿＿＿＿＿＿＿＿＿＿＿＿＿

e. 我们部门仅负责人事管理。

解释：＿＿＿＿＿＿＿＿＿＿＿＿＿＿＿＿＿＿

f. 中国人民银行在中国金融体系中起了决定性的作用。

解释：＿＿＿＿＿＿＿＿＿＿＿＿＿＿＿＿＿＿

g. 这台电脑已经使了5年了，该升级了。

解释：＿＿＿＿＿＿＿＿＿＿＿＿＿＿＿＿＿＿

h. 中国人民银行调高利率后，各商业银行也随着调高了利率。

解释：＿＿＿＿＿＿＿＿＿＿＿＿＿＿＿＿＿＿

i. 整个公司的出差费用相当大，<u>仅</u>交通费就达到4万元。

解释：_____

# 4. 用"随着"完成下列句子并翻译：
Complete the following sentences with "随着" and translate the sentences into English:

a. 随着改革的深入，_____

翻译：_____

b. 随着经济的发展，_____

翻译：_____

c. _____，产品的价格会下降。

翻译：_____

d. _____，银行的商业职能越来越大。

翻译：_____

# 5. 用"及"或"以及"改写下列句子：
Rewrite the following sentences with "及" or "以及"：

a. 这家跨国公司规模很大，在美国、日本、德国、中国都有它的分支机构。

_____

b. 各部门经理和家属都被邀请参加舞会。

_____

   c. 出差时的住宿费、交通费、伙食费、其它各种费用都可以报销。

_____

   d. 从改革开放到设立自由贸易区、金融贸易区，上海发生了巨大的变化。

_____

## 6. 选词填空：
Fill in each blank with the most appropriate word:

展开　开展　发展

a. 早上公司宣布全面降价后，整个行业的价格战便_____了序幕。

b. 证券公司员工_____了如何提高利润率的讨论。

c. 随着外资的不断涌入，中国的金融业在迅速地_____。

d. 为了增加员工间的团结，公司经常_____集体活动。

## 7. 阅读理解并判断正确与错误：
Read the following paragraph and indicate whether the statements below are TRUE or FALSE:

根据在加入WTO谈判中所答应的条件，中国将在一定时候取消设立外资银行的地域限制，允许更多的外资银行开展人民币业务和进一步扩大人民币业务的范围。从日前定出的开放人民币业务的时间表来看，人民币业务开放速度将超出多数人的预期。

a. (　　　)中国政府将放宽外资银行在华业务的限制。

b. (　　　)银行业是中国政府垄断的行业。

c. (　　　)中国政府将允许外资银行在中国开办人民币业务。

d. (　　　)人民币业务开放速度将达不到大多数人的预期。

# 8. 问题与探讨:
Questions and Exploration:

a. 中国银行体系是否包括投资银行？

b. 目前中国商业银行可否由私人开办？

c. 外资银行的客户是否只限于三资企业？其发展方向是什么？

d. 外资银行可否在中国发行信用卡？

e. 中国政府对外资金融机构进入中国市场的资产标准是什么？

f. 外资银行会给中国经济建设带来什么影响及作用？

# 2.2 练习

## 1. 根据课文内容填入正确的词语：

Fill in each blank with the most appropriate word according to the text reading for this lesson:

a. 在经济过热的情况下，政府通常会＿＿＿＿银根来抑制通胀。

b. SAFE ("State Administration of Foreign Exchange")是中国国家外汇
＿＿＿＿局的简称。

c. 当本币＿＿＿＿时，进口商品的价格将下降。

d. 利率影响＿＿＿＿的价格。

e. 利率和汇率是两个非常重要的经济＿＿＿＿。

f. 汇率的＿＿＿＿会影响一个国家资本的流动。

## 2. 选词填空：

Fill in each blank with the most appropriate word:

a. 变化　变动

1）气象预报无法准确预知天气＿＿＿＿。

2）最近由于公司重组，财务部门的人事＿＿＿＿比较多。

3）股市行情＿＿＿＿多端。

4）合同正本不需要做任何文字＿＿＿＿。

b. 欲望　愿望

1）佛教的教义主张人们放弃一切＿＿＿＿。

2) 维护和平是全世界人民的共同＿＿＿。

3) 他向领导提出调动工作的＿＿＿。

4) 广告可以刺激人们的消费＿＿＿。

c. 表示　表达　表明

1) 这部影片＿＿＿了人类对太空的好奇。

2) 总经理在大会上＿＿＿公司不会裁员。

3) 董事会表决结果现在是3:3，就等董事长最后＿＿＿立场了。

4) 政府已经明确＿＿＿了支持高科技产业发展的政策。

d. 抑制　控制

1) 他用理智＿＿＿了冲动，使他能冷静地分析目前的形势。

2) 中方代表最终＿＿＿了整个谈判局势。

3) 他＿＿＿不住心中的怒火，向老板提出辞职。

4) 高血压患者要严格＿＿＿饮食。

e. 鼓励　勉励

1) 得到经理的＿＿＿后，职员们更加努力工作了。

2) ＿＿＿比批评更能使人进步。

3) 政府总理＿＿＿科技人员不断创新。

4) 他以"克服困难、争取成功"来自我＿＿＿。

f. 防止　避免

1) 谈判双方应尽量克制情绪，＿＿＿发生冲突。

2) 打预防针可以＿＿＿得病。

3）政府调整利率是为了＿＿＿＿通货膨胀。

4）孕妇应该＿＿＿＿抽烟、喝酒。

## 3. 用"既 ... 也 ... "或"既 ... 又 ... "改写下列句子：
Rewrite the following sentences with "既 ... 也 ... " or "既 ... 又 ... ":

a. 对待员工不但要批评，也要鼓励。

_____

b. 消费者喜欢选择质量好价格低的商品。

_____

c. 生产力的提高可以促进经济增长，还可以抑制通货膨胀。

_____

d. 大多数决策都有不利的一面和有利的一面。

_____

## 4. 解释划线词语的意思并翻译：
Explain the underlined words or phrases and translate the sentences into English:

a. "而"

1）价廉而物美的产品最受消费者欢迎。

解释：_____

翻译：_____

2) 这次比赛他赢了，但他胜而不骄，非常谦虚。

解释：＿＿＿＿＿＿＿＿＿＿＿＿＿＿＿＿＿＿＿＿＿＿＿

翻译：＿＿＿＿＿＿＿＿＿＿＿＿＿＿＿＿＿＿＿＿＿＿＿

3) 中国古代有许多美丽而动人的传说。

解释：＿＿＿＿＿＿＿＿＿＿＿＿＿＿＿＿＿＿＿＿＿＿＿

翻译：＿＿＿＿＿＿＿＿＿＿＿＿＿＿＿＿＿＿＿＿＿＿＿

4) 有些外国人认为中国不是发展中国家，而中国人认为自己是发展中国家。

解释：＿＿＿＿＿＿＿＿＿＿＿＿＿＿＿＿＿＿＿＿＿＿＿

翻译：＿＿＿＿＿＿＿＿＿＿＿＿＿＿＿＿＿＿＿＿＿＿＿

b. "之"

1) 对方公司退出竞争，我们正求之不得。

解释：＿＿＿＿＿＿＿＿＿＿＿＿＿＿＿＿＿＿＿＿＿＿＿

翻译：＿＿＿＿＿＿＿＿＿＿＿＿＿＿＿＿＿＿＿＿＿＿＿

2) 由于总经理犯了错误，他现已被副总经理取而代之了。

解释：＿＿＿＿＿＿＿＿＿＿＿＿＿＿＿＿＿＿＿＿＿＿＿

翻译：＿＿＿＿＿＿＿＿＿＿＿＿＿＿＿＿＿＿＿＿＿＿＿

3) 我们之间有深厚的友谊。

解释：＿＿＿＿＿＿＿＿＿＿＿＿＿＿＿＿＿＿＿＿＿＿＿

翻译：＿＿＿＿＿＿＿＿＿＿＿＿＿＿＿＿＿＿＿＿＿＿＿

4) 在公司转型之际，我们更需要员工的支持。

解释 ：＿＿＿＿＿＿＿＿＿＿＿＿＿＿＿＿＿＿＿＿＿＿＿

翻译 ：＿＿＿＿＿＿＿＿＿＿＿＿＿＿＿＿＿＿＿＿＿＿＿

5) 旅行社现在推出的黄山之旅价格很便宜。

解释 ：＿＿＿＿＿＿＿＿＿＿＿＿＿＿＿＿＿＿＿＿＿＿＿

翻译 ：＿＿＿＿＿＿＿＿＿＿＿＿＿＿＿＿＿＿＿＿＿＿＿

c. "如何"

1) 如何提高本公司的利润率是这次会议首先要解决的问题。

解释 ：＿＿＿＿＿＿＿＿＿＿＿＿＿＿＿＿＿＿＿＿＿＿＿

翻译 ：＿＿＿＿＿＿＿＿＿＿＿＿＿＿＿＿＿＿＿＿＿＿＿

2) 天已经黑了，看来我们是无论如何都来不及了。

解释 ：＿＿＿＿＿＿＿＿＿＿＿＿＿＿＿＿＿＿＿＿＿＿＿

翻译 ：＿＿＿＿＿＿＿＿＿＿＿＿＿＿＿＿＿＿＿＿＿＿＿

3) 比赛很激烈，胜负如何现在还很难预料。

解释 ：＿＿＿＿＿＿＿＿＿＿＿＿＿＿＿＿＿＿＿＿＿＿＿

翻译 ：＿＿＿＿＿＿＿＿＿＿＿＿＿＿＿＿＿＿＿＿＿＿＿

4) 你刚听过气象预报，明天的天气如何？

解释 ：＿＿＿＿＿＿＿＿＿＿＿＿＿＿＿＿＿＿＿＿＿＿＿

翻译 ：＿＿＿＿＿＿＿＿＿＿＿＿＿＿＿＿＿＿＿＿＿＿＿

## 5. 用 " 反之 " 完成下列句子 :

Complete the following sentences with " 反之 " :

a. 利率的上升会带动汇率的上升，_____

b. 货币贬值会促进出口，_____

c. 利率降低时，股票价格会上升，_____

d. 物体受热后会膨胀，_____

## 6. 阅读理解并判断正确与错误 :

Read the following paragraph and indicate whether the statements below are TRUE or FALSE:

> 90年代中期以来，中国的宏观经济政策由治理通货膨胀转向刺激需求、调整结构和保持经济增长速度。中国的利率调整对汇率是零效应，甚至是负效应。但利率政策对汇率的影响会以其它方式表现出来，如资本外逃、外汇黑市的波动等。这些都会对人民币汇率的稳定造成很大的影响。

a. (　　) 中国自90年代中期以来，一直为治理通胀而努力。

b. (　　) 在中国，利率下降，汇率也会随着下降。

c. (　　) 中国宏观经济政策一直是先刺激需求再治理通胀。

d. (　　) 利率下降对汇率没有明显影响。

e. (　　) 资本外逃对人民币汇率的稳定有压力。

## 7. 问题与探讨：
Questions and Exploration:

a. 为什么中国政府在1998-1999年期间连续降低利率？

b. 目前人民币在国际金融市场的地位如何？

# 2.3 练习

**1. 根据课文内容填入正确的词语：**
Fill in each blank with the most appropriate word according to the text reading for this lesson:

a. 中国早先发行的股票是100元人民币_____的票据。

b. 中国的A股和B股、H股和N股具有不同的_____。

c. _____在香港的地位相当于美国的蓝筹股。

d. 中国股市的发展还处于初级_____。

e. 发行股票可以在市场上_____资金。

f. 中资企业在香港有_____的实力。

g. 中国证券市场的制度还不_____。

h. 中国在80年代中期_____了股票买卖。

**2. 选词填空：**
Fill in each blank with the most appropriate word:

a. 缺少　缺乏

　　1)证券分析师是每个证券公司都不可_____的人才。

　　2)沙漠地带水源比较_____。

　　3)他因_____专业知识而没有被录用。

　　4)由于_____资金，这项工程无法进行。

　b. 紧密　密切

　　1)合资企业双方需要_____合作。

　　2)已经连续四个小时了，他仍在_____关注股票的走势。

　　3)网络与人们日常生活的关系越来越_____了。

　c. 概念　观念

　　1)要投资股市，必须先了解一些有关股票的基本_____。

　　2)消费_____会随着收入水平的提高而改变。

　　3)中国股民的投资_____还不是很成熟。

　　4)很多人对股票指数没有清楚的_____。

　d. 相关　有关

　　1)要买卖股票必须先到证券交易所办理_____手续。

　　2)很多时候，股价的波动和券商炒作_____。

　　3)创办公司需要得到_____部门的许可。

　　4)国家的宏观政策与经济发展密切_____。

# 3. 解释划线词语的意思并造句：

Explain the underlined words and use those words to make an additional sentence:

　a.　由于政府接连发布了几条利好消息，股民恢复了对股票市场的信心。

　　解释：_____

　　造句：_____

b. 喝了水，休息了一阵后，他觉得自己的体力慢慢<u>恢复</u>了。

解释：_____

造句：_____

c. 中国先后在1997年和1999年<u>恢复</u>了对香港和澳门行使主权。

解释：_____

造句：_____

d. <u>通过</u>银行贷款，公司筹足了项目建设的经费。

解释：_____

造句：_____

e. 经过激烈的讨论，董事会终于<u>通过</u>了派息方案。

解释：_____

造句：_____

f. 我们<u>通过</u>长长的走廊来到他的房间。

解释：_____

造句：_____

g. H股是<u>指</u>在香港上市的中国股票。

解释：_____

造句：_____

h. 老师<u>指</u>着幻灯片向学生讲解计算机的构造。

解释：＿＿＿＿＿＿＿＿＿＿＿＿＿＿＿＿＿＿＿＿＿＿＿＿＿

造句：＿＿＿＿＿＿＿＿＿＿＿＿＿＿＿＿＿＿＿＿＿＿＿＿＿

## 4. 用"而"把A、B、C中合适的部分搭配起来：

Match the phrases in column A with the corresponding phrases in column B and column C and indicate where "而" belongs in the sentence:

| A | B | C |
|---|---|---|
| 这个项目 | 需要根据供求关系 | 被迫停工 |
| 许多误解 | 因文化差异 | 决定 |
| 产品的产量 | 随着政策变动 | 产生 |
| 股价 | 因经费不足 | 上下波动 |

## 5. 阅读理解并判断正确与错误：

Read the following paragraph and indicate whether the statements below are TRUE or FALSE:

> B股对国内投资者开放以后，在沪深两市如期开盘。由于市场没有取消涨停限制，两市100多只股票全部被钉在"涨停板"上，而买盘依旧不断增加。深交所行情只能显示1亿股以内的买盘。许多股票的买盘超过了1亿股，只能显示其最大数字999,999手。沪市最大的买盘居然有3亿多股。两地市场同时趋向疯狂。

a. (　　　)B股对国内投资者开放以后，市场反应并不热烈。

b. (　　　)取消涨停限制后，很多公司被钉在了"涨停板"上。

c. (　　　)上海交易所行情可以显示1亿股以上的买盘。

d. (　　　)中国境内的中国人可以投资B股。

# 6. 问题与探讨：
Questions and Exploration:

a. B股对境内投资者开放后，对中国股票市场有何影响？

b. 根据你的知识与判断，谈谈对海外上市的中国股票的展望。

# 2.4 练习

## 1. 选择适当的动词填空：
Fill in each blank with the most appropriate verb:

> 惊人　充足　云集　美称　成绩
>
> 坚实　优秀　繁荣　基础　雄厚

a. 多年苦读使他在金融学方面打下了_____的基础。

b. 1999财富论坛在上海举行，国内外企业_____一方。

c. 上海很早就有"东方明珠"的_____。

d. 上海的工业基础_____，商业经济_____，人口素质_____，资金供应_____。

e. 高新技术产业是上海持续发展的_____。

f. 陆家嘴金融中心取得了_____的发展。


## 2. 选词填空：
Fill in each blank with the most appropriate word:

a. 此外　另外　另

　1) 他投资地产证券，_____再没有别的投资。

　2) 证券投资一方面可以带来高收入，_____一方面也带来高风险。

　3) 有关项目的进度问题，我们改天_____讨论。

　4) 东方明珠电视塔、金茂大厦、上海证券交易所，_____还有一些其它著名建筑都位于陆家嘴。

b. 注目　瞩目

1)她穿着一件大红袍子，非常引人＿＿＿。

2)中国改革开放的成就举世＿＿＿。

c. 焦点　热点

1)B股市场的开放是日前的＿＿＿问题。

2)由于董事长请假，总经理在会议中成为＿＿＿人物。

3)这次讨论的＿＿＿是客户关系管理。

4)上海是亚洲的投资＿＿＿城市之一。

d. 保证　保障

1)中央银行的监督是金融市场健康运作的＿＿＿。

2)在得到总工程师的＿＿＿后，总经理在计划书上签了字。

3)企业退休计划为退休员工提供了生活＿＿＿。

4)政府的政策支持是上海得以发展的＿＿＿。

# 3. 用括号里的词语完成句子：
Complete the following sentences with the words given in parentheses:

a. 券商违规会造成严重后果，＿＿＿＿＿＿＿＿＿＿。（乃至）

b. ＿＿＿＿＿＿＿＿＿＿＿，同事们都对他另眼相看。（取得）

c. ＿＿＿＿＿＿＿＿＿＿＿，不适合竞争的需要。（规模）

d. 由于上海在金融产业建设上的成就，＿＿＿＿＿＿。（博得）

e. 国有银行与外资银行各有优势，＿＿＿＿＿＿。（并驾齐驱）

## 4. 阅读理解并判断正确与错误：
Read the following paragraph and indicate whether the statements below are TRUE or FALSE:

目前，上海浦东的产业结构包括以金融、保险为支柱的第三产业，以信息技术、医药和汽车为主体的第二产业和以农业为基础的第一产业。此外，金融贸易功能也日渐增强。外高桥保税区已成为国内最大的保税区和新建港口，从而强化了国际贸易、保税仓储和出口加工三大功能。张江高科技园区已发展成上海技术创新的重要平台。金桥出口加工区吸引了340多家中资和外资企业，成为建设上海新兴工业的又一动力。

a.　（　　　）浦东已成功发展了第一、二、三产业。

b.　（　　　）金融业是第一产业。

c.　（　　　）张江高科技园区已发展成上海的重要出口加工区。

d.　（　　　）浦东的金融贸易功能正在一天一天地加强。

e.　（　　　）外高桥保税区强化了国际贸易、保险服务和出口加工三大功能

## 5. 问题与探讨：
Questions and Exploration:

a.　谈谈陆家嘴金融贸易区自建立以来所取得的发展。

b.　上海能否建成与香港同等地位的世界商业金融中心？

# 3.1 练习

## 1. 选择适当的动词填空：
Fill in each blank with the most appropriate verb:

传递　收集　推销　促销　进行

掌握　预测　制定　面临　增加

a. (　　　　)销售额　　　f. (　　　　)产品

b. (　　　　)信息　　　　g. (　　　　)情报

c. (　　　　)策略　　　　h. (　　　　)资料

d. (　　　　)手段　　　　i. (　　　　)评估

e. (　　　　)需求量　　　j. (　　　　)困难

## 2. 选词填空：
Fill in each blank with the most appropriate word:

a. 面临　面对

1) 金融领域引入国际竞争机制以后，中国的金融业将＿＿＿巨大的挑战。

2) 我们要＿＿＿现实，制定可行的方案，以度过目前的难关。

3) ＿＿＿强大的竞争对手，我们公司只能不断降价以保持市场占有率。

4) 由于经济衰退，许多公司都＿＿＿倒闭。

5) ＿＿＿业绩下降的问题，董事会决定关闭几家分公司。

6) 投资者有权知道公司所＿＿＿＿＿的困难。

b.　广泛　广大

1) ＿＿＿＿＿市民踊跃参加了昨天的抽奖活动。

2) 他的建议得到了＿＿＿＿＿的支持。

3) 为了推出适销对路的产品，公司开展了＿＿＿＿＿的市场调查，以了解消费者需求。

4) 中国西部＿＿＿＿＿地区正面临沙漠化的威胁。

c.　把握　掌握

1) 当主管，我还没有＿＿＿＿＿。

2) 作为公司总会计师，你要＿＿＿＿＿丰富的财务理论知识。

3) 通过调查问卷及电话访谈，我们＿＿＿＿＿了第一手资料。

4) 他认真钻研，终于＿＿＿＿＿了这门技术。

5) 他有＿＿＿＿＿竞选成功。

d.　靠　依靠　依赖

1) 仅＿＿＿＿＿广告促销是不够的，有时还要采用降价、送礼品和抽奖等其它方式。

2) 沿海地区＿＿＿＿＿有利的地理位置发展外向型经济。

3) 日本的自然资源短缺，只能＿＿＿＿＿进口解决原材料问题。

4) 他＿＿＿＿＿养牛发了大财。

e.　关心　关注

1) 大家都密切＿＿＿＿＿局势的发展。

2)全社会都应该_____青少年的成长。

3)治理环境污染是全世界共同_____的话题。

4)很多公司都在_____股票市场的动向。

## 3. 选择划线词语的正确解释：
Choose the word or phrase that best explains the meaning of the underlined word or phrase:

a. 他在国外<u>受</u>过良好的教育。

　1)接受　　　2)遭受　　　3)承受

b. 他<u>受</u>到了不公正的待遇。

　1)接受　　　2)遭受　　　3)承受

c. 总工程师是执行这个项目的<u>关键</u>人物。

　1)有关系的　2)重要的　3)特殊的

d. 这批货幸亏<u>卖得及时</u>。

　1)卖得很快　2)卖得正是时候　3)马上卖掉

e. 接到通知后他<u>及时</u>赶到了现场。

　1)很早　　　2)马上　　　3)来不及

f. 为达到个人目的，他往往<u>不择手段</u>。

　1)不仔细选择方法　　　2)不选择任何方法
　3)不管用什么方法

## 4. 完成下列句子并翻译：
Complete the following sentences and translate into English:

a. 尽管做了周密的市场调查，_____

翻译：_____

b. 获取市场信息的手段很多，例如_____

翻译：_____

c. 他做出的市场预测很准确，因为他及时_____

翻译：_____

d. 这则广告成功的关键是_____

翻译：_____

e. 这次的降价促销不太成功，关键是_____

翻译：_____

f. 尽管市场调研只是近年来才在中国开始实行，_____

翻译：_____

## 5. 用括号里的词语完成句子：
Complete the following sentences with the words given in parentheses:

a. _____，新产品的上市还是很成功。（尽管）

b. 商品的销售除了与质量有关之外，还_____。（受）

c. 公司_____，在激烈的竞争中保持领先地位。（及时）

d. 他＿＿＿＿＿＿＿＿＿＿＿＿＿＿＿＿＿＿，所以业绩非常优秀。（手段）

## 6. 阅读理解并回答问题：
Read the following paragraph and answer the questions below:

> 中国第一家以"公司"命名的专业市场调研机构—广州市场研究公司于1987年7月正式注册成立。之后，大量的调研机构纷纷于1992-1993期间成立。
>
> 中国市场调研的发展与跨国公司在中国市场上的营销活动有密切关系。举例来说，宝洁、联合利华等公司对消费者意见的高度关注为市场调研公司的出现奠定了需求的基础。另外，伴随着跨国公司进入中国，一批为之服务的国际调查集团，如盖洛普、SRG等先后在中国设立了分支机构。

a. 1987年以前中国有没有市场调研公司？

b. 1992-1993年期间，中国为什么出现了大量的调研公司？

c. 中国市场调研的发展与什么有密切关系？

d. 宝洁为什么能为市场调研公司奠定需求的基础？

e. 中国第一家市场调研公司是在什么城市成立的？

## 7. 问题与探讨：
Questions and Exploration:

a. 请列出中国人均 GDP 水平和主要城市的人口总数。

b. 除了可口可乐公司以外，还有哪些外国公司是因为在进入中国市场以前市场调研工作做得充分而成功的呢？

c. 在中国专门从事市场调研的公司有几家？

d. 调研人员一般通过哪些方式收集资料？

# 3.2 练习

## 1. 选择适当的动词填空：
Fill in each blank with the most appropriate verb:

建立　　面向　　树立

营销　　达到　　推动

a. (　　　　)目的　　　　　d. (　　　　)市场

b. (　　　　)形象　　　　　e. (　　　　)转变

c. (　　　　)体系　　　　　f. (　　　　)方式

## 2. 选择适当的词语填空：
Fill in each blank with the most appropriate word:

目的、序、中心、导向、代表、标准

a. 以到达先后为_____

b. 以消费者为_____

c. 以市场为_____

d. 以盈利为_____

e. 以业绩为_____

## 3. 选词填空：
Fill in each blank with the most appropriate word:

a. 逐步　　逐渐

1) 他＿＿＿＿适应了国外的生活。

2) 这种新产品首先在北京试销，如果成功的话，再＿＿＿＿向其它城市推广。

3) 中美两国人民随着文化交流活动的增多，＿＿＿＿加深了相互之间的了解。

4) 由于采用了先进的管理方式，并配合灵活的促销手段，这种产品的销售量＿＿＿＿增长了。

b. 采用　采取

1) 目前，产品质量不断下降。如果不＿＿＿＿适当措施，后果会很严重。

2) 工厂＿＿＿＿了日本式的管理方法。

3) 他提出的人事方案没有被人事部门＿＿＿＿。

4) 针对竞争对手的促销方案，我们及时＿＿＿＿行动，加大了促销力度。

c. 实践　实行　实现

1) 自从＿＿＿＿"五天工作制"以来，旅游商品成为消费热点，商家应根据这种情况及时调整营销策略。

2) 中国从1979年起开始＿＿＿＿经济体制改革。

3) 在＿＿＿＿中发现问题并改正是一种非常有效的工作方法。

4) 他一直为＿＿＿＿当教师的愿望而努力。

d. 策略　战略

　1)市场营销是一门讲＿＿＿＿的学问。

　2)公司在新形势下必须制定新的＿＿＿＿。

　3)市场部门的职责之一是制定营销＿＿＿＿。

e. 建立　树立

　1)经过多年努力，公司已＿＿＿＿了完善的销售渠道。

　2)他的表现为大家＿＿＿＿了榜样。

　3)这个公司是他与哥哥共同＿＿＿＿的。

# 4. 根据课文内容完成句子：
Complete the following sentences according to the text reading for this lesson:

a. 市场营销是＿＿＿＿＿＿＿＿＿＿＿＿＿＿＿＿＿＿＿＿＿＿的桥梁。

b. "4P"是指＿＿＿＿＿＿＿＿＿＿＿＿＿＿＿＿＿＿＿＿＿＿。

c. "优惠券"是指＿＿＿＿＿＿＿＿＿＿＿＿＿＿＿＿＿＿＿＿。

d. 采用促销手段是为了达到＿＿＿＿＿＿＿＿＿＿＿＿＿的目的。

## 5. 阅读理解并回答问题：
Read the following paragraph and answer the questions below:

> 市场营销渠道和分销渠道是两个不同的概念。市场营销渠道包括产品的产、供、销过程中所有的企业和个人，如供应商、生产者、中间商、代理商、辅助商以及最后消费者或用户等。以消费品行业为例，市场营销渠道包括生产者、收购商、其它供应商、各种代理商、批发商、零售商和消费者等。分销渠道则包括加工商、批发商、代理商、零售商和消费者等。

a. 试将下列中英文词语配对：
Match each Chinese term with its English equivalent:

| | |
|---|---|
| 市场营销渠道 | users |
| 分销渠道 | agent |
| 供应商 | supplier |
| 生产者 | marketing channel |
| 中间商 | producer |
| 代理商 | distribution channel |
| 辅助商 | middle man |
| 用户 | facilitator |

b. 营销渠道和分销渠道到底有何不同？

c. 试以你熟悉的行业为例，指出营销渠道包括的具体环节。

## 6. 问题与探讨：
Questions and Exploration:

a. 如果你将来可能从事市场营销工作，那么在"现代营销方式"的四个环节中，你对哪个环节的工作最感兴趣？

b. 你认为电子商务会在中国成为主要的市场营销方式吗？

# 3.3 练习

**1. 选择适当的动词填空：**
Fill in each blank with the most appropriate verb:

转变　存在　满足　获得　占稳

开发　进入　提高　销售　具有

a. (　　　　　)水平　　　　e. (　　　　　)观念

b. (　　　　　)问题　　　　f. (　　　　　)技术

c. (　　　　　)成功　　　　g. (　　　　　)需求

d. (　　　　　)市场　　　　h. (　　　　　)潜力

**2. 解释划线词语的意思并造句：**
Explain the underlined words or phrases and use those words to make an additional sentence:

a. 这几年公司的业绩<u>一般</u>。

　　解释：＿＿＿＿＿＿＿＿＿＿＿＿＿＿＿＿＿＿＿＿＿＿＿

　　造句：＿＿＿＿＿＿＿＿＿＿＿＿＿＿＿＿＿＿＿＿＿＿＿

b. 我们的产品质量和竞争对手<u>一般</u>高。

　　解释：＿＿＿＿＿＿＿＿＿＿＿＿＿＿＿＿＿＿＿＿＿＿＿

　　造句：＿＿＿＿＿＿＿＿＿＿＿＿＿＿＿＿＿＿＿＿＿＿＿

  c. 他们的交情不是<u>一般</u>的雇主与雇员的关系。

    解释：_____

    造句：_____

  d. 他刚进公司不久<u>便</u>被提升为部门经理。

    解释：_____

    造句：_____

  e. 人们的收入增加后，<u>便</u>会有购买高档名牌产品的欲望。

    解释：_____

    造句：_____

# 3. 完成句子并翻译：
Complete the following sentences and translate the sentences into English:

  a. 所谓"皇帝的女儿不愁嫁"指的是_____

    翻译：_____

  b. 只有_____，才能创造出真正的名牌产品。

    翻译：_____

  c. 许多跨国知名企业在做生意的同时，_____

    翻译：_____

  d. 中国只有加入WTO_____

    翻译：_____

e. 新产品刚研制成功便＿＿＿＿＿＿＿＿＿＿＿＿＿＿＿＿＿＿＿＿＿＿

   翻译：＿＿＿＿＿＿＿＿＿＿＿＿＿＿＿＿＿＿＿＿＿＿＿＿＿＿＿＿＿＿

# 4. 选词填空：
Fill in each blank with the most appropriate word:

a. 意识　认识

　1) 运动员一般都有很强的竞争＿＿＿＿。

　2) 通过竞争，他们才＿＿＿＿到自己的缺点。

　3) 商家通过广告宣传加深了消费者对其产品的＿＿＿＿。

　4) 她的女儿就快生产了，可她一点儿也没有当奶奶的＿＿＿＿。

　5) 现在越来越多的企业＿＿＿＿到树立品牌＿＿＿＿的重要性。

　6) 我们很早就＿＿＿＿了。

　7) 老师刚一开口，他就＿＿＿＿到他的答案错了。

b. 获得　取得

　1) 尽管已经＿＿＿＿了很大的成绩，他仍然不断地努力。

　2) 今年公司在产品出口上＿＿＿＿了巨大收益，这个成绩的＿＿＿＿
　　　是与全体员工的努力分不开的。

　3) 新产品的质量＿＿＿＿行家的一致赞扬。

c. 转变　转化

　1) 中国正努力完成向市场经济的＿＿＿＿。

　2) 压力有时可以＿＿＿＿为动力。

　3) 总经理一来，他的态度马上就＿＿＿＿了。

　　d. 均衡　平衡

　　　1)社会财富不＿＿＿＿会带来严重的社会问题。

　　　2)公司的收入与支出应该保持＿＿＿＿。

　　　3)不公平地对待员工会造成员工心里不＿＿＿＿。

　　e. 普遍　普及　遍及

　　　1)大城市中的家庭已经＿＿＿＿使用空调。

　　　2)政府正在努力＿＿＿＿科学文化知识。

　　　3)公司的销售网络已＿＿＿＿全国各地。

## 5. 阅读理解并判断正确与错误：

Read the following paragraph and indicate whether the statements below are TRUE or FALSE:

---

　　　健力宝是中国的一个民族品牌。它"支持中国体育事业，致力国民素质提高"的产品定位曾为其销售立下汗马功劳。在极短的时间内，健力宝的品牌响遍全国，老少皆知。但是，随着社会的发展，消费者的观念也起了变化。而健力宝仍紧抓原先的定位不放，致使其品牌意识减弱。如何拓展现有的企业文化重塑企业形象是健力宝首先要解决的问题。

---

a. （　　）健力宝是中国的一个品牌。

b. （　　）健力宝的市场定位适合当今中国消费者的观念。

c. （　　）健力宝急需重新塑造企业形象及市场定位。

d. （　　　）健力宝 "支持中国体育事业，致力国民素质提高"
的定位未在市场销售中起到应有的作用。

e. （　　　）健力宝的销售方式有问题。

## 6. 问题与探讨：
Questions and Exploration:

a. 请分析知名品牌在中国受欢迎的原因。

b. 你认为一般中国人或亚洲人品牌意识比较高吗？这跟什么文
化背景有关系？

# 3.4 练习

## 1. 选择适当的动词填空：
Fill in each blank with the most appropriate verb:

利用　出口　面临　影响

降低　形成　损害　存在

a. (　　　　　)挑战　　　e. (　　　　　)价格

b. (　　　　　)威胁　　　f. (　　　　　)差距

c. (　　　　　)优势　　　g. (　　　　　)形象

d. (　　　　　)汇率　　　h. (　　　　　)商品

## 2. 选词填空：
Fill in each blank with the most appropriate word:

a. 严重　严峻　严肃

1) 国有企业在中国加入WTO后将面临_____的挑战。

2) 面对如此_____的挑战，我们更要_____纪律。

3) 公司存在_____的销售问题，应该尽快制定新的销售方案，从而增加销售量。

4) 当总经理谈到目前_____的形势时，面容是_____的。

b. 形成　成形

1) 中国目前的金融市场尚未_____。

2)通过与国外公司广泛合作，我们产品的国际营销已经＿＿＿＿了一定规模。

3)随着生产及管理技术水平的提高，生产一辆汽车从制造零配件到组装＿＿＿＿只需要短短几天的时间。

c. 注重　注意　重视

1)边远地区的居民一般对教育都不够＿＿＿＿。

2)引进技术后如何消化是一个值得＿＿＿＿的问题。

3)要＿＿＿＿研发力量的投入，才能不断推出新产品。

4)中国人以前买东西只讲究"实惠"，不＿＿＿＿包装。

d. 损害　伤害　危害　损坏

1)在公共场所吸烟会＿＿＿＿他人健康。

2)＿＿＿＿公物就是＿＿＿＿公众的利益。

3)警察的职责是保护民众不受＿＿＿＿。

4)吸毒不但会＿＿＿＿自身的健康，还会＿＿＿＿整个社会的安定。

5)低价甩卖不仅会损失利润，而且会＿＿＿＿公司信誉，因为对有些人来说，低价就等于低质量。

6)生产玻璃的企业一般在当地销售，因为玻璃容易＿＿＿＿，不适于长途运输。

7)石油的价格波动会对某些工业造成很大＿＿＿＿，但对食品、医药等行业的影响则相对较小。

e.　取代　代替

　　1)电脑已经_____了打字机，成为文字处理的工具。

　　2)总经理这个月去休假了，由副总经理_____履行他的职责。

　　3)他年轻有为，刚来不久便_____了厂长的地位。

f.　大力发展　大力推动　大力支持　大力宣传

　　1)在_____经济的同时，也要避免环境污染。

　　2)科技发展_____了社会的进步。

　　3)绿化运动得到国家的_____。

　　4)_____环境保护政策得到了社会各界的广泛支持。

**3. 阅读理解并判断正确与错误：**
Read the following paragraph and indicate whether the statements below are TRUE or FALSE:

> 　　目前中国外贸结构中一个十分突出的问题是出口产品加工程度低，附加值不高。如果不在短期内解决这个问题，将可能使加工工业变为一种"无根工业"，而且有可能由于劳动力成本和政策性优势的消失而导致出口产品的国际竞争力严重下降，从而丧失加工工业的发展条件和贸易机会。

a.　(　　　) 中国出口产品加工程度及附加值都很高。

b.　(　　　) 中国外贸结构并无任何突出问题。

c.　(　　　) 无根工业是中国加工工业的现状。

d. （　　　）中国出口产品失去国际竞争力的原因在于劳动
力成本和政策性优势的消失。

## 4. 问题与探讨：
Questions and Exploration:

a. 中国出口额最大的商品是什么？最主要目的地是哪儿？

b. 影响中国出口产业发展的因素是什么？

練習

# 1.1練習

## 1. 選擇適當的動詞填空：
Fill in each blank with the most appropriate verb:

促進 吸引 建立 成立 克服

實行 看好 鼓勵 分配 充滿

a. (　　　　)困難　　　　f. (　　　　)公司

b. (　　　　)發展　　　　g. (　　　　)資源

c. (　　　　)外資　　　　h. (　　　　)市場

d. (　　　　)信心　　　　i. (　　　　)生產

e. (　　　　)體制　　　　j. (　　　　)改革


## 2. 選詞填空：
Fill in each blank with the most appropriate word:

a. 中國有可能＿＿＿經濟大國嗎？

　　1)成爲　　　2)變爲　　　3)轉爲


b. 因爲長期虧損，我們只好把公司＿＿＿了。

　　1)倒閉　　　2)關閉　　　3)關門


c. 改革的步伐應該再＿＿＿一點兒。

　　1)加快　　　2)加速　　　3)加強

d. 政府應該趕快＿＿＿＿下崗職工再就業。

　　1) 指導　　　2) 領導　　　3) 引導

e. 目前哪一個國家的失業問題最＿＿＿＿呢？

　　1) 嚴重　　　2) 嚴厲　　　3) 嚴格

f. 中國從1979年開始＿＿＿＿經濟體制改革，剛開始＿＿＿＿的時候，遇到很多困難。

　　1) 推行　　　2) 實行　　　3) 實施

g. 你們公司的管理＿＿＿＿很現代化嗎？

　　1) 體制　　　2) 制度　　　3) 體係

h. 我們要把不利的條件＿＿＿＿有利的條件。

　　1) 變爲　　　2) 成爲　　　3) 轉變爲

## 3. 完成句子並翻譯：
Complete the following sentences and translate the sentences into English:

a. 在領導的鼓勵下，＿＿＿＿＿＿＿＿＿＿＿＿＿＿＿＿＿＿

　　翻譯：＿＿＿＿＿＿＿＿＿＿＿＿＿＿＿＿＿＿＿＿＿＿＿

b. 爲了降低失業率，＿＿＿＿＿＿＿＿＿＿＿＿＿＿＿＿＿＿

　　翻譯：＿＿＿＿＿＿＿＿＿＿＿＿＿＿＿＿＿＿＿＿＿＿＿

c. 公司分了兩個月的獎金，此外，＿＿＿＿＿＿＿＿＿＿＿＿

　　翻譯：＿＿＿＿＿＿＿＿＿＿＿＿＿＿＿＿＿＿＿＿＿＿＿

d. 中國實行計劃經濟政策是為了 ＿＿＿＿＿＿＿＿＿＿＿＿＿＿＿＿

　　翻譯：＿＿＿＿＿＿＿＿＿＿＿＿＿＿＿＿＿＿＿＿＿＿＿＿＿

e. 為了公平起見，＿＿＿＿＿＿＿＿＿＿＿＿＿＿＿＿＿＿＿＿＿

　　翻譯：＿＿＿＿＿＿＿＿＿＿＿＿＿＿＿＿＿＿＿＿＿＿＿＿＿

f. ＿＿＿＿＿＿，從而促使美國公司進一步擴大在中國的投資。

　　翻譯：＿＿＿＿＿＿＿＿＿＿＿＿＿＿＿＿＿＿＿＿＿＿＿＿＿

g. 越來越多的 ＿＿＿＿＿＿＿＿＿＿＿＿＿＿＿＿＿＿＿＿＿＿＿

　　翻譯：＿＿＿＿＿＿＿＿＿＿＿＿＿＿＿＿＿＿＿＿＿＿＿＿＿

h. 經過多年的努力，他已經成為＿＿＿＿＿＿＿＿＿＿＿＿＿＿＿

　　翻譯：＿＿＿＿＿＿＿＿＿＿＿＿＿＿＿＿＿＿＿＿＿＿＿＿＿

## 4. 翻譯：
Translate into Chinese/English:

a. Besides Taiwanese and Hong Kong business people, there are also business people coming from all over the world to invest in China.

＿＿＿＿＿＿＿＿＿＿＿＿＿＿＿＿＿＿＿＿＿＿＿＿＿＿＿＿＿＿＿

b. Under the planned economic system, productivity is very low.

＿＿＿＿＿＿＿＿＿＿＿＿＿＿＿＿＿＿＿＿＿＿＿＿＿＿＿＿＿＿＿

c. The members of the delegation were selected by the Ministry of Foreign Affairs.

_____

d. More and more privately-owned enterprises have purchased state-owned enterprises.

_____

e. Which company will become the world's largest manufacturer of laptops?

_____

f. Before Nixon visited China, the diplomatic relationship between the U.S. and China had not been officially formed.

_____

g. He still can not change his opinion.

_____

h. 所有的員工都由此進出。

_____

i. 國有企業的經營方式正在轉變。

_____

j. 這家軟件公司在世界各地都建立了子公司。

_____

## 5. 問題與探討：
Questions and Exploration:

a. 外國投資者可不可以收購中國的國有企業？

b. 處理國有企業資產的主要困難是什麼？

c. 多數下崗職工的再就業有什麼問題？

d. 中國政府怎樣解決失業問題？

# 1.2練習

## 1. 選擇適當的動詞填空：
Fill in each blank with the most appropriate verb:

涉及　擴大　公布　得到

從事　允許　取得　頒布

a. (　　　　)成績 　　e. (　　　　)名單

b. (　　　　)領域 　　f. (　　　　)規模

c. (　　　　)法規 　　g. (　　　　)認可

d. (　　　　)活動 　　h. (　　　　)改革


## 2. 解釋以下句子中 " 以 " 的用法並翻譯：
Explain the different meanings of " 以 " in the following sentences and translate the sentences into English:

a. 公司應以公平的原則對待員工。

解釋 : _____

翻譯 : _____


b. 以你現在的健康狀況來說，不適合長途旅行。

解釋 : _____

翻譯 : _____

c. 私有經濟在沿海地區發展迅速，<u>以</u>深圳來說，多數企業都是私有企業。

解釋：_____

翻譯：_____

d. <u>以</u>人口來說，中國是世界上第一大國。

解釋：_____

翻譯：_____

## 3. 用"甚至"改寫下列句子：
Rewrite the following sentences with "甚至"：

a. 國企被私有企業併購後，有些減少了虧損，有些還有盈利。

_____

b. 有些私有企業規模不斷擴大，不但在國內擁有子公司，而且在國外成立辦事處或分公司。

_____

c. 他工作很忙，忘了吃飯。

_____

d. 在中國的計劃經濟體制下，中央政府統一分配資源，統一組織生產，還統一銷售。

_____

e. 現在不僅年輕人和中年人用電腦，老年人也用。

_____

## 4. 用 " 不僅 " 改寫下列句子：
Rewrite the following sentences with " 不僅 " :

a. 這次會議沒有解決問題，卻加深了矛盾。

_____

b. 近年來，中國的私有企業數量增多，規模擴大。

_____

c. 中國加入WTO以後，國有企業要和國內其它企業競爭，也要和外國的企業競爭。

_____

d. 中國政府改革了稅收和金融體制，也改革了外貿體制。

_____

## 5. 選詞填空：
Fill in each blank with the most appropriate word:

a. 認可　許可　允許

1)企業要得到對外經濟貿易合作部的正式_____才能從事進出口業務。

2)中國政府_____一部分人先富起來的政策促進了中國的私有經濟。

3)這項計劃已經得到生產部門的_____了。

4)很多國際航班都不＿＿＿＿＿乘客吸煙。

b. 領域　　領土

1)過了這條河，就是另一個國家的＿＿＿＿＿了。

2)私有經濟已經進軍高科技＿＿＿＿＿了。

3)這個公司的經營範圍很廣，已經在房地產、金融和貿易等多個＿＿＿＿＿進行投資。

4)現在香港是中國的＿＿＿＿＿了。

c. 頒布　　公布

1)下個月將正式＿＿＿＿＿得獎名單。

2)自從政府＿＿＿＿＿新的投資法以來，到這裏來投資的外商越來越多。

3)比賽的結果還沒＿＿＿＿＿。

4)總統＿＿＿＿＿禁嚴令，宣布整個城市進入緊急戰爭狀態。

d. 擴大　　擴充

1)經過幾年的發展，私有企業逐步＿＿＿＿＿了經營範圍。

2)在這個行業，目前每個公司都在努力＿＿＿＿＿研發實力。

3)我們公司不僅要＿＿＿＿＿規模，而且要＿＿＿＿＿設備。

e. 方式　　方法

1)承包是國有企業改革中經常採用的＿＿＿＿＿之一。

2)他們夫妻倆的生活＿＿＿＿＿不一樣。

3) 在生活中，我們要用科學的_____解決問題。

4) 他用各種_____算這道題，幾個小時過後仍然找不到答案。

## 6. 用括號裏的詞語完成句子並翻譯：

Complete the following sentences with the words given in parentheses and translate the sentences into English:

a. _____，這裏的氣溫就一直很高。（以來）

   翻譯：_____

b. _____，他才到會場。（直到）

   翻譯：_____

c. 公司上半年的業績，_____。（令）

   翻譯：_____

d. 私有企業的規模不斷擴大，_____。（甚至）

   翻譯：_____

e. 他_____參加了這次會議。（以）

   翻譯：_____

f. 他的銷售額總是第一，實在_____。（令）

   翻譯：_____

## 7. 翻譯：

Translate the following sentences into English:

a. 自從引進先進的技術以來，工廠的效益就不斷提高。

_____

b. 私有企業在中國存在的時間不長，但已取得了令人矚目的成就。

_____

c. 這個項目要是經理不認可，就無法進行。

_____

d. 政府壟斷的行業不允許私有企業介入。

_____

e. 中國鼓勵發展多種經濟形式，以私有經濟來說，就有個體、合伙及有限責任公司等多種形式。

_____

## 8. 問題與探討：

Questions and Exploration:

a. 私有企業對中國經濟發展有什麼作用？

b. 中國哪一省的私有企業最多？它們多半從事什麼行業？

c. 中國將來是否有可能允許私有企業經營銀行業？

# 1.3 練習

## 1. 選擇適當的動詞填空：
Fill in each blank with the most appropriate verb:

建立　　製造　　扶植　　提高

給予　　吸引　　提供　　推動

a. (　　　　) 投資　　　　　d. (　　　　) 資金

b. (　　　　) 優惠　　　　　e. (　　　　) 特區

c. (　　　　) 企業　　　　　f. (　　　　) 飛機

## 2. 選詞填空：
Fill in each blank with the most appropriate word:

a. 會議開始十分鐘後還有代表＿＿＿＿入場。

　　1) 連續　　　2) 陸續　　　3) 繼續

b. 公司已經＿＿＿＿虧損三年了。

　　1) 連續　　　2) 陸續　　　3) 繼續

c. 中國廣闊的市場＿＿＿＿了越來越多的外國投資者。

　　1) 吸引　　　2) 吸收　　　3) 吸取

d. 很多發達國家政府向本國企業＿＿＿＿出口信貸，鼓勵出口。

　　1) 提供　　　2) 供給　　　3) 供應

e. 國家＿＿＿＿＿了專門基金，解決貧困地區的教育問題。

    1)建立　　　 2)設立　　　 3)成立

f. 你認爲這個理論能＿＿＿＿＿嗎？

    1)建立　　　 2)設立　　　 3)成立

g. 中國與世界上大多數國家都＿＿＿＿＿了正式的外交關係。

    1)建立　　　 2)設立　　　 3)成立

# 3. 將指定的詞語插入適當的位置並翻譯：

Indicate where each designated word belongs in the sentence and translate the sentences into English:

a. 起

   1)公司從下半年開始實行新的獎懲制度。

   翻譯：＿＿＿＿＿＿＿＿＿＿＿＿＿＿＿＿＿＿＿＿＿＿＿＿＿

   2)長城自山海關一直延續了幾個省份。

   翻譯：＿＿＿＿＿＿＿＿＿＿＿＿＿＿＿＿＿＿＿＿＿＿＿＿＿

b. 以　　以便

   1)希望消費者多提意見，我們改進產品質量。

   翻譯：＿＿＿＿＿＿＿＿＿＿＿＿＿＿＿＿＿＿＿＿＿＿＿＿＿

   2)政府制定了許多優惠政策，吸引外資。

   翻譯：＿＿＿＿＿＿＿＿＿＿＿＿＿＿＿＿＿＿＿＿＿＿＿＿＿

3) 公司設有食堂，方便員工用餐。

翻譯：＿＿＿＿＿＿＿＿＿＿＿＿＿＿＿＿＿＿＿＿＿

c. 紛紛

1) 幾家公司看好他的設計，找他合作。

翻譯：＿＿＿＿＿＿＿＿＿＿＿＿＿＿＿＿＿＿＿＿＿

d. 先後

1) 考察團參觀了幾個工廠。

翻譯：＿＿＿＿＿＿＿＿＿＿＿＿＿＿＿＿＿＿＿＿＿

2) 請大家按順序進入會場。

翻譯：＿＿＿＿＿＿＿＿＿＿＿＿＿＿＿＿＿＿＿＿＿

e. 以上

1) 我想對發言作個總結。

翻譯：＿＿＿＿＿＿＿＿＿＿＿＿＿＿＿＿＿＿＿＿＿

2) 我列出了投資環境比較好的幾個城市。

翻譯：＿＿＿＿＿＿＿＿＿＿＿＿＿＿＿＿＿＿＿＿＿

## 4. 解釋劃線詞語的意思並翻譯：
Explain the underlined words or phrases and translate the sentence into English:

a. 為了吸引外資，中國政府為外國投資者提供了理想的投資環境。

解釋：＿＿＿＿＿＿＿＿＿＿＿＿＿＿＿＿＿＿＿＿＿

翻譯：_____

b. 對這項改革方案，大家意見<u>紛紛</u>。

解釋：_____

翻譯：_____

c. 公司降低工資<u>以</u>減少生產成本。

解釋：_____

翻譯：_____

d. 中國從1979年<u>起</u>實行市場經濟政策。

解釋：_____

翻譯：_____

e. 大學畢業生找工作<u>以</u>計算機專業最吃香。

解釋：_____

翻譯：_____

## 5. 用括號裏的詞語完成句子並翻譯：

Complete the following sentences with the words given in parentheses and translate the sentences into English:

a. 爲了引進先進技術，中國企業_____。（紛紛）

翻譯：_____

b. 人們對政府降息的計劃，_____。（紛紛）

翻譯：_____

c. _____，中國政府降低外商所得稅稅率。（爲了 ）

翻譯：_____

d. 中國政府_____開始推行經濟體制改革。（從...起 ）

翻譯：_____

## 6. 問題與探討：
Questions and Exploration:

a. 經濟特區的主要特點和作用。

b. 經濟特區吸引外資是否主要靠優惠政策？

c. 中國最大的經濟技術開發區在哪個城市？

d. 爲什麼中國政府將在政策上側重開發大西部？具體措施有哪些？探討目前中國西北部開發區的發展狀況。

# 1.4練習

## 1. 選擇適當的動詞填空：
Fill in each blank with the most appropriate verb:

制定　分享　協助　承擔　轉換

獲得　分配　分擔　取代　加速

a. (　　　　　) 利潤　　　　e. (　　　　　) 改革

b. (　　　　　) 伙伴　　　　f. (　　　　　) 機制

c. (　　　　　) 風險　　　　g. (　　　　　) 責任

d. (　　　　　) 經驗　　　　h. (　　　　　) 政策

## 2. 選詞填空：
Fill in each blank with the most appropriate word:

a. 形式　形狀

1) 這個工廠生產各種_____的鐘錶。

2) 在政府的鼓勵下，投資_____多樣化。

3) 那朵雲的_____像隻狗。

4) 這兩個方案_____不同，但內容是一樣的。

b. 對　對於

1) 公司_____項目的回報率要求很高。

2) 開發新產品_____一個企業非常重要。

3)＿＿＿＿中方來説，引進資金才是他們建立合資企業的眞正目的。

4)年終決算時各個部門需要與財務部門＿＿＿＿帳。

c. 分享　分擔

1)科研小組共同＿＿＿＿研究成果。

2)這次旅行的費用，我們彼此＿＿＿＿。

3)總公司同意＿＿＿＿這項投資的損失。

4)全體員工都能＿＿＿＿公司所得。

# 3. 用 " 則 " 把 A、B 中合適的部分搭配起來：
Match the phrases in column A with the corresponding phrases in column B and indicate where " 則 " belongs in the sentence:

| A | B |
| --- | --- |
| 如果資金短缺 | 内地發展緩慢 |
| 計劃經濟不改革 | 人們的生活水準無法提高 |
| 中國人想到外國去做生意 | 這個項目無法完成 |
| 沿海城市經濟發展迅速 | 外國人想到中國投資 |

# 4. 用 " 來 " 把 A、B 中合適的部分搭配起來 :
Match the phrases in column A with the corresponding phrases in column B
and indicate where " 來 " belongs in the sentence:

| A | B |
|---|---|
| 外商採用與中方合資的方式 | 慶祝公司周年慶 |
| 公司引進先進技術 | 分配利潤 |
| 你們用什麼方式 | 提高競爭力 |
| 合資公司一般按投資比例 | 進入中國市場 |

# 5. 用 " ～化 " 填空 :
Use " ～化 " to fill in the blanks:

a. 爲了提高生產效率，生產流程應該_____。

b. 上海已成爲_____的城市。

c. 我們應該不斷_____改革。

d. 我們要_____環境，_____城市。

# 6. 在以下含有 " ～則 " 的句子中填空 :
Fill in the blanks in the following sentences containing " ～則 " :

a. 如果投資失敗，輕則_____，重則_____。

b. 合作期限一般不會太長，少則_____，多則_____。

# 7. 解釋劃線詞語的意思並翻譯 :
Explain the underlined words or phrases and translate the sentences into English:

a. 香港被稱爲 " 東方之珠 " 。

解釋：_____

翻譯：_____

b. 年輕人都要有所作<u>爲</u>。

解釋：_____

翻譯：_____

c. 經營企業不應該僅以賺錢<u>爲</u>目的。

解釋：_____

翻譯：_____

d. 這裏保姆的工資是<u>按</u>月計算的。

解釋：_____

翻譯：_____

e. 如果政府早一點實行改革開放政策，<u>或者</u>中國的經濟會更加強大。

解釋：_____

翻譯：_____

f. 特區裏不論軟環境<u>或者</u>硬環境都已達到國際標準。

解釋：_____

翻譯：_____

g. 過去我們對他一直不太了解，只是從最近的報道中才知道<u>其</u>人<u>其</u>事。

解釋：_____

翻譯：_____

h. 爲了讓大家了解這個項目的重要性，他不厭<u>其</u>煩地作解釋。

解釋：_____

翻譯：_____

## 8. 用括號裏的詞語完成句子：
Complete the following sentences by using the words given in parentheses:

a. _____，這個項目太難了。( 對於...而言 )

b. 到中國開辦網路公司是_____。( 爲 )

c. 在美國，距離是_____。( 按 )

d. 如果中國不設立經濟特區，_____。( 則 )

e. 我們可以投資到中國建廠，_____。( 或者 )

## 9. 翻譯：
Translate the following sentences into English/Chinese:

a. 你所建議的投資計劃已被董事會批准。

_____

b. 他們所關心的問題是提高生產力。

_____

c.　As far as investors are concerned, financial return is the most important issue.

_____

d.　Whether you approve or disapprove, you must make your decision.

_____

e.　We are not in charge of the foreign investment. Perhaps MOFTEC can help.

_____


# 10.　問題與探討：
Questions and Exploration:

a.　中國政府爲何會允許外商在中國設立獨資企業？獨資企業對中國的發展有何作用？

b.　中國爲保護國內企業，是否會對外商採取一些限制性措施？

# 2.1 練習

## 1. 選擇適當的動詞填空：
Fill in each blank with the most appropriate verb:

壟斷　分離　獲准　承擔　自負

執行　發揮　確定　扶持　自主

a. (　　　　　)作用　　　　f. (　　　　　)市場

b. (　　　　　)利率　　　　g. (　　　　　)任務

c. (　　　　　)營業　　　　h. (　　　　　)盈虧

d. (　　　　　)職能　　　　i. (　　　　　)責任

e. (　　　　　)政策　　　　j. (　　　　　)經營

## 2. 根據課文內容填入正確的詞語：
Fill in each blank with the most appropriate word according to the text reading for this lesson:

a. 銀行與保險公司都屬於_____機構。

b. 子公司成立后將自主_____，_____盈虧。

c. 銀行在中國經濟發展中發揮的_____越來越大。

d. 銀行業是金融體係中重要的_____部分。

e. 中國銀行體制的改革重點是分離銀行的_____和_____職能。

f. 花旗銀行是最早進入中國市場的_____銀行之一。

# 3. 解釋劃線詞語的意思：

Explain the underlined words or phrases:

a. 他<u>隨著</u>參觀者進入了會場。

解釋：＿＿＿＿＿＿＿＿＿＿＿＿＿＿＿＿＿＿＿＿＿＿＿＿＿＿

b. 他的強硬態度<u>使</u>人難以接受。

解釋：＿＿＿＿＿＿＿＿＿＿＿＿＿＿＿＿＿＿＿＿＿＿＿＿＿＿

c. 這<u>起</u>車禍使他不得不住院三個月。

解釋：＿＿＿＿＿＿＿＿＿＿＿＿＿＿＿＿＿＿＿＿＿＿＿＿＿＿

d. 改革開放以後，中國的經濟<u>起</u>了很大的變化。

解釋：＿＿＿＿＿＿＿＿＿＿＿＿＿＿＿＿＿＿＿＿＿＿＿＿＿＿

e. 我們部門<u>僅</u>負責人事管理。

解釋：＿＿＿＿＿＿＿＿＿＿＿＿＿＿＿＿＿＿＿＿＿＿＿＿＿＿

f. 中國人民銀行在中國金融體系中<u>起</u>了決定性的作用。

解釋：＿＿＿＿＿＿＿＿＿＿＿＿＿＿＿＿＿＿＿＿＿＿＿＿＿＿

g. 這台電腦已經<u>使</u>了5年了，該升級了。

解釋：＿＿＿＿＿＿＿＿＿＿＿＿＿＿＿＿＿＿＿＿＿＿＿＿＿＿

h. 中國人民銀行調高利率後，各商業銀行也<u>隨著</u>調高了利率。

解釋：＿＿＿＿＿＿＿＿＿＿＿＿＿＿＿＿＿＿＿＿＿＿＿＿＿＿

i. 整個公司的出差費用相當大，<u>僅</u>交通費就達到4萬元。

解釋：＿＿＿＿＿＿＿＿＿＿＿＿＿＿＿＿＿＿＿＿＿＿＿＿＿＿＿＿


# 4. 用＂隨著＂完成下列句子並翻譯：
Complete the following sentences with＂隨著＂and translate the sentences into English:

a. 隨著改革的深入，＿＿＿＿＿＿＿＿＿＿＿＿＿＿＿＿＿＿＿＿＿

翻譯：＿＿＿＿＿＿＿＿＿＿＿＿＿＿＿＿＿＿＿＿＿＿＿＿＿＿＿＿


b. 隨著經濟的發展，＿＿＿＿＿＿＿＿＿＿＿＿＿＿＿＿＿＿＿＿＿

翻譯：＿＿＿＿＿＿＿＿＿＿＿＿＿＿＿＿＿＿＿＿＿＿＿＿＿＿＿＿


c. ＿＿＿＿＿＿＿＿＿＿＿＿＿＿＿＿＿＿＿＿＿＿，產品的價格會下降。

翻譯：＿＿＿＿＿＿＿＿＿＿＿＿＿＿＿＿＿＿＿＿＿＿＿＿＿＿＿＿


d. ＿＿＿＿＿＿＿＿＿＿＿＿＿＿＿＿＿＿＿，銀行的商業職能越來越大。

翻譯：＿＿＿＿＿＿＿＿＿＿＿＿＿＿＿＿＿＿＿＿＿＿＿＿＿＿＿＿


# 5. 用＂及＂或＂以及＂改寫下列句子：
Rewrite the following sentences with＂及＂or＂以及＂：

a. 這家跨國公司規模很大，在美國、日本、德國、中國都有它的分支機構。

＿＿＿＿＿＿＿＿＿＿＿＿＿＿＿＿＿＿＿＿＿＿＿＿＿＿＿＿＿＿＿


b. 各部門經理和家屬都被邀請參加舞會。

＿＿＿＿＿＿＿＿＿＿＿＿＿＿＿＿＿＿＿＿＿＿＿＿＿＿＿＿＿＿＿

　　c. 出差時的住宿費、交通費、伙食費、其它各種費用都可以報銷。

_____

　　d. 從改革開放到設立自由貿易區、金融貿易區，上海發生了巨大的變化。

_____

# 6. 選詞填空：

Fill in each blank with the most appropriate word:

展開　開展　發展

　　a. 早上公司宣布全面降價后，整個行業的價格戰便_____了序幕。

　　b. 證券公司員工_____了如何提高利潤率的討論。

　　c. 隨著外資的不斷湧入，中國的金融業在迅速地_____。

　　d. 爲了增加員工間的團結，公司經常_____集體活動。

# 7. 閱讀理解並判斷正確與錯誤：

Read the following paragraph and indicate whether the statements below are TRUE or FALSE:

> 　　根據在加入WTO談判中所答應的條件，中國將在一定時候取消設立外資銀行的地域限制，允許更多的外資銀行開展人民幣業務和進一步擴大人民幣業務的範圍。從日前定出的開放人民幣業務的時間表來看，人民幣業務開放速度將超出多數人的預期。

a. (　　　)中國政府將放寬外資銀行在華業務的限制。

b. (　　　)銀行業是中國政府壟斷的行業。

c. (　　　)中國政府將允許外資銀行在中國開辦人民幣業務。

d. (　　　)人民幣業務開放速度將達不到大多數人的預期。

## 8. 問題與探討：
Questions and Exploration:

a. 中國銀行體系是否包括投資銀行？

b. 目前中國商業銀行可否由私人開辦？

c. 外資銀行的客戶是否只限於三資企業？其發展方向是什麼？

d. 外資銀行可否在中國發行信用卡？

e. 中國政府對外資金融機構進入中國市場的資產標準是什麼？

f. 外資銀行會給中國經濟建設帶來什麼影響及作用？

# 2.2 練習

**1.** 根據課文內容填入正確的詞語：

Fill in each blank with the most appropriate word according to the text reading for this lesson:

a. 在經濟過熱的情況下，政府通常會＿＿＿＿銀根來抑制通脹。

b. SAFE ( State Administration of Foreign Exchange) 是中國國家外匯 ＿＿＿＿局的簡稱。

c. 當本幣＿＿＿＿時，進口商品的價格將下降。

d. 利率影響＿＿＿＿的價格。

e. 利率和匯率是兩個非常重要的經濟＿＿＿＿。

f. 匯率的＿＿＿＿會影響一個國家資本的流動。

**2.** 選詞填空：

Fill in each blank with the most appropriate word:

a. 變化　變動

1) 氣象預報無法準確預知天氣＿＿＿＿。

2) 最近由於公司重組，財務部門的人事＿＿＿＿比較多。

3) 股市行情＿＿＿＿多端。

4) 合同正本不需要做任何文字＿＿＿＿。

b. 欲望　願望

1) 佛教的教義主張人們放棄一切＿＿＿＿。

2)維護和平是全世界人民的共同＿＿＿＿。

3)他向領導提出調動工作的＿＿＿＿。

4)廣告可以刺激人們的消費＿＿＿＿。

c. 表示　表達　表明

1)這部影片＿＿＿＿了人類對太空的好奇。

2)總經理在大會上＿＿　公司不會裁員。

3)董事會表決結果現在是3:3，就等董事長最後＿＿＿＿立場了。

4)政府已經明確＿＿＿＿了支持高科技產業發展的政策。

d. 抑制　控制

1)他用理智＿＿＿＿了衝動，使他能冷靜地分析目前的形勢。

2)中方代表最終＿＿＿＿了整個談判局勢。

3)他＿＿＿＿不住心中的怒火，向老板提出辭職。

4)高血壓患者要嚴格＿＿＿＿飲食。

e. 鼓勵　勉勵

1)得到經理的＿＿＿＿後，職員們更加努力工作了。

2)＿＿＿＿比批評更能使人進步。

3)政府總理＿＿＿＿科技人員不斷創新。

4)他以"克服困難、爭取成功"來自我＿＿＿＿。

f. 防止　避免

1)談判雙方應盡量克制情緒，＿＿＿＿發生衝突。

2)打預防針可以＿＿＿＿得病。

3)政府調整利率是為了＿＿＿通貨膨脹。

4)孕婦應該＿＿＿抽煙、喝酒。

## 3. 用 " 既 ... 也 ... " 或 " 既 ... 又 ... " 改寫下列句子：
Rewrite the following sentences with " 既 ... 也 ... " or " 既 ... 又 ... " :

a. 對待員工不但要批評，也要鼓勵。

_____

b. 消費者喜歡選擇質量好價格低的商品。

_____

c. 生產力的提高可以促進經濟增長，還可以抑制通貨膨脹。

_____

d. 大多數決策都有不利的一面和有利的一面。

_____

## 4. 解釋劃線詞語的意思並翻譯：
Explain the underlined words or phrases and translate the sentences into English:

a. " 而 "

1) 價廉而物美的產品最受消費者歡迎。

解釋：_____

翻譯：_____

2) 這次比賽他贏了，但他勝<u>而</u>不驕，非常謙虛。

解釋：＿＿＿＿＿＿＿＿＿＿＿＿＿＿＿＿＿＿＿＿＿＿＿

翻譯：＿＿＿＿＿＿＿＿＿＿＿＿＿＿＿＿＿＿＿＿＿＿＿

3) 中國古代有許多美麗<u>而</u>動人的傳說。

解釋：＿＿＿＿＿＿＿＿＿＿＿＿＿＿＿＿＿＿＿＿＿＿＿

翻譯：＿＿＿＿＿＿＿＿＿＿＿＿＿＿＿＿＿＿＿＿＿＿＿

4) 有些外國人認為中國不是發展中國家，<u>而</u>中國人認為自己是發展中國家。

解釋：＿＿＿＿＿＿＿＿＿＿＿＿＿＿＿＿＿＿＿＿＿＿＿

翻譯：＿＿＿＿＿＿＿＿＿＿＿＿＿＿＿＿＿＿＿＿＿＿＿

b.　"之"

1) 對方公司退出競爭，我們正求<u>之</u>不得。

解釋：＿＿＿＿＿＿＿＿＿＿＿＿＿＿＿＿＿＿＿＿＿＿＿

翻譯：＿＿＿＿＿＿＿＿＿＿＿＿＿＿＿＿＿＿＿＿＿＿＿

2) 由於總經理犯了錯誤，他現已被副總經理取而代<u>之</u>了。

解釋：＿＿＿＿＿＿＿＿＿＿＿＿＿＿＿＿＿＿＿＿＿＿＿

翻譯：＿＿＿＿＿＿＿＿＿＿＿＿＿＿＿＿＿＿＿＿＿＿＿

3) 我們<u>之</u>間有深厚的友誼。

解釋：＿＿＿＿＿＿＿＿＿＿＿＿＿＿＿＿＿＿＿＿＿＿＿

翻譯：＿＿＿＿＿＿＿＿＿＿＿＿＿＿＿＿＿＿＿＿＿＿＿

4) 在公司轉型<u>之</u>際，我們更需要員工的支持。

解釋：＿＿＿＿＿＿＿＿＿＿＿＿＿＿＿＿＿＿＿＿＿＿

翻譯：＿＿＿＿＿＿＿＿＿＿＿＿＿＿＿＿＿＿＿＿＿＿

5) 旅行社現在推出的黃山<u>之</u>旅價格很便宜。

解釋：＿＿＿＿＿＿＿＿＿＿＿＿＿＿＿＿＿＿＿＿＿＿

翻譯：＿＿＿＿＿＿＿＿＿＿＿＿＿＿＿＿＿＿＿＿＿＿

c. "如何"

1) <u>如何</u>提高本公司的利潤率是這次會議首先要解決的問題。

解釋：＿＿＿＿＿＿＿＿＿＿＿＿＿＿＿＿＿＿＿＿＿＿

翻譯：＿＿＿＿＿＿＿＿＿＿＿＿＿＿＿＿＿＿＿＿＿＿

2) 天已經黑了，看來我們是無論<u>如何</u>都來不及了。

解釋：＿＿＿＿＿＿＿＿＿＿＿＿＿＿＿＿＿＿＿＿＿＿

翻譯：＿＿＿＿＿＿＿＿＿＿＿＿＿＿＿＿＿＿＿＿＿＿

3) 比賽很激烈，勝負<u>如何</u>現在還很難預料。

解釋：＿＿＿＿＿＿＿＿＿＿＿＿＿＿＿＿＿＿＿＿＿＿

翻譯：＿＿＿＿＿＿＿＿＿＿＿＿＿＿＿＿＿＿＿＿＿＿

4) 你剛聽過氣象預報，明天的天氣<u>如何</u>？

解釋：＿＿＿＿＿＿＿＿＿＿＿＿＿＿＿＿＿＿＿＿＿＿

翻譯：＿＿＿＿＿＿＿＿＿＿＿＿＿＿＿＿＿＿＿＿＿＿

## 5. 用 " 反之 " 完成下列句子：
Complete the following sentences with " 反之 "：

a. 利率的上升會帶動匯率的上升，_____

b. 貨幣貶值會促進出口，_____

c. 利率降低時，股票價格會上升，_____

d. 物體受熱後會膨脹，_____

## 6. 閱讀理解並判斷正確與錯誤 ：
Read the following paragraph and indicate whether the statements below are TRUE or FALSE:

> 　　90年代中期以來，中國的宏觀經濟政策由治理通貨膨脹轉向刺激需求、調整結構和保持經濟增長速度。中國的利率調整對匯率是零效應，甚至是負效應。但利率政策對匯率的影響會以其它方式表現出來，如資本外逃、外匯黑市的波動等。這些都會對人民幣匯率的穩定造成很大的影響。

a. (　　　) 中國自90年代中期以來，一直爲治理通脹而努力。

b. (　　　) 在中國，利率下降，匯率也會隨着下降。

c. (　　　) 中國宏觀經濟政策一直是先刺激需求再治理通脹。

d. (　　　) 利率下降對匯率沒有明顯影響。

e. (　　　) 資本外逃對人民幣匯率的穩定有壓力。

# 7. 問題與探討：

Questions and Exploration:

a. 爲什麽中國政府在1998-1999年期間連續降低利率？

b. 目前人民幣在國際金融市場的地位如何？

# 2.3 練習

## 1. 根據課文內容填入正確的詞語：

Fill in each blank with the most appropriate word according to the text reading for this lesson:

a. 中國早先發行的股票是100元人民幣＿＿＿＿的票據。

b. 中國的A股和B股、H股和N股具有不同的＿＿＿＿。

c. ＿＿＿＿在香港的地位相當於美國的藍籌股。

d. 中國股市的發展還處於初級＿＿＿＿。

e. 發行股票可以在市場上＿＿＿＿資金。

f. 中資企業在香港有＿＿＿＿的實力。

g. 中國證券市場的制度還不＿＿＿＿。

h. 中國在80年代中期＿＿＿＿了股票買賣。

## 2. 選詞填空：

Fill in each blank with the most appropriate word:

a. 缺少　缺乏

1) 證券分析師是每個證券公司都不可＿＿＿＿的人才。

2) 沙漠地帶水源比較＿＿＿＿。

3) 他因＿＿＿＿專業知識而沒有被錄用。

4) 由於＿＿＿＿資金，這項工程無法進行。

b. 緊密　密切

1) 合資企業雙方需要＿＿＿＿合作。

2) 已經連續四個小時了，他仍在＿＿＿＿關注股票的走勢。

3) 網絡與人們日常生活的關係越來越＿＿＿＿了。

c. 概念　觀念

1) 要投資股市，必須先了解一些有關股票的基本　＿＿＿。

2) 消費＿＿＿＿會隨著收入水平的提高而改變。

3) 中國股民的投資＿＿＿＿還不是很成熟。

4) 很多人對股票指數沒有清楚的＿＿＿＿。

d. 相關　有關

1) 要買賣股票必須先到證券交易所辦理＿＿＿＿手續。

2) 很多時候，股價的波動和券商炒作＿＿＿＿。

3) 創辦公司需要得到＿＿＿＿部門的許可。

4) 國家的宏觀政策與經濟發展密切＿＿＿＿。

# 3. 解釋劃線詞語的意思並造句：
Explain the underlined words and use those words to make an additional sentence:

a. 由於政府接連發布了幾條利好消息，股民恢復了對股票市場的信心。

解釋：＿＿＿＿＿＿＿＿＿＿＿＿＿＿＿＿＿＿＿＿＿＿＿＿＿

造句：＿＿＿＿＿＿＿＿＿＿＿＿＿＿＿＿＿＿＿＿＿＿＿＿＿

b. 喝了水，休息了一陣後，他覺得自己的體力慢慢恢復了。

解釋：＿＿＿＿＿＿＿＿＿＿＿＿＿＿＿＿＿＿＿＿＿＿＿

造句：＿＿＿＿＿＿＿＿＿＿＿＿＿＿＿＿＿＿＿＿＿＿＿

c. 中國先後在1997年和1999年恢復了對香港和澳門行使主權。

解釋：＿＿＿＿＿＿＿＿＿＿＿＿＿＿＿＿＿＿＿＿＿＿＿

造句：＿＿＿＿＿＿＿＿＿＿＿＿＿＿＿＿＿＿＿＿＿＿＿

d. 通過銀行貸款，公司籌足了項目建設的經費。

解釋：＿＿＿＿＿＿＿＿＿＿＿＿＿＿＿＿＿＿＿＿＿＿＿

造句：＿＿＿＿＿＿＿＿＿＿＿＿＿＿＿＿＿＿＿＿＿＿＿

e. 經過激烈的討論，董事會終於通過了派息方案。

解釋：＿＿＿＿＿＿＿＿＿＿＿＿＿＿＿＿＿＿＿＿＿＿＿

造句：＿＿＿＿＿＿＿＿＿＿＿＿＿＿＿＿＿＿＿＿＿＿＿

f. 我們通過長長的走廊來到他的房間。

解釋：＿＿＿＿＿＿＿＿＿＿＿＿＿＿＿＿＿＿＿＿＿＿＿

造句：＿＿＿＿＿＿＿＿＿＿＿＿＿＿＿＿＿＿＿＿＿＿＿

g. H股是指在香港上市的中國股票。

解釋：＿＿＿＿＿＿＿＿＿＿＿＿＿＿＿＿＿＿＿＿＿＿＿

造句：＿＿＿＿＿＿＿＿＿＿＿＿＿＿＿＿＿＿＿＿＿＿＿

h.老師指著幻燈片向學生講解計算機的構造。

解釋：_____

造句：_____

## 4. 用 " 而 " 把 A、B、C中合適的部分搭配起來：
Match the phrases in column A with the corresponding phrases in column B and column C and indicate where " 而 " belongs in the sentence:

| A | B | C |
|---|---|---|
| 這個項目 | 需要根據供求關係 | 被迫停工 |
| 許多誤解 | 因文化差異 | 決定 |
| 產品的產量 | 隨著政策變動 | 產生 |
| 股價 | 因經費不足 | 上下波動 |

## 5. 閱讀理解並判斷正確與錯誤：
Read the following paragraph and indicate whether the statements below are TRUE or FALSE:

> 　　B股對國內投資者開放以後，在滬深兩市如期開盤。由於市場沒有取消漲停限制，兩市100多只股票全部被釘在 " 漲停板 " 上，而買盤依舊不斷增加。深交所行情只能顯示1億股以內的買盤。許多股票的買盤超過了1億股，只能顯示其最大數字999,999手。滬市最大的買盤居然有3億多股。 兩地市場同時趨向瘋狂。

a. (　　　　)B股對國內投資者開放以後，市場反應並不熱烈。

b.　(　　　　)取消漲停限制後，很多公司被釘在了 " 漲停板 " 上。

c.　(　　　　)上海交易所行情可以顯示1億股以上的買盤。

d.　(　　　　)中國境內的中國人可以投資B股。


## 6. 問題與探討 :
Questions and Exploration:

a.　B股對境內投資者開放后，對中國股票市場有何影響？

b.　根據你的知識與判斷，談談對海外上市的中國股票的展望。

# 2.4 練習

## 1. 選擇適當的動詞填空：
Fill in each blank with the most appropriate verb:

驚人　充足　雲集　美稱　成績

堅實　優秀　繁榮　基礎　雄厚

a. 多年苦讀使他在金融學方面打下了＿＿＿的基礎。

b. 1999財富論壇在上海舉行，國內外企業＿＿＿一方。

c. 上海很早就有"東方明珠"的＿＿＿。

d. 上海的工業基礎＿＿＿，商業經濟＿＿＿，人口素質＿＿＿，資金供應＿＿＿。

e. 高新技術產業是上海持續發展的＿＿＿。

f. 陸家嘴金融中心取得了＿＿＿的發展。


## 2. 選詞填空：
Fill in each blank with the most appropriate word:

a. 此外　另外　另

1)他投資地產證券，＿＿＿再沒有別的投資。

2)證券投資一方面可以帶來高收入，＿＿＿一方面也帶來高風險。

3)有關項目的進度問題，我們改天＿＿＿討論。

4)東方明珠電視塔、金茂大廈、上海證券交易所，＿＿＿還有一些其它著名建築都位於陸家嘴。

　　b．注目　矚目

　　　1)她穿着一件大紅袍子，非常引人_____。

　　　2)中國改革開放的成就舉世_____。


　　c．焦點　熱點

　　　1)B股市場的開放是日前的_____問題。

　　　2)由於董事長請假，總經理在會議中成爲_____人物。

　　　3)這次討論的_____是客戶關係管理。

　　　4)上海是亞洲的投資_____城市之一。


　　d．保證　保障

　　　1)中央銀行的監督是金融市場健康運作的_____。

　　　2)在得到總工程師的_____後，總經理在計劃書上簽了字。

　　　3)企業退休計劃爲退休員工提供了生活_____。

　　　4)政府的政策支持是上海得以發展的_____。


# 3. 用括號裏的詞語完成句子：
Complete the following sentences with the words given in parentheses:

　　a．券商違規會造成嚴重後果，_____。（乃至）

　　b．_____，同事們都對他另眼相看。（取得）

　　c．_____，不適合競爭的需要。（規模）

　　d．由於上海在金融產業建設上的成就，_____。（博得）

　　e．國有銀行與外資銀行各有優勢，_____。（並駕齊驅）

# 4. 閱讀理解並判斷正確與錯誤：

Read the following paragraph and indicate whether the statements below are TRUE or FALSE:

目前，上海浦東的產業結構包括以金融、保險為支柱的第三產業，以信息技術、醫藥和汽車為主體的第二產業和以農業為基礎的第一產業。此外，金融貿易功能也日漸增強。外高橋保稅區已成為國內最大的保稅區和新建港口，從而強化了國際貿易、保稅倉儲和出口加工三大功能。張江高科技園區已發展成上海技術創新的重要平台。金橋出口加工區吸引了340多家中資和外資企業，成為建設上海新興工業的又一動力。

a. (　　　)浦東已成功發展了第一、二、三產業。

b. (　　　)金融業是第一產業。

c. (　　　)張江高科技園區已發展成上海的重要出口加工區。

d. (　　　)浦東的金融貿易功能正在一天一天地加強。

e. (　　　)外高橋保稅區強化了國際貿易、保險服務和出口加工三大功能

# 5. 問題與探討：

Questions and Exploration:

a. 談談陸家嘴金融貿易區自建立以來所取得的發展。

b. 上海能否建成與香港同等地位的世界商業金融中心？

# 3.1 練習

## 1. 選擇適當的動詞填空：
Fill in each blank with the most appropriate verb:

傳遞　收集　推銷　促銷　進行

掌握　預測　制定　面臨　增加

a. (　　　　)銷售額　　　　f. (　　　　)產品

b. (　　　　)信息　　　　　g. (　　　　)情報

c. (　　　　)策略　　　　　h. (　　　　)資料

d. (　　　　)手段　　　　　i. (　　　　)評估

e. (　　　　)需求量　　　　j. (　　　　)困難

## 2. 選詞填空：
Fill in each blank with the most appropriate word:

a. 面臨　面對

1) 金融領域引入國際競爭機制以後，中國的金融業將＿＿＿巨大的挑戰。

2) 我們要＿＿＿現實，制定可行的方案，以度過目前的難關。

3) ＿＿＿強大的競爭對手，我們公司只能不斷降價以保持市場佔有率。

4) 由於經濟衰退，許多公司都＿＿＿倒閉。

5) ＿＿＿業績下降的問題，董事會決定關閉幾家分公司。

6) 投資者有權知道公司所＿＿＿＿＿的困難。

b. 廣泛　廣大

1) ＿＿＿＿＿市民踴躍參加了昨天的抽獎活動。

2) 他的建議得到了＿＿＿＿＿的支持。

3) 爲了推出適銷對路的產品，公司開展了＿＿＿＿＿的市場調查，以了解消費者需求。

4) 中國西部＿＿＿＿＿地區正面臨沙漠化的威脅。

c. 把握　掌握

1) 當主管，我還沒有＿＿＿＿＿。

2) 作爲公司總會計師，你要＿＿＿＿＿豐富的財務理論知識。

3) 通過調查問卷及電話訪談，我們＿＿＿＿＿了第一手資料。

4) 他認眞鑽研，終於＿＿＿＿＿＿了這門技術。

5) 他有＿＿＿＿＿競選成功。

d. 靠　依靠　依賴

1) 僅＿＿＿＿＿廣告促銷是不夠的，有時還要採用降價、送禮品和抽獎等其它方式。

2) 沿海地區＿＿＿＿＿有利的地理位置發展外向型經濟。

3) 日本的自然資源短缺，只能＿＿＿＿＿進口解決原材料問題。

4) 他＿＿＿＿＿養牛發了大財。

e. 關心　關注

1) 大家都密切＿＿＿＿＿局勢的發展。

2)全社會都應該_____青少年的成長。

3)治理環境污染是全世界共同_____的話題。

4)很多公司都在_____股票市場的動向。

## 3. 選擇劃線詞語的正確解釋：

Choose the word or phrase that best explains the meaning of the underlined word or phrase:

a. 他在國外<u>受</u>過良好的教育。

　　1)接受　　　2)遭受　　　3)承受

b. 他<u>受</u>到了不公正的待遇。

　　1)接受　　　2)遭受　　　3)承受

c. 總工程師是執行這個項目的<u>關鍵</u>人物。

　　1)有關係的　　2)重要的　　3)特殊的

d. 這批貨幸虧<u>賣得及時</u>。

　　1)賣得很快　　2)賣得正是時候　　3)馬上賣掉

e. 接到通知後他<u>及時</u>趕到了現場。

　　1)很早　　　2)馬上　　　3)來不及

f. 爲達到個人目的，他往往<u>不擇手段</u>。

　　1)不仔細選擇方法　　　2)不選擇任何方法
　　3)不管用什麼方法

## 4. 完成下列句子並翻譯：
Complete the following sentences and translate into English:

a. 儘管做了周密的市場調查，＿＿＿＿＿＿＿＿＿＿＿＿＿＿＿＿＿＿＿

翻譯：＿＿＿＿＿＿＿＿＿＿＿＿＿＿＿＿＿＿＿＿＿＿＿＿＿＿＿＿

b. 獲取市場信息的手段很多，例如＿＿＿＿＿＿＿＿＿＿＿＿＿＿＿＿

翻譯：＿＿＿＿＿＿＿＿＿＿＿＿＿＿＿＿＿＿＿＿＿＿＿＿＿＿＿＿

c. 他做出的市場預測很準確，因爲他及時＿＿＿＿＿＿＿＿＿＿＿＿＿

翻譯：＿＿＿＿＿＿＿＿＿＿＿＿＿＿＿＿＿＿＿＿＿＿＿＿＿＿＿＿

d. 這則廣告成功的關鍵是＿＿＿＿＿＿＿＿＿＿＿＿＿＿＿＿＿＿＿＿

翻譯：＿＿＿＿＿＿＿＿＿＿＿＿＿＿＿＿＿＿＿＿＿＿＿＿＿＿＿＿

e. 這次的降價促銷不太成功，關鍵是＿＿＿＿＿＿＿＿＿＿＿＿＿＿＿

翻譯：＿＿＿＿＿＿＿＿＿＿＿＿＿＿＿＿＿＿＿＿＿＿＿＿＿＿＿＿

f. 儘管市場調研只是近年來才在中國開始實行，＿＿＿＿＿＿＿＿＿

翻譯：＿＿＿＿＿＿＿＿＿＿＿＿＿＿＿＿＿＿＿＿＿＿＿＿＿＿＿＿

## 5. 用括號裏的詞語完成句子：
Complete the following sentences with the words given in parentheses:

a. ＿＿＿＿＿＿＿＿＿＿＿＿＿，新產品的上市還是很成功。（儘管）

b. 商品的銷售除了與質量有關之外，還＿＿＿＿＿＿＿。（受）

c. 公司＿＿＿＿＿＿＿，在激烈的競爭中保持領先地位。（及時）

d. 他＿＿＿＿＿＿＿＿＿＿＿＿＿＿＿＿＿＿＿，所以業績非常優秀。（手段）

## 6. 閱讀理解並回答問題：
Read the following paragraph and answer the questions below:

> 　　中國第一家以 " 公司 " 命名的專業市場調研機構—廣州市場研究公司於1987年7月正式注冊成立。之後，大量的調研機構紛紛於1992-1993期間成立。
>
> 　　中國市場調研的發展與跨國公司在中國市場上的營銷活動有密切關係。舉例來說，寶潔、聯合利華等公司對消費者意見的高度關注爲市場調研公司的出現奠定了需求的基礎。另外，伴隨著跨國公司進入中國，一批爲之服務的國際調查集團，如蓋洛普、SRG等先後在中國設立了分支機構。

a. 1987年以前中國有沒有市場調研公司？

b. 1992-1993年期間，中國爲什麼出現了大量的調研公司？

c. 中國市場調研的發展與什麼有密切關係？

d. 寶潔爲什麼能爲市場調研公司奠定需求的基礎？

e. 中國第一家市場調研公司是在什麼城市成立的？

## 7. 問題與探討：
Questions and Exploration:

a. 請列出中國人均 GDP 水平和主要城市的人口總數。

b. 除了可口可樂公司以外，還有哪些外國公司是因爲在進入中國市場以前市場調研工作做得充分而成功的呢？

c. 在中國專門從事市場調研的公司有幾家？

d. 調研人員一般通過哪些方式收集資料？

# 3.2 練習

**1. 選擇適當的動詞填空：**
Fill in each blank with the most appropriate verb:

建立　　面向　　樹立

營銷　　達到　　推動

a. (　　　　　)目的　　　　d. (　　　　　)市場

b. (　　　　　)形象　　　　e. (　　　　　)轉變

c. (　　　　　)體系　　　　f. (　　　　　)方式

**2. 選擇適當的詞語填空：**
Fill in each blank with the most appropriate word:

目的、序、中心、導向、代表、標准

a. 以到達先後為＿＿＿＿＿

b. 以消費者為＿＿＿＿＿

c. 以市場為＿＿＿＿＿

d. 以盈利為＿＿＿＿＿

e. 以業績為＿＿＿＿＿

**3. 選詞填空：**
Fill in each blank with the most appropriate word:

a. 逐步　　逐漸

1)他＿＿＿適應了國外的生活。

2)這種新產品首先在北京試銷，如果成功的話，再＿＿＿向其它城市推廣。

3)中美兩國人民隨著文化交流活動的增多，＿＿＿加深了相互之間的了解。

4)由於採用了先進的管理方式，並配合靈活的促銷手段，這種產品的銷售量＿＿＿增長了。

b. 採用　採取

1)目前，產品質量不斷下降。如果不＿＿＿適當措施，後果會很嚴重。

2)工廠＿＿＿了日本式的管理方法。

3)他提出的人事方案沒有被人事部門＿＿＿。

4)針對競爭對手的促銷方案，我們及時＿＿＿行動，加大了促銷度。

c. 實踐　實行　實現

1)自從＿＿＿"五天工作制"以來，旅游商品成爲消費熱點，商家應根據這種情況及時調整營銷策略。

2)中國從1979年起開始＿＿＿經濟體制改革。

3)在＿＿＿中發現問題並改正是一種非常有效的工作方法。

4)他一直爲＿＿＿當教師的願望而努力。

d. 策略　戰略

1)市場營銷是一門講＿＿＿＿的學問。

2)公司在新形勢下必須制定新的＿＿＿＿。

3)市場部門的職責之一是制定營銷＿＿＿＿。


e. 建立　樹立

1)經過多年努力，公司已＿＿＿＿了完善的銷售管道。

2)他的表現爲大家＿＿＿＿了榜樣。

3)這個公司是他與哥哥共同＿＿＿＿的。


# 4. 根據課文內容完成句子：
Complete the following sentences according to the text reading for this lesson:

a. 市場營銷是 ＿＿＿＿＿＿＿＿＿＿＿＿＿＿＿＿的橋梁。

b. “4P”是指＿＿＿＿＿＿＿＿＿＿＿＿＿＿＿＿。

c. “優惠券”是指＿＿＿＿＿＿＿＿＿＿＿＿＿＿。

d. 採用促銷手段是爲了達到＿＿＿＿＿＿＿＿的目的。

# 5. 閱讀理解並回答問題：

Read the following paragraph and answer the questions below:

> 市場營銷管道和分銷管道是兩個不同的概念。市場營銷管道包括產品的產、供、銷過程中所有的企業和個人，如供應商、生產者、中間商、代理商、輔助商以及最後消費者或用戶等。以消費品行業為例，市場營銷管道包括生產者、收購商、其它供應商、各種代理商、批發商、零售商和消費者等。分銷管道則包括加工商、批發商、代理商、零售商和消費者等。

a. 試將下列中英文詞語配對：
   Match each Chinese term with its English equivalent:

| 市場營銷管道 | user |
|---|---|
| 分銷管道 | agent |
| 供應商 | supplier |
| 生產者 | marketing channel |
| 中間商 | producer |
| 代理商 | distribution channel |
| 輔助商 | middleman |
| 用戶 | facilitator |

b. 營銷管道和分銷管道到底有何不同？

c. 試以你熟悉的行業為例，指出營銷管道包括的具體環節。

## 6. 問題與探討：
Questions and Exploration:

a. 如果你將來可能從事市場營銷工作，那麼在＂現代營銷方式＂的四個環節中，你對哪個環節的工作最感興趣？

b. 你認爲電子商務會在中國成爲主要的市場營銷方式嗎？

# 3.3 練習

## 1. 選擇適當的動詞填空：
Fill in each blank with the most appropriate verb:

轉變　存在　滿足　獲得　占穩

開發　進入　提高　銷售　具有

a. (　　　　　)水平　　　　e. (　　　　　)觀念

b. (　　　　　)問題　　　　f. (　　　　　)技術

c. (　　　　　)成功　　　　g. (　　　　　)需求

d. (　　　　　)市場　　　　h. (　　　　　)潛力


## 2. 解釋劃線詞語的意思並造句：
Explain the underlined words or phrases and use those words to make an additional sentence:

a. 這幾年公司的業績一般。

解釋：_____

造句：_____


b. 我們的產品質量和競爭對手一般高。

解釋：_____

造句：_____

c. 他們的交情不是<u>一般</u>的雇主與雇員的關係。

解釋：_____

造句：_____

d. 他剛進公司不久<u>便</u>被提升為部門經理。

解釋：_____

造句：_____

e. 人們的收入增加後，<u>便</u>會有購買高檔名牌產品的欲望。

解釋：_____

造句：_____

# 3. 完成句子並翻譯：
Complete the following sentences and translate the sentences into English:

a. 所謂 " 皇帝的女兒不愁嫁 " 指的是_____

翻譯：_____

b. 只有_____，才能創造出真正的名牌產品。

翻譯：_____

c. 許多跨國知名企業在做生意的同時，_____

翻譯：_____

d. 中國只有加入WTO_____

翻譯：_____

e. 新產品剛研制成功便＿＿＿＿＿＿＿＿＿＿＿＿＿＿＿＿＿＿＿＿

　　翻譯：＿＿＿＿＿＿＿＿＿＿＿＿＿＿＿＿＿＿＿＿＿＿＿＿＿＿

# 4. 選詞填空：
Fill in each blank with the most appropriate word:

a. 意識　認識

　1) 運動員一般都有很強的競爭＿＿＿＿。

　2) 通過競爭，他們才＿＿＿到自己的缺點。

　3) 商家通過廣告宣傳加深了消費者對其產品的＿＿＿＿。

　4) 她的女兒就快生產了，可她一點兒也沒有當奶奶的＿＿＿＿。

　5) 現在越來越多的企業＿＿＿＿到樹立品牌＿＿＿＿的重要性。

　6) 我們很早就＿＿＿＿了。

　7) 老師剛一開口，他就＿＿＿＿到他的答案錯了。

b. 獲得　取得

　1) 儘管已經＿＿＿＿了很大的成績，他仍然不斷地努力。

　2) 今年公司在產品出口上＿＿＿＿了巨大收益，這個成績的＿＿＿＿
　　是與全體員工的努力分不開的。

　3) 新產品的質量＿＿＿＿行家的一致贊揚。

c. 轉變　轉化

　1) 中國正努力完成向市場經濟的＿＿＿＿。

　2) 壓力有時可以＿＿＿＿為動力。

　3) 總經理一來，他的態度馬上就＿＿＿＿了。

    d. 均衡　平衡

        1) 社會財富不_____會帶來嚴重的社會問題。

        2) 公司的收入與支出應該保持_____。

        3) 不公平地對待員工會造成員工心裏不_____。

    e. 普遍　普及　遍及

        1) 大城市中的家庭已經_____使用空調。

        2) 政府正在努力_____科學文化知識。

        3) 公司的銷售網絡已_____全國各地。

## 5. 閱讀理解並判斷正確與錯誤：

Read the following paragraph and indicate whether the statements below are TRUE or FALSE:

> 　　健力寶是中國的一個民族品牌。它 " 支持中國體育事業，致力國民素質提高 " 的產品定位曾爲其銷售立下汗馬功勞。在極短的時間內，健力寶的品牌響遍全國，老少皆知。但是，隨著社會的發展，消費者的觀念也起了變化。而健力寶仍緊抓原先的定位不放，致使其品牌意識減弱。如何拓展現有的企業文化重塑企業形象是健力寶首先要解決的問題。

a. （　　）健力寶是中國的一個品牌。

b. （　　）健力寶的市場定位適合當今中國消費者的觀念。

c. （　　）健力寶急需重新塑造企業形象及市場定位。

d. （　　　）健力寶 " 支持中國體育事業，致力國民素質提高 "
　　　的定位未在市場銷售中起到應有的作用。

e. （　　　）健力寶的銷售方式有問題。

## 6. 問題與探討：
Questions and Exploration:

a. 請分析知名品牌在中國受歡迎的原因。

b. 你認為一般中國人或亞洲人品牌意識比較高嗎？這跟什麼文
化背景有關係？

# 3.4 練習

## 1. 選擇適當的動詞填空：
Fill in each blank with the most appropriate verb:

利用　出口　面臨　影響

降低　形成　損害　存在

a. (　　　　)挑戰　　　　e. (　　　　)價格

b. (　　　　)威脅　　　　f. (　　　　)差距

c. (　　　　)優勢　　　　g. (　　　　)形象

d. (　　　　)匯率　　　　h. (　　　　)商品

## 2. 選詞填空：
Fill in each blank with the most appropriate word:

a. 嚴重　嚴峻　嚴肅

1) 國有企業在中國加入WTO後將面臨＿＿＿的挑戰。

2) 面對如此＿＿＿的挑戰，我們更要＿＿＿紀律。

3) 公司存在＿＿＿的銷售問題，應該盡快制定新的銷售方案，從而增加銷售量。

4) 當總經理談到目前＿＿＿的形勢時，面容是＿＿＿的。

b. 形成　成形

1) 中國目前的金融市場尚未＿＿＿。

2)通過與國外公司廣泛合作，我們產品的國際營銷已經_____
了一定規模。

3)隨著生產及管理技術水平的提高，生產一輛汽車從製造零
配件到組裝_____只需要短短幾天的時間。

c. 注重　注意　重視

1)邊遠地區的居民一般對教育都不夠_____。

2)引進技術後如何消化是一個值得_____的問題。

3)要_____研發力量的投入，才能不斷推出新產品。

4)中國人以前買東西只講究“實惠”，不_____包裝。

d. 損害　傷害　危害　損壞

1)在公共場所吸煙會_____他人健康。

2)_____公物就是_____公眾的利益。

3)警察的職責是保護民眾不受_____。

4)吸毒不但會_____自身的健康，還會_____整個社會的安定。

5)低價甩賣不僅會損失利潤，而且會_____公司信譽，因爲對有
些人來說，低價就等於低質量。

6)生產玻璃的企業一般在當地銷售，因爲玻璃容易_____，不
適於長途運輸。

7)石油的價格波動會對某些工業造成很大_____，但對食品、
醫藥等行業的影響則相對較小。

e. 取代　代替

　　1)電腦已經_____了打字機，成為文字處理的工具。

　　2)總經理這個月去休假了，由副總經理_____履行他的職責。

　　3)他年輕有為，剛來不久便_____了廠長的地位。

f. 大力發展　大力推動　大力支持　大力宣傳

　　1)在_____經濟的同時，也要避免環境污染。

　　2)科技發展_____了社會的進步。

　　3)綠化運動得到國家的_____。

　　4)_____環境保護政策得到了社會各界的廣泛支持。

# 3. 閱讀理解並判斷正確與錯誤：
Read the following paragraph and indicate whether the statements below are TRUE or FALSE:

　　　　目前中國外貿結構中一個十分突出的問題是出口產品加工程度低，附加值不高。如果不在短期內解決這個問題，將可能使加工工業變為一種"無根工業"，而且有可能由於勞動力成本和政策性優勢的消失而導致出口產品的國際競爭力嚴重下降，從而喪失加工工業的發展條件和貿易機會。

a. (　　　) 中國出口產品加工程度及附加值都很高。

b. (　　　) 中國外貿結構並無任何突出問題。

c. (　　　) 無根工業是中國加工工業的現狀。

d. (　　　) 中國出口產品失去國際競爭力的原因在於勞動
　　　　　力成本和政策性優勢的消失。


# 4. 問題與探討：
Questions and Exploration:

a. 中國出口額最大的商品是什麼？最主要目的地是哪兒？

b. 影響中國出口產業發展的因素是什麼？

# 练习答案

# 1.1 练习答案

**1.** **a.** 克服　　**b.** 鼓励　　**c.** 吸引　　**d.** 充满　　**e.** 建立

　　**f.** 成立　　**g.** 分配　　**h.** 看好　　**i.** 促进　　**j.** 实行

**2.** **a.** 1）成为　　　　　　　　**b.** 2）关闭

　　**c.** 1）加快　　　　　　　　**d.** 3）引导

　　**a.** 1）加快　　　　　　　　**d.** 3）引导

　　**e.** 1）严重　　　　　　　　**f.** 2）实行 1）推行

　　**g.** 2）制度　　　　　　　　**h.** 3）转变为

# 1.2 练习答案

**1.** **a.** 取得　　**b.** 涉及　　**c.** 颁布　　**d.** 从事

　　**e.** 公布　　**f.** 扩大　　**g.** 得到　　**h.** 允许

**3.** **a.** 国企被私有企业并购后，有些减少了亏损，有些甚至还有盈利。

　　**b.** 有些私有企业规模不断扩大，不但在国内拥有子公司，甚至在国外成立办事处或分支公司。

　　**c.** 他工作很忙，甚至忘了吃饭。

　　**d.** 在中国的计划经济体制下，中央政府统一分配资源，统一组织生产，甚至还统一销售。

　　**e.** 现在不仅年轻人和中年人用电脑，甚至老年人也用。

**4.** **a.** 这次会议不仅没有解决问题，反而加深了矛盾。

    **b.** 近年来，中国的私有企业不仅数量增多，而且规模扩大。

    **c.** 中国加入WTO以后，国有企业不仅要和国内其它企业竞争，而且要和外国的企业竞争。

    **d.** 中国政府不仅改革了税收和金融体制，而且也改革了外贸体制。

**5.** **a.** 1)许可　　2)允许　　3)认可　　4)允许

    **b.** 1)领土　　2)领域　　3)领域　　4)领土

    **c.** 1)公布　　2)颁布　　3)公布　　4)颁布

    **d.** 1)扩大　　2)扩充　　3)扩大／扩充

    **e.** 1)方式　　2)方式　　3)方法　　4)方法

# 1.3 练习答案

**1.** **a.** 吸引　　**b.** 给予　　**c.** 扶植

    **d.** 提供　　**e.** 建立　　**f.** 制造

**2.** **a.** 2)陆续　　**b.** 1)连续　　**c.** 1)吸引

    **d.** 1)提供　　**e.** 2)设立　　**f.** 3)成立

    **g.** 1)建立

**3.** **a.** 1)　公司从下半年起开始实行新的奖惩制度。

      2)　长城自山海关起一直延续了几个省份。

**b.** 1) 希望消费者多提意见，以便我们改进产品质量。

2) 政府制定了许多优惠政策以吸引外资。

3) 公司设有食堂以方便员工用餐。

**c.** 1) 几家公司看好他的设计，纷纷找他合作。

**d.** 1) 考察团先后参观了几个工厂。

2) 请大家按先后顺序进入会场。

**e.** 1) 我想对以上发言作个总结。

2) 我以上列出了投资环境比较好的几个城市。

# 1.4 练习答案

**1.** **a.** 分享　　　**b.** 协助　　　**c.** 分担　　　**d.** 获得

　　**e.** 加速　　　**f.** 转换　　　**g.** 承担　　　**h.** 制定

**2.** **a.** 1)形状　　2)形式　　3)形状　　4)形式

　　**b.** 1)对　　　2)对于　　3)对于　　4)对

　　**c.** 1)分享　　2)分担　　3)分担　　4)分享

**3.** 如果资金短缺，这个项目则无法完成。

　　计划经济不改革，人们的生活水平则无法提高。

　　中国人想到外国去做生意，外国人则想到中国投资。

　　沿海城市经济发展迅速，内地则发展缓慢。

4. 外商采用与中方合资的方式来进入中国市场。

   公司引进先进技术来提高竞争力。

   你们用什么方式来庆祝公司周年庆？

   合资公司一般按投资比例来分配利润。

5. a. 自动化

   b. 现代化

   c. 深化

   d. 绿化、美化

# 2.1 练习答案

**1.** **a.** 发挥    **b.** 确定    **c.** 获准    **d.** 分离    **e.** 扶持

     **f.** 垄断    **g.** 执行    **h.** 自负    **i.** 承担    **j.** 自主

**2.** **a.** 金融                 **b.** 经营、自负

     **c.** 作用                 **d.** 组成

     **e.** 政策、商业         **f.** 外资

**5.** **a.** 这家跨国公司规模很大，在美国、日本、德国以及中国都有它的分支机构。

     **b.** 各部门经理及其家属都被邀请参加舞会。

     **c.** 出差时的住宿费、交通费、伙食费以及其它各种费用都可以报销。

     **d.** 从改革开放到设立自由贸易区以及金融贸易区，上海发生了巨大的变化。

**6.** **a.** 展开                 **b.** 展开

     **c.** 发展                 **d.** 开展

**7.** **a.** T                 **b.** T

     **c.** T                 **d.** F

# 2.2 练习答案

**1.** **a.** 紧缩　　　　　　**b.** 管理　　　　　　**c.** 升值

　　 **d.** 货币　　　　　　**e.** 指标　　　　　　**f.** 变动

**2.** **a.** 1)变化　　　2)变动　　　3)变化　　　4)变动

　　 **b.** 1)欲望　　　2)愿望　　　3)愿望　　　4)欲望

　　 **c.** 1)表达　　　2)表示　　　3)表明　　　4)表明

　　 **d.** 1)抑制　　　2)控制　　　3)抑制　　　4)控制

　　 **e.** 1)鼓励　　　2)鼓励　　　3)鼓励　　　4)勉励

　　 **f.** 1)避免　　　2)防止　　　3)防止　　　4)避免

**3.** **a.** 对待员工既要批评，也要鼓励。

　　 **b.** 消费者喜欢选择质量既好，价格又低的商品。

　　 **c.** 生产力的提高既可以促进经济增长，又可以抑制通货膨胀。

　　 **d.** 大多数决策都既有不利的一面，也有有利的一面。

**6.** **a.** F　　　　　　　　**b.** F

　　 **c.** F　　　　　　　　**d.** T

　　 **e.** T

# 2.3 练习答案

1. **a.** 面值　　　　**b.** 上市地点　　**c.** 红筹股　　　**d.** 阶段
　　　　　　　　　　和投资者

　 **e.** 筹集　　　　**f.** 雄厚　　　　**g.** 健全　　　　**h.** 恢复

2. **a.** 1)缺少　　　2)缺乏　　　　3)缺乏　　　　4)缺少

　 **b.** 1)密切　　　2)密切　　　　3)紧密

　 **c.** 1)概念　　　2)观念　　　　3)观念　　　　4)概念

　 **d.** 1)相关　　　2)有关　　　　3)有关　　　　4)相关

4. 　　这个项目因经费不足而被迫停工。

　　　　许多误解因文化差异而产生。

　　　　产品的产量需要根据供求关系而决定。

　　　　股价随着政策变动而上下波动。

5. **a.** F　　　　　　　　　　**b.** F

　 **c.** T　　　　　　　　　　**d.** T

# 2.4 练习答案

1. **a.** 坚实　　　　**b.** 云集　　　　**c.** 美称

　 **d.** 雄厚、繁荣　**e.** 基础　　　　**f.** 惊人
　　　优秀、充足

**2.** **a.** 1) 此外　　2) 另　　3) 另外　　4) 另外

　　 **b.** 1) 注目　　2) 瞩目

　　 **c.** 1) 热点　　2) 焦点　　3) 焦点　　4) 热点

　　 **d.** 1) 保障　　2) 保证　　3) 保障　　4) 保障

**4.** **a.** T　　　　　　　　**b.** F

　　 **c.** F　　　　　　　　**d.** T

　　 **e.** F

# 3.1 练习答案

**1.** **a.** 预测　　**b.** 传递　　**c.** 制定　　**d.** 促销　　**e.** 增加

　　**f.** 推销　　**g.** 收集　　**h.** 掌握　　**i.** 进行　　**j.** 面临

**2.** **a.** 1)面临　2)面对　3)面临　4)面临　5)面对　6)面临

　　**b.** 1)广大　2)广泛　3)广泛　4)广大

　　**c.** 1)把握　2)掌握　3)掌握　4)掌握　5)把握

　　**d.** 1)靠　　2)依靠　3)依赖　4)靠

　　**e.** 1)关注　2)关心　3)关心　4)关注

**3.** **a.** 1)接受　　　　　　　**b.** 2)遭受

　　**c.** 2)重要的　　　　　　**d.** 2)卖得正是时候

　　**e.** 2)马上　　　　　　　**f.** 3)不管用什么方法

# 3.2 练习答案

**1.** **a.** 达到　　　　　**b.** 树立　　　　　**c.** 建立

　　**d.** 面向　　　　　**e.** 推动　　　　　**f.** 营销

**2.** 　a.序　　　b.中心　　　c.导向　　　d.目的　　　e.标准

**3.** **a.** 1)逐渐　　　2)逐步　　　3)逐渐　　　4)逐步

**b.** 1) 采取     2) 采用     3) 采用     4) 采取

**c.** 1) 实行     2) 实行     3) 实践     4) 实现

**d.** 1) 策略     2) 战略     3) 策略

**e.** 1) 建立     2) 树立     3) 建立

**4.** **a.** 一个产品或一个品牌通向市场、成为商品

     **b.** 产品、价格、分销和促销

     **c.** 降价和折扣券等现代促销方式

     **d.** 薄利多销、扩大市场占有率

**5.** **a.**

| | |
|---|---|
| 市场营销渠道 | marketing channel |
| 分销渠道 | distribution channel |
| 供应商 | supplier |
| 生产商 | producer |
| 中间商 | middle man |
| 代理商 | agent |
| 辅助商 | facilitator |
| 用户 | user |

# 3.3 练习答案

**1.** **a.** 提高    **b.** 存在    **c.** 获得    **d.** 占稳

     **e.** 转变    **f.** 开发    **g.** 满足    **h.** 具有

**4.** **a.** 1) 意识　　　2) 认识　　　3) 认识　　　4) 意识

　　　　5) 认识/意识　6) 认识　　　7) 意识

　　**b.** 1) 取得　　　2) 获得/取得　3) 取得

　　**c.** 1) 转变　　　2) 转化　　　3) 转变

　　**d.** 1) 均衡　　　2) 平衡　　　3) 平衡

　　**e.** 1) 普遍　　　2) 普及　　　3) 遍及

**5.** **a.** T　　　　　　　　　　**b.** F

　　**c.** T　　　　　　　　　　**d.** F

　　**e.** F

# 3.4 练习答案

**1.** **a.** 面临　　**b.** 形成　　**c.** 利用　　**d.** 降低

　　**e.** 影响　　**f.** 存在　　**g.** 损害　　**h.** 出口

**2.** **a.** 1) 严峻　　　2) 严峻/严肃　3) 严重　　　4) 严峻/严肃

　　**b.** 1) 成形　　　2) 形成　　　3) 成形

　　**c.** 1) 重视　　　2) 注意　　　3) 注重　　　4) 注重

　　**d.** 1) 危害　　　2) 损坏/损害　3) 伤害　　　4) 危害/危害

　　　　5) 损害　　　6) 损坏　　　7) 损害

　　**e.** 1) 取代　　　2) 代替　　　3) 取代

　　**f.** 1) 大力发展　2) 大力推动　3) 大力支持　4) 大力宣传

**3.** **a.** F                    **b.** F

**c.** F                    **d.** T

Exercise Answers

# 練習答案

## 1.1 練習答案

1.  a.  克服　　b.  鼓勵　　c.  吸引　　d.  充滿　　e.  建立
    f.  成立　　g.  分配　　h.  看好　　i.  促進　　j.  實行

2.  a.  1)成爲　　　　　　　　b.  2)關閉
    c.  1)加快　　　　　　　　d.  3)引導
    e.  1)嚴重　　　　　　　　f.  2)實行 1)推行
    g.  2)制度　　　　　　　　h.  3)轉變爲

## 1.2 練習答案

1.  a.  取得　　b.  涉及　　c.  頒布　　d.  從事
    e.  公布　　f.  擴大　　g.  得到　　h.  允許

3.  a.  國企被私有企業併購后，有些減少了虧損，有些甚至還有盈利。
    b.  有些私有企業規模不斷擴大，不但在國內擁有子公司，甚至在國外成立辦事處或分支公司。
    c.  他工作很忙，甚至忘了吃飯。
    d.  在中國的計劃經濟體制下，中央政府統一分配資源，統一組織生產，甚至還統一銷售。
    e.  現在不僅年輕人和中年人用電腦，甚至老年人也用。

4. a. 這次會議不僅沒有解決問題，反而加深了矛盾。

b. 近年來，中國的私有企業不僅數量增多，而且規模擴大。

c. 中國加入WTO以後，國有企業不僅要和國內其它企業競爭，而且要和外國的企業競爭。

d. 中國政府不僅改革了稅收和金融體制，而且也改革了外貿體制。

5. a.　1)許可　　　2)允許　　　3)認可　　　4)允許

b.　1)領土　　　2)領域　　　3)領域　　　4)領土

c.　1)公布　　　2)頒布　　　3)公布　　　4)頒布

d.　1)擴大　　　2)擴充　　　3)擴大/擴充

e.　1)方式　　　2)方式　　　3)方法　　　4)方法


# 1.3 練習答案

1. a.　吸引　　　　b.　給予　　　　c.　扶植

d.　提供　　　　e.　建立　　　　f.　制造

2. a.　2)陸續　　　b.　1)連續　　　c.　1)吸引

d.　1)提供　　　e.　2)設立　　　f.　3)成立

g.　1)建立

3. a.　1)　公司從下半年起開始實行新的獎懲制度。

2)　長城自山海關起一直延續了幾個省份。

b.　1)　希望消費者多提意見，以便我們改進產品質量。

　　2)　政府制定了許多優惠政策以吸引外資。

　　3)　公司設有食堂以方便員工用餐。

c.　1)　几家公司看好他的設計，紛紛找他合作。

d.　1)　考察團先後參觀了幾個工廠。

　　2)　請大家按先後順序進入會場。

e.　1)　我想對以上發言作個總結。

　　2)　我以上列出了投資環境比較好的幾個城市。

# 1.4 練習答案

1.　a.　分享　　　b.　協助　　　c.　分擔　　　d.　獲得

　　e.　加速　　　f.　轉換　　　g.　承擔　　　h.　制定

2.　a.　1)形狀　　2)形式　　3)形狀　　4)形式

　　b.　1)對　　　2)對于　　3)對于　　4)對

　　c.　1)分享　　2)分擔　　3)分擔　　4)分享

3.　如果資金短缺，這個項目則無法完成。

　　計劃經濟不改革，人們的生活水平則無法提高。

　　中國人想到外國去做生意，外國人則想到中國投資。

　　沿海城市經濟發展迅速，內地則發展緩慢。

4. 外商採用與中方合資的方式來進入中國市場。

   公司引進先進技術來提高競爭力。

   你們用什么方式來慶祝公司周年慶？

   合資公司一般按投資比例來分配利潤。

5. a. 自動化

   b. 現代化

   c. 深化

   d. 綠化、美化

# 2.1 練習答案

1. a. 發揮　　b. 確定　　c. 獲准　　d. 分離　　e. 扶持

   f. 壟斷　　g. 執行　　h. 自負　　i. 承擔　　j. 自主

2. a. 金融　　　　　　　　　b. 經營、自負

   c. 作用　　　　　　　　　d. 組成

   e. 政策、商業　　　　　　f. 外資

5. a. 這家跨國公司規模很大，在美國、日本、德國以及中國都有它的分支機構。

   b. 各部門經理及其家屬都被邀請參加舞會。

   c. 出差時的住宿費、交通費、伙食費以及其它各種費用都可以報銷。

   d. 從改革開放到設立自由貿易區以及金融貿易區，上海發生了巨大的變化。

6. a. 展開　　　　　　　　　b. 展開

   c. 發展　　　　　　　　　d. 開展

7. a. T　　　　　　　　　　b. T

   c. T　　　　　　　　　　d. F

# 2.2 練習答案

1. a. 緊縮　　　b. 管理　　　c. 升值
   d. 貨幣　　　e. 指標　　　f. 變動

2. a. 1)變化　2)變動　3)變化　4)變動
   b. 1)欲望　2)願望　3)願望　4)欲望
   c. 1)表達　2)表示　3)表明　4)表明
   d. 1)抑制　2)控制　3)抑制　4)控制
   e. 1)鼓勵　2)鼓勵　3)鼓勵　4)勉勵
   f. 1)避免　2)防止　3)防止　4)避免

3. a. 對待員工既要批評，也要鼓勵。
   b. 消費者喜歡選擇質量既好，價格又低的商品。
   c. 生產力的提高既可以促進經濟增長，又可以抑制通貨膨脹。
   d. 大多數決策都既有不利的一面，也有有利的一面。

6. a. F　　　　b. F
   c. F　　　　d. T
   e. T

## 2.3 練習答案

1. a. 面值　　　　b. 上市地點　　c. 紅籌股　　　d. 階段
　　　　　　　　　　和投資者

　　e. 籌集　　　　f. 雄厚　　　　g. 健全　　　　h. 恢復

2. a. 1)缺少　　　2)缺乏　　　　3)缺乏　　　　4)缺少

　　b. 1)密切　　　2)密切　　　　3)緊密

　　c. 1)概念　　　2)觀念　　　　3)觀念　　　　4)概念

　　d. 1)相關　　　2)有關　　　　3)有關　　　　4)相關

4. 　　　這個項目因經費不足而被迫停工。

　　　　許多誤解因文化差異而產生。

　　　　產品的產量需要根據供求關系而決定。

　　　　股價隨著政策變動而上下波動。

5. a. F　　　　　　　　　　b. F
　　c. T　　　　　　　　　　d. T

## 2.4 練習答案

1. a. 堅實　　　　　b. 雲集　　　　c. 美稱
　　d. 雄厚、繁榮　　e. 基礎　　　　f. 驚人
　　　優秀、充足

2.    a.    1)此外      2)另          3)另外        4)另外

       b.    1)注日      2)矚目

       c.    1)熱點      2)焦點        3)焦點        4)熱點

       d.    1)保障      2)保證        3)保障        4)保障

4.    a.    T               b.    F

       c.    F               d.    T

       e.    F

# 3.1 練習答案

1. a. 預測　　b. 傳遞　　c. 制定　　d. 促銷　　e. 增加

   f. 推銷　　g. 收集　　h. 掌握　　i. 進行　　j. 面臨

2. a. 1)面臨　2)面對　3)面臨　4)面臨　5)面對　6)面臨

   b. 1)廣大　2)廣泛　3)廣泛　4)廣大

   c. 1)把握　2)掌握　3)掌握　4)掌握　5)把握

   d. 1)靠　　2)依靠　3)依賴　4)靠

   e. 1)關注　2)關心　3)關心　4)關注

3. a. 1)接受　　　　　　　　　　b. 2)遭受

   c. 2)重要的　　　　　　　　　d. 2)賣得正是時候

   e. 2)馬上　　　　　　　　　　f. 3)不管用什么方法

# 3.2 練習答案

1. a. 達到　　　　　　b. 樹立　　　　　　c. 建立

   d. 面向　　　　　　e. 推動　　　　　　f. 營銷

2. a.序　　　b.中心　　c.導向　　d.目的　　e.標準

3. a. 1)逐漸　　　2)逐步　　　3)逐漸　　　4)逐步

b. 1)採取　2)採用　3)採用　4)採取
c. 1)實行　2)實行　3)實踐　4)實現
d. 1)策略　2)戰略　3)策略
e. 1)建立　2)樹立　3)建立

4. a. 一個產品或一個品牌通向市場、成為商品
   b. 產品、價格、分銷和促銷
   c. 降價和折扣券等現代促銷方式
   d. 薄利多銷、擴大市場佔有率

5. a. 市場營銷渠道　　　　marketing
   分銷渠道　　　　　　distribution channel
   供應商　　　　　　　supplier
   生產商　　　　　　　producer
   中間商　　　　　　　middle man
   代理商　　　　　　　agent
   輔助商　　　　　　　facilitator
   用戶　　　　　　　　user

# 3.3 練習答案

1. a. 提高　　b. 存在　　c. 獲得　　d. 占穩
   e. 轉變　　f. 開發　　g. 滿足　　h. 具有

4.　a.　1)意識　　　2)認識　　　3)認識　　　4)意識

　　　　5)認識／意識　6)認識　　　7)意識

　　b.　1)取得　　　2)獲得／取得　3)取得

　　c.　1)轉變　　　2)轉化　　　3)轉變

　　d.　1)均衡　　　2)平衡　　　3)平衡

　　e.　1)普遍　　　2)普及　　　3)遍及


5.　a.　T　　　　　　　　b.　F

　　c.　T　　　　　　　　d.　F

　　e.　F


# 3.4 練習答案

1.　a.　面臨　　　b.　形成　　　c.　利用　　　d.　降低

　　e.　影響　　　f.　存在　　　g.　損害　　　h.　出口


2.　a.　1)嚴峻　　　2)嚴峻／嚴肅　3)嚴重　　　4)嚴峻／嚴肅

　　b.　1)成形　　　2)形成　　　3)成形

　　c.　1)重視　　　2)注意　　　3)注重　　　4)注重

　　d.　1)危害　　　2)損壞／損害　3)傷害　　　4)危害／危害

　　　　5)損害　　　6)損壞　　　7)損害

　　e.　1)取代　　　2)代替　　　3)取代

　　f.　1)大力發展　2)大力推動　3)大力支持　4)大力宣傳